Social Psychology, Past and Present

AN INTEGRATIVE ORIENTATION

Social Psychology, Past and Present

AN INTEGRATIVE ORIENTATION

JAY M. JACKSON

Taylor & Francis Group
New York London

First published by Lawrence Erlbaurn Associates, Inc., Publishers

Published 2017 by Routledge
711 Third Avenue, New York, NY 10017, USA
2 Park Square, Milton Park, Abingdon, Oxon OX14 4RN

First issued in hardback 2017

Routledge is an imprint of the Taylor & Francis Group, an informa business

Copyright © Lawrence Erlbaurn Associates, Inc., 1988

All rights reserved. No part of this book may be reprinted or reproduced or utilised in any form or by any electronic, mechanical, or other means, now known or hereafter invented, including photocopying and recording, or in any information storage or retrieval system, without permission in writing from the publishers.

Notice:
Product or corporate names may be trademarks or registered trademarks, and are used only for identification and explanation without intent to infringe.

Library of Congress Cataloging-in-Publication Data

Jackson, Jay M.
Social psychology, past and present

Bibliography: p.
Includes index.
1. Social psychology. I. Title.
HM251.J26 1988 302 88-11255
ISBN 0-8058-1572-4

Publisher's Note
The publisher has gone to great lengths to ensure the quality of this reprint but points out that some imperfections in the original may be apparent.

ISBN 13: 978-0-8058-1572-6 (pbk)
ISBN 13: 978-1-1384-6740-8 (hbk)

Contents

PREFACE ix

1
EARLY THINKING ABOUT SOCIAL PERSONS 1

The Heritage From Antiquity *3*
Questions and Answers From Classical Philosophy *5*

2
INFLUENCES FROM THE RECENT PAST 21

The Impact of Darwin *21*
Physiological and Experimental Psychology *25*
Gestalt Psychology and Phenomenology *29*
The Freudian Revolution *32*
Cultural Anthropology *36*
"Sociological" Sociology *40*
American Pragmatism and "Psychological" Sociology *41*

3
THE FORMATIVE YEARS OF SCIENTIFIC SOCIAL PSYCHOLOGY 45

Resolution of the Great Controversies   *46*
Demonstrating that Social Psychology was Scientific   *52*

4
CONTEMPORARY SOCIAL PSYCHOLOGY: THE EARLY DECADES 62

Social Psychology and the Second World War   *63*
Interdisciplinary Optimism   *65*
Interdisciplinary Disillusionment   *69*
Social Psychology's Early Accomplishments   *70*

5
THE CRISIS IN SOCIAL PSYCHOLOGY 82

Criticism and Confusion in Social Psychology   *83*
Perspectives and Positions   *89*
Responses to the Crisis   *92*
Proposals for Major Changes in Orientation   *94*

6
CURRENT TRENDS IN SOCIAL PSYCHOLOGY 98

The Crisis: Ten Years Later   *98*
Current Trends in Research, Theory, and Metatheory   *103*
From a Cognitive to an Integrative Theoretical Orientation   *113*

7
AN INTEGRATIVE THEORETICAL ORIENTATION 116

Prerequisites for an Integrative Orientation   *116*
The Social Act as a Unit of Analysis   *119*
Normative Processes in the Social Act   *123*

Identity Processes in the Social Act *126*
Reference Processes in the Social Act *129*
Implications of the Integrative
Theoretical Orientation *131*

REFERENCES 137

AUTHOR INDEX 161

SUBJECT INDEX 168

Preface

You probably have heard the cliché that someone who is ignorant of history is doomed to repeat the mistakes of the past. Like most aphorisms, it is either unclear or false. Who can say with any assurance that a scientific endeavor is mistaken? Scientists probably learn more from their "mistakes" than they do from their successes. Scientific ideas go through cycles, from initial excitement and adulation to eventual apathy, skepticism, or rejection, and sometimes then to resurrection and renovation. At each stage they are conceived somewhat differently by a new generation of thinkers and investigators. History is always being rewritten from the perspective of the present and that of the particular historian. Otherwise, historians and would-be historians would suffer a higher rate of unemployment.

Philosophers of history are still arguing about whether "objective facts" occur. I think that misses the point. We can agree and document that a particular event occurred but disagree completely about its meaning in historical context or for contemporary affairs. In many well-known studies in social psychology—which is the subject of this book—even though the data are unquestioned, entirely different theoretical interpretations are advanced to explain them. Facts or data do not speak for themselves but must be placed within a framework of understanding. Different frameworks compete based on their ability to make sense of the available data and relate them to "knowns."

The quest for understanding of human affairs goes back to the beginnings of human thought. Many of the problems are still with us although our conceptual and methodological resources for attacking them are infinitely greater. The accumulated results of systematic empirical research have refined and redefined the issues, if not resolved them.

Contemporary social psychology is a scientific approach to understanding social conduct. It is a massive, diversified, international endeavor by professional scholars and practitioners to advance understanding and to alleviate human problems, by research, teaching, and application. The accumulated literature of social psychology is immense and spreads across every conceivable area of human endeavor. Like most scientists in the modern world, social psychologists become specialists in order to focus on and master specific problem areas. It becomes increasingly difficult, therefore, to obtain more than a superficial view of the whole field and to appreciate particular contributions within a larger context, both contemporary and historical.

The increasing popularization of social psychology has introduced it—under various names—into all of the areas of application that involve social activity, for example, education, business, government, health and welfare, sports, politics, jurisprudence, and architecture. There is an almost inevitable tendency to seize upon and accept the most dramatic or best-publicized ideas and research from social psychology without sufficient awareness of their antecedents or limitations.

This book is offered to serious students of social psychology, both those preparing for professional careers—undergraduate and graduate students—and also all those in fields of application who struggle daily with the most puzzling and intractable problem, dealing with the intricacies of human social relations and conduct. Hopefully, some of my colleagues also may read it. I have tried to make it intelligible to any interested, educated person, with a minimum of technical background.

It has always seemed to me that short books that have something to say are preferable to long ones—even though they are harder to write—and I have kept the exposition brief. It is a story rather than a catalogue of the history and development of social psychology. This has been particularly desirable in view of my objective, to provide the reader with a scholarly overview of the whole field without becoming bogged down in details or esoteric parochial controversies, so that contemporary problems might be understood within a broader and historical context. There are a great many sources that can be consulted for fine-tuning one's knowledge of specific special questions or events.

A large majority of social psychologists today have received their professional training in psychology and identify with that discipline, but they are not unaware of a minority "version" or subdiscipline of social psychology populated by sociologists. Among the majority, social psychology is viewed as a subdivision or even an application of psychology. Sociologists also lay claim to the discipline, however, in view of their historical contributions and distinctive emphases.

The orientation of this work is integrative, in a number of different respects. It looks to the roots of social psychology's central ideas and problems in classical philosophy. It attempts to identify and trace the contributions to the development of contemporary social psychology by scholars from many different disciplines, not only psychology and sociology, but also anthropology, psychiatry, political science, business administration, and others. An integrative social psychology is seen as a possibly independent scientific discipline that could unite all those "doing" social psychology, regardless of their other professional identities.

In recent decades, dissatisfaction among some social psychologists has led to a fractionation of the discipline. Scholars and practitioners with specialized interests, perspectives, or methods have tended to form their own subdisciplines, such as Environmental (Social) Psychology, Cross-Cultural (Social) Psychology, Applied Social Psychology, and Humanistic (Social) Psychology. Our interpretation of the developing trends in contemporary social psychology is that an integrative orientation is emerging that could re-unite these various subdivisions and permit their adherents to make their contributions within a unified discipline.

I do not pretend that what you are about to read is the "truth." It is my interpretation, reflecting 30 years of research, teaching, and working with practitioners in the professions, government, and industry. I became acquainted with social psychology immediately after World War II, at the beginning of its contemporary expansion and consolidation as a scientific discipline. My perspective gradually has changed and developed as I have attempted to answer for myself and my students questions such as: What is social psychology all about? How can it be both individual and social? How can it be applied to our everyday human and social problems? How much can we trust a particular theory or research result and how can we make use of it? Especially in the latter chapters dealing with contemporary social psychology, my perspective is not the standard or "mainstream" one, although I am convinced that it accurately reflects significant developments and thinking in the field. At every stage I have leaned heavily on authoritative secondary sources. Naturally, my selection of material and evidence has been selective. Although I have attempted a balanced consideration of issues, clearly my own viewpoint, and the brevity of the work, have weighted the presentation. In the final chapter I have attempted to project into the future a model of an integrative orientation, as one possible culmination of contemporary trends in social psychology.

ACKNOWLEDGMENTS

It is not really possible to express my indebtedness to all those from whom I have learned about social psychology. I have been especially fortunate in having associated with some outstanding thinkers and persons. My first introduction to research and the fragility of theory was in Telecommunications Research Establishment at Malvern, England, with the "back-room boys," the pioneers of radar during World War II. My group leader, Ryle, now a famous radio-astronomer, provided some timely encouragement to my budding scientific ability. Oswald Hall in sociology at McGill University first excited me about the possibilities of systematic, quantitative field research. Robert MacLeod in psychology seduced me into social psychology with his illuminating teaching, contagious enthusiasm, and awesome scholarship.

Assisting Donald Hebb forced me into the paths of logically rigorous scientific thought wedded to imaginative theory (and also into a reluctant detailed acquaintance with the cerebral cortex!). George Ferguson at McGill and Clyde Coombs at Michigan unveiled the realities and the beauty of statistical reasoning and measurement theory. During the first years of Bethel, the National Training Laboratory for Group Development, the staff provided acquaintance and association with a cross-section of outstanding social scientists and stimulated a vision of an integrated and applicable social psychology. This was fostered during my years at the University of Michigan, in Newcomb's interdisciplinary doctoral program, and in the Institute for Social Research with so many brilliant colleagues. Although I disagreed with Leon Festinger's approach, assisting him in research forced me to think analytically about research procedures.

My years guiding the graduate social psychology program at the University of Kansas psychology department provided the privilege of association and friendship with Heider, Barker, the Wrights (Beatrice, Erik, and Herbert), Martin Scheerer, Bert Kaplan, and many others. Even the years in the embattled University of Oregon sociology department deepened my awareness of alternative metatheoretical perspectives. Finally, there have been so many unmentioned stimulating colleagues and students, each of whom has taught me something important and to whom I am grateful.

Time present and time past
Are both perhaps present in time future
And time future contained in time past

—T. S. Eliot, BURNT NORTON
(From "Four Quartets")

Chapter 1
Early Thinking About Social Persons

A graduate student in a seminar at the University of Kansas once asked Fritz Heider how and when the famous contemporary social psychologist had begun to develop his influential balance theory. This was in 1958 shortly after the publication of Heider's modern classic, *The Psychology of Interpersonal Relations*. With characteristic humility, Heider replied: "Why, it's all in Spinoza!"

Does this mean that the writings of early philosophers and theologians are replete with theoretical nuggets awaiting discovery by social psychological prospectors? Not unless one brings to the exploration the scholarship and insight of a Heider. Nor is there any direct and clear path from these classical speculations, no matter how profound, to contemporary social psychological theories and research. What, then, can be found in early thinking about social persons, and how much investment should be made in examining these ancient lodes?

Some would say that the student of contemporary social psychology has little to gain by such studies. After all, the phenomena to be observed and explained vary from one era to another, just as they do among different societies and regions of the world. The relationships between master and servant or between husband and wife surely were different in ancient Greece than in San Francisco today. What could be observed in the agora of Athens would not correspond to the sights and sounds at Fisherman's Wharf.

The topics of social psychology, those categories by which the subject matter is classified in textbooks and technical publications, also have undergone continuous change from the early writings to the latest. Even in any particular year, they vary widely among different publications. These reflect not only the cross winds of political concerns and the fads, fashions and foibles of the era, but also divergent theoretical and methodological assumptions regarding the nature of social life and how to study it. In the 1950s, the fearful era of Senator Joseph McCarthy bred a concern with conformity and resistance. It was followed, once the crisis had passed, by a focus on topics like independence, counter-conformity, and creativity. At one time leadership was almost a mandatory topic, but it has waned in popularity. It now appears in most textbooks, if at all, tucked into the corner of some other category such as social influence, attitudes, or the social psychology of organizations.

An especially ingenious or striking experiment or program of research can mesmerize the field temporarily, introducing a new "required" topic; or at times spread across several topics, to the degree that its basic issues are not readily apparent.

There seem to be an endless number of ways of cutting up the subject matter of social psychology into "topics." Is this just an arbitrary matter of interest and preference? Are some topics obsolete because of advances in knowledge? Or does each topic include subject matter that requires different principles of explanation? And if so, in the light of such fragmentation, where lies the justification for a unified field of scientific inquiry called social psychology?

Kenneth Gergen, an eminent and controversial social psychologist, has argued that social psychology should not aspire to be a unified science, but rather a field of historical inquiry, recounting and attempting to interpret the flow of varied social phenomena, the ever-changing patterns of customs and activities within their shifting cultural, social, and technological historical contexts.

An alternative perspective is that there are generic problems in the understanding of social persons and social living that date back to the beginnings of human thought, for example: What is the nature of a social person? How does one person's activity affect another's? What is the basis of organized social life?

To see social psychology as a whole, we must recognize the persistent, universal issues reflected in particular phenomena or topics of social psychology, because throughout its history they continue to reappear in novel guises with fresh identities. Although emphasis on the cultural, situational, and technological contexts of social conduct is essential, it does not nullify the traditional aspiration of social psychologists to construct a unified science. Rather, it presents a challenge to be met and imperatives to be accepted in progress toward that objective.

Just as the experience of living makes us wiser, hopefully, in that we recognize a recurrent problem and how we attempted to deal with it previously, so each issue that reappears in social psychology presents a somewhat modified problem and the potential for improved attempted solutions. In all of science and in social psychology there is a continuous challenge to identify the persistent issues embedded in novel formulations and phraseology, and also to create possible answers more general, more complete, and more compatible with the existing state of theoretical and methodological understanding.

To achieve such awareness, the student fortunately does not have to become an historical scholar, familiar with the innumerable contributions to human thought from antiquity to the present. Our focus can remain on the contents of contemporary social psychology. Past thinking can be examined selectively where it can broaden, deepen and refine our understanding of current issues.

THE HERITAGE FROM ANTIQUITY

Plato and Aristotle

In every part of the world there have been ancient societies and mature cultures whose scholars pondered over humanity and its problems. Unfortunately, almost all of their intellectual heritage has been lost to us. The first systematic discussions readily available to western students are by the twin giants of ancient Greek philosophy, Plato (420–348 B.C.) and his pupil Aristotle (384–322 B.C.). Their joint influence permeates all of western culture. Although clearly it is impossible to prove direct influence on any particular contemporary development, the roots of social psychology can be traced back to their writings.

These two great thinkers differed in their intellectual methods and assumptions. Plato believed that the truest realities were not revealed by the senses. The ultimate reality resided in the idea of the good. The aim of all science was to attain knowledge of this absolute good—the essential meaning and unity of all things. His method of inquiry was deductive: he began with assumptions about reality and logically derived from these his thinking about persons and society. Today we would call him a theorist.

Aristotle assumed that observation and inductive reasoning would ultimately reveal the essential reality, or *entelechy*, of each phenomenon. He arrived at his conclusions about persons and society by a systematic scrutiny of the "facts" around him. His method of investigation was empirical.

Plato's and Aristotle's contrasting orientations toward scientific inquiry—the emphasis on theoretical constructions from which "true" hypotheses could be derived, as against the belief that truth would gradually emerge from the accumulation of facts by an unbiased observer—have influenced generations of scientists. They are reflected, for example, in the different approaches of the behaviorist and cognitive orientations in contemporary social psychology. The first emphasizes detailed observation of overt social behavior; the second stresses the significance of the inner (subjective) meanings of sense data.

Because their philosophical writings are both profound and encyclopaedic, it is not difficult to find in Plato and Aristotle anticipations of developments in contemporary social psychology. They seem to have thought of almost everything! For example, the basic conceptions of need theory, learning theory, and cognitive theory, as reflected in social psychology, can be found in Plato's writings. Aristotle's famous theory of persuasion that discusses the organization of arguments, the effect of an audience, and the source credibility of a communicator, anticipates modern theory and research (Hovland, Janis, & Kelley, 1953). His views that bonds of association between persons form the basic fabric of society, and that similarity leads to friendship, are not too different from contemporary thinking about the similarity-attraction problem.

Our most striking inheritance from Plato and Aristotle is apparent on nearly every campus in America where social psychology is taught. Courses on the same subject, often by the same name, are offered both within departments of psychology and sociology. This academic anomaly surely must arouse the curiosity of students. It probably generates feelings of dissonance among many of the discipline's practitioners.

The bifurcation of social psychology between a majority group, psychologists, and a smaller but intellectually vigorous minority group of sociologists, is no recent occurrence. The first acknowledged textbooks in the subject were published in 1908 by a sociologist, Edward Ross, and by a psychologist William McDougall. The schism can be traced back ultimately to Plato and Aristotle and their contrasting views of "the key problem of social psychology" (Allport, 1954), the social nature of a human being.

Plato assumed a biological individual with a physiological and psychological nature. Psychological processes arose from the functioning of particular parts of the organism: intellect from the head, volition from the heart, and appetite from the stomach. Individuals initiated cooperative activity in order to satisfy their diverse needs. For Plato, social behavior arose out of individual psychological processes: Society was secondary to the individual.

One can recognize this basic position in psychology's social psychology. In spite of theoretical diversity, "psychological" social psychologists assume that social psychology is a branch or application of the principles of general psychology, itself resting firmly on physiology. The biological individual with its cognitive, conative, and affective processes is the primary locus of explanation for social behavior.

On the basis of his observations of social life, Aristotle arrived at the opposite conclusion: Human nature was primarily social and only secondarily biological. An individual was born into a society and social situations with an inherent tendency to be gregarious and affiliative, an inborn need of human society. One accounted for social activity primarily by observing social conditions and only secondarily by studying psychological states of the individual.

The path from Aristotle to the founder of sociology, Auguste Comte, can be traced via the Greek Stoic philosophers, Cicero, St. Augustine, and St. Thomas Aquinas. Essentially, the same orientation is found among contemporary "sociological" social psychologists: A socially isolated or deprived individual does not become a "person." The essentially social nature of a person is actualized by interaction with others. To account for social behavior, one looks first to the social situation in which the activity occurs and only secondarily to a person's individual psychological processes.

You may object that the differences today between psychological and sociological approaches to social psychology are more apparent than real. No psychologist would deny the importance of social environment and socialization in the normal development of a person. No sociologist would deny that humans are members of a biological species and that physiological, neurological, and genetic processes contribute to their development and activity. All social psychologists agree that a person's social behavior is the product of interaction between physical and social forces—internal and external influences. Which comes first, the physical or the social? Is this just another version of the "chicken-and-the-egg" question? Where is the basis for disagreement and the bifurcation of the discipline?

However, let us review the undeniable realities in present-day social psychology. There are parallel courses called "social psychology" taught in colleges and universities throughout the country, often strikingly different in orientations and contents. Textbooks, technical books, and journals are published primarily for each discipline and are only of secondary interest to some members of the other. The two groups of social psychologists belong to separate, active professional societies with their attendant political–economic activities; although a small minority of each also belongs to both. The overriding fact is that a powerful ingroup–outgroup phenomenon dictates membership and professional identity as either a "psychological" or "sociological" social psychologist.

At the heart of this schism are somewhat different orientations toward the phenomena of social life, conceptual and theoretical constructions, methods of research, and emphases in principles of explanation. Although social psychologists in both disciplines make valiant efforts to understand the "outgroup" and attempt to incorporate its contributions, there are powerful barriers. This bifurcation is a fact of contemporary social psychology. Its genesis can be found in Plato's and Aristotle's contrasting assumptions about human nature.

QUESTIONS AND ANSWERS FROM CLASSICAL PHILOSOPHY

When we say that an idea in prescientific social thought anticipated a theoretical or research development in contemporary social psychology, we state an interpretation, not a fact. There is an essential difference between the methods of speculative philosophy and modern science. In the hands of different classical philosophers, the "same" concept's significance can vary greatly, because its meaning is contextual, derived from its place in a system of thought (Northrop, 1949). In scientific social psychology, ideally, the meaning of a concept is specified either by precise measurement operations, operational definition, or by construct validity, logically interrelated predictions to observables.

We also must not minimize the distinction between speculative philosophical or theoretical statements, no matter how prophetic or profound, and statements of hypotheses in forms that can be tested empirically; or even more, conclusions from data obtained and analyzed under scientific controls.

With these "caveats" in mind, however, it is possible to identify questions and answers in philosophy addressed to persistent problems of contemporary social psychology. Two interrelated questions dominated classical social thought: What is the nature of a person? and How is society possible? These two questions really were inseparable, because an answer to one of them implied a corresponding answer to the other. For example, the American founding fathers constructed a blueprint for a new state upon assumptions about human nature and society provided by 17th and 18th century social philosophers.

Early Hedonism: The Selfish Person

The most pervasive answer to the first question was the doctrine of *hedonism*: a person acts to avoid pain and attain pleasure. The thesis can be traced back at least to Aristippus (430–360 B.C.), a student of Socrates, whose Cyrenaics emphasized sensual enjoyment, and to Epicurus (342–270 B.C.), whose Epicurean school stressed spiritual pleasure—freedom from want and pain, and tranquility of mind. Hedonism in its various forms is implicit in many early social philosophies.

Thomas Hobbes: Egoism and Power. Thomas Hobbes (1588–1679) was one of the great philosophical system builders of the 17th century who believed that knowledge of natural science should be the foundation of all knowledge of existence. Copernicus, Kepler, Galilei, and Harvey had constructed the foundations of modern physical science. Hobbes attempted to continue the naturalistic movement initiated by them and to extend it to ethics and politics.

Hobbes was an early hedonist who believed that the greatest source of pleasure was the possession of power. In his famous work, *Leviathan* (1651), he theorized that a person's egoism and desire for self-preservation were the primary impulses in determining social behavior. The person's struggle for survival entailed achievement of as much personal power as possible to defend against others' power, because the state of nature was a "war of all against all."

If left to their own resources, however, people frequently were engulfed by catastrophe and disaster. When worn down by the insecurity of the incessant struggle, they were willing to exchange their personal power for protection by a Leviathan or super-being, whether a God, a strong leader, or the State, to exercise supreme authority in the suppression of anarchy. This "social contract" was the genesis of the all-powerful central state.

Hobbes had been close to the aristocracy all of his life, and had become apprehensive at the turmoil and potential excesses of the English civil war. His theory reflected his ultra-conservative political sympathies. But his social thinking provided an example of the relationship between assumptions about human nature and about the nature of society. Human nature was egotistical and power-seeking (for self-protection and survival): From this he derived the centralized state with delegated absolute power.

Hobbes' doctrine can be traced down through intellectual history but can be discerned in contemporary social psychology, if at all, only in attenuated and fragmentary forms. His was an attempted unitary explanation of social life, one of Allport's (1954) "simple and sovereign theories." Social psychologists today have recognized that one-factor explanations of social behavior are inadequate. Human motivation is complex and changeable, depending on personal, cultural, and situational contexts.

The best examples of Hobbes' view of human nature are found in Freud's instinctual thinking. He postulated that individuals were inherently selfish and aggressive. One finds in psychoanalytic theories of leadership an essentially Hobbesian conception, that leader–follower relations in the social group (which includes society and its major institutions) are dominant–submissive, based on *father-figure* emotional transference (Bion, 1948–1951; Freud, 1922). The theory and research on *authoritarian personality* (Adorno, Frenkel-Brunswik, Levinson, & Sanford 1950), was derived directly from psychoanalytic theory: it explains racial bigotry as the product of abnormalities of the human psyche, not as a manifestation of universal human nature. Freud's theories have been modified and "socialized" by his followers, as we discuss in chapter 2, and it is the resultant, more "benign" view of human nature in psychoanalytic thinking rather than that of the orthodox theory that has been more acceptable to and influential in contemporary social psychology.

For a long period in the modern era of psychology and derived social psychology, the *self* and related processes were frowned upon by theorists as too "mentalistic" and speculative. In recent decades, however, especially with the primacy of the cognitive orientation, they have become quite fashionable and have assumed a significant place in contemporary social psychology. An early redirection of the focus was in the psychology of *ego involvement* (Allport, 1943; Sherif & Cantril, 1947), which asserted the relationship between a person's central attitudes and self-processes. There followed research on *self-image* (Lecky, 1945), *self-concept* (Wylie, 1961), *self-schema* (Markus, 1977), *self-awareness* (Duval &

Wicklund, 1972), *self-monitoring* (Snyder, 1979), and *self-presentation* (Goffman, 1959). These contemporary contributions are reviewed in chapter 3.

With the exception of work on *self-esteem* (Coopersmith, 1967), which owes something to Freud's theory, self-theories in contemporary social psychology are a far cry from Hobbes' view of human nature. The *self* has become cognitive, rational, and socialized. It reflects more of James' genteel *social self* (see chapter 2) than of Hobbes' elemental drive for power and survival.

Power theories in contemporary social psychology reflect even less of Hobbes' egocentric urge. The phenomenon of power, so obvious and pervasive in the "real world" of government, industry, and even academia, had been avoided by social psychologists until Cartwright (1959) called attention to its importance. As discussed later, however, it has remained "soft," in contrast with its treatment in sociology or political science. In social psychology, power is subjective: only in the eyes of the beholder. It is a source of influence depending on how it is perceived. Even *coercive power* (French & Raven, 1959; Raven, 1965), which sounds as if it is conceptualizing some of the realities of a Hobbesian world, is a perception—whether accurate or mistaken—that another person has the potential to punish one.

The small amount of research on power has focused on its relative effectiveness as an influence technique rather than on power as a motive. The exception is research on the *need for power* (McClelland, 1961), using the Thematic Apperception Test (TAT), a projective technique that asks subjects to respond with spontaneous imagery to a series of pictures. A person's relative need for power is assessed by McClelland and his co-workers by content analysis. Following Henry Murray's (1938) theory, *n power* is assumed to be an individual's personality trait, responsive to both internal and external pressures. However, McClelland has provided little theoretical elaboration and used the technique meagerly, as an adjunct to his research on *need for achievement*.

There also is hardly any reflection of Hobbes' social contract theory in contemporary social psychology. The discipline has been individualistic in its formulations and has tended to avoid, at least explicitly, dealing with the question of the societal context of social behavior. In the 1960s, Berkowitz and his associates did some scattered research on a *norm of responsibility*, conceived as regulating the relations between powerful and powerless members of society (Berkowitz & Daniels, 1963, 1964). The sociological concept, *legitimate authority*, which recognizes the objective power of a position in social structure, becomes the "perception of legitimacy" in social psychology and has been used sparsely.

The *Zeitgeist* of our era finds the Hobbesian doctrine repugnant. For example, in studies of small problem-solving groups, a member's striving for individual prominence, or behavior coded by observers as expressing *self- oriented needs,* was frowned on by other group members and led to conflict and lower productivity of the group (Kelley & Thibaut, 1969). The theory of *self-actualiza-*

tion (Fromm, 1947; Maslow, 1954), similar to Hobbes' *egoism,* asserts that an individual should not permit social convention to inhibit self-interest. It has been castigated by Berkowitz (1964) for lack of empirical support and for being deleterious to child rearing that can "facilitate social progress and promote domestic tranquility."

One must conclude that Hobbes' view of human nature and his theory in its original form have not been influential in contemporary social psychology, for a number of apparent reasons. First, unitary explanations of social phenomena are outdated. Social life is recognized by social psychologists as a dynamic product of many forces and contingencies. Second, the implicit model of human nature preferred is very much an "oversocialized" and "other-directed" one (Riesman, 1950; Wrong, 1961). With some exceptions, to be mentioned later, it minimizes genetic, instinctual, or internal bases of social behavior and emphasizes external sources: socialization, social learning, influence by peers and public opinion. Third, today's social psychology is primarily a product of American society and cultural values: democratic, humane, reflecting the Judao-Christian ethical value system. Even social psychologists in other lands have been trained in America or strongly influenced by its preeminent theoretical and research accomplishments. This has produced a scientific bias in the formulation of theories and selection of appropriate research questions. As discussed in the next section, social psychologists for the most part are more interested in explaining why people refuse to help rather than why they do, why they are aggressive rather than amiable, and why they hate rather than love.

The vast majority of the world's people live under extremely different conditions than do Americans. Their governments and leaders are authoritarian, exercising absolute authority. They experience coercion, privation, and a terrible struggle for sheer survival. Their conditions may approximate those to which the Hobbesian doctrine applies. This raises the question of the adequacy of contemporary social psychology to generalize about all of social life, an issue discussed in some detail in chapter 5.

The Benevolent Person

Critical philosophers, such as Bacon, Hobbes, Locke, Hume, and Adam Smith, who explored the empirical bases of all knowledge, were denounced in England as skeptics and radicals. Hobbes' view of human nature and society was seen as a direct attack on the Church. The opposition was centered among the theological scholars at Oxford and Cambridge. The Cambridge school merged Plato's philosophy with Christian theology. It held that sense data of experience revealed only phenomenal appearances, not real causes: All Truth came from a knowledge and acceptance of God. Persons were not dominated by egoism and power, but by benevolence. Because self-interest was only an elementary stage and soon supplanted by generous impulses, or *self-esteem (generositas)* (Cumberland, 1672), no social contract was necessary.

Sympathy: Empirical Arguments. One of the great English critical philosophers, David Hume (1711–1776), also disagreed with Hobbes. He believed that the study of human nature would reveal the foundations of all knowledge. He concluded that because people sometimes approve of actions that do not benefit them personally, they must be guided by more than just egoism, by both their own and others' interests. He called this unselfish motive "fellow-feeling," or *sympathy*, "the first virtuous motive which bestows a merit on any action." Hume explained sympathy in terms of a fundamental principle of human knowledge, that people when aware of others' joy or pain experience the same feelings themselves.

Adam Smith (1723–1790) was Hume's successor in philosophical eminence. When he was at Oxford he was reprimanded for reading Hume, and his copy of the *Treatise* was confiscated. Although Smith is famous for his *The Wealth of Nations* (1776) and its utilitarian, laissez-faire economic theory, he agreed with Hume that there was no necessary conflict between self-interest and sympathetic concern with others' well-being. In his earlier work, *The Theory of Moral Sentiments* (1759), he had explained a wide range of social behavior by *sympathy*, from a person's sense of justice to a sense of propriety or "good taste."

He distinguished between two types of sympathy, a spontaneous feeling and a reflective one. In one you immediately experienced another's emotions; in the other, after consideration of the other's situation, you understood the feelings whether or not you felt the same way yourself. Allport (1954) explained the first as probably a "conditioned-reflex" and the second as "cognitive."

Among a number of late 19th and early 20th century thinkers, a view of human nature that emphasized the benevolent and social impulses was predominant. Sympathy was "sovereign" among only a few, however, and hardly ever "simple." Herbert Spencer (1820–1903) identified essentially the same two types of sympathy that Adam Smith had, and added a third. Spencer could hardly be termed a humanist, because both his view of human nature and his social philosophy emphasized harsh self-interest in the evolutionary struggle for survival and a laissez-faire society that permitted the fittest to emerge. But he viewed sympathy as a minor mutation in evolutionary development, needed to account for people's social tendencies, but to be confined to family circles and not permitted to intrude on public policy. A German psychologist contributed the most thorough and subtle analysis of sympathy, dissecting it into eight distinct types, each with its own German appellation (Scheler, 1923).

Sympathy: A Social Instinct. For some, the idea became a social instinct. The sociologist Giddings (1896) explained the development of society and its institutions by a universal *consciousness of kind*. The French psychologist Ribot (1897) also viewed sympathy as basic to all social life. The famous revolutionary and anarchist Prince Kropotkin (1902) in his book *Mutual Aid* posited an instinct of *human solidarity* that accounted for human evolution better than individual self-interest. William McDougall (1908), who wrote one of the first systematic social psychology texts, described a number of social instincts, including *gregariousness*. However, for him sympathy was a person's general tendency to reproduce another's emotions rather than a specific instinct. These and other instinct theorists, such as Trotter (1916), whose chauvinistic war-time work glorified the English social instincts over the German, were discredited when social psychology, after extensive critical examination of the instinctual thesis, rejected it almost unanimously (see chapter 3).

Sympathy in Modern Social Psychology. Empirical research on sympathy and its constituent feelings and motives, such as benevolence, empathy, affiliation, and cooperation, began in the 1930s. Its humanistic impetus was the hardship suffered by many Americans during the Great Depression (Allport, 1954, 1968). Public funds supported scholarly compilations of what was known about cooperative behavior from early empirical studies (May & Doob, 1937) and from anthropological evidence (Mead, 1937). Lois Murphy in the same year, (1937) published her systematic field observations of nursery school children and found frequent occurrence of sympathetic acts, although not as prevalent as aggressive behavior.

Interest in sympathy raised questions of *empathy:* To what degree does one person experience another person's emotional feelings? How is a person able to recognize another's emotions? The issue had been initiated in Darwin's (1872) classical work (see chapter 2) and explored by early experimental social psychologists. During the 1940s and 1950s the topic of *social perception,* or what became *person perception,* was a favorite one for experimenters, primarily because it was easy to design a laboratory study involving one person's behavior, judgments, feelings, or attitudes, and the *accuracy* of another person's "perceptions" of those events (Bruner & Tagiuri, 1954; Tagiuri, 1969). However, the problem as narrowly formulated—the accuracy of one person's perception of another—foundered upon the exposure of crippling flaws of method that invalidated most of the accumulated findings (Cronbach, 1955; Crow & Hammond, 1957). Even though more sophisticated and valid methods have been designed, it has never regained the favor of those days. As we see in later chapters, the larger topic of person perception has been developed as a major one in contemporary social psychology.

A different path toward recognition of a person's social nature— often equated, although mistakenly, with Hume's sympathy rather than with Hobbes' selfishness—derived from George Mead's (1924–1925, 1934) theoretical exposition of the development of the *self.* His theory that a person was inherently social because the self-system developed out of the ability to assume another's perspective, to *take the role of the other,* and Cooley's related work (see chapter 2), became well-known and influential among social psychologists but generated little empirical research.

During the period of optimism and expansion immediately following World War II, (see chapter 4), the humanistic, benign view of human nature was dominant in much research by social psychologists, for example, in the areas of group dynamics and human relations. Findings that *democratic leadership* was preferable to *authoritarian* (Lippitt, 1940), *group learning* superior to *individual* (Perlmutter & de Montmollin, 1952), and *cooperation* more productive than *competition* (Deutsch, 1949), for example, tended to reaffirm that view.

Gregariousness often had been coupled with sympathy in this model of human nature, just as an individual alone or aloof could be assumed to be selfish or egotistical. The issue reemerged in Schachter's (1959) extensive research on *affiliative behavior*, which provided experimental evidence of the social and personal antecedents of the desire to be with others. Another influential reesearch contribution with a similar implicit view of human nature was Latané and Darley's (1968) landmark study of helping behavior, prompted initially by the unresponsive witnesses to a notorious brutal murder.

These and other pioneering studies have expanded into a general and highly diversified area of contemporary social psychology often referrred to as *pro-social behavior*, a designation that clearly reflects its heritage from Hume's sympathy.

Enlightened Hedonism: The Utilitarians

Influenced by Adam Smith's (1776) great treatise on economic theory and its central principle of the pursuit of self-interest, Jeremy Bentham (1748–1832) made hedonism the foundation of his philosophical system. He applied it to the understanding of all forms of social activity and proclaimed that pain and pleasure are our "sovereign masters." He believed that the degree of pleasure or pain could be measured in comparable units. His "hedonistic calculus" analyzed the dimensions of various feelings, such as their intensity, duration and purity, in order to predict a person's reaction to situations.

It would be a mistake to conclude that Smith, Bentham, and other *utilitarians* assumed that a person's essential nature was "selfish" and that they neglected others' well-being in the pursuit of their own pleasure. Their principle of *utility*, the tendency to produce the greatest possible happiness of the greatest number, distinguished among various feelings of happiness. It evaluated a person's motives as good or bad, depending on whether they led to harmony between one's own and others' interests, or to disunity. In his major work, Bentham (1789) said that "the dicates of utility are neither more nor less than the dictates of the most extensive and enlightened benevolence."

In the political struggles of the times, Bentham was neither a conservative nor a revolutionary: The principle of utility was his criterion in efforts to reform legislature, to improve the penal system, and to make the British constitution more democratic by the introduction of universal suffrage. He opposed the existing assumptions that a "contract" existed between princes with their natural rights and subjects who were bound to obey in exchange for protection. But he also rejected the French revolutionaries' proclamations of the "universal rights of man," regardless of the well-being of society (Höffding, 1955).

The utilitarian thesis, based on a hedonist view of human nature, had general implications for the form of society. Essentially it implied a liberal free-enterprise democracy, with a policy of laissez-faire, or minimum government interference in an individual's pursuit of happiness. With certain safeguards, such as the right to criticize existing institutions, the greatest good of the greatest number would automatically be achieved. It was no accident that these principles were built into the American constitution (Parrington, 1927).

Utilitarianism in Contemporary Social Psychology. The utilitarian view of human nature is well represented in the theories and research of contemporary social psychology. Utility theory and the concept of *economic man*, so important in economics, also have been utilized to account for social behavior: as in *exchange theory's* assumption that interpersonal relations develop in terms of expectations of relative rewards and costs. A number of distinctive areas of inquiry assume that persons attempt to avoid unpleasant states: theories of *reinforcement, tension reduction, stress avoidance,* and *dissonance reduction.*

In the simplest terms, *reinforcement theories* of social psychology substitute the concepts of reward and punishment, or positive and negative reinforcement, for the concept of pleasure with its dualistic, mind–body connotations (Dollard & Miller, 1950). Depending on whether social behavior is positively or negtively reinforced, its reoccurrence under similar circumstances becomes more or less probable. Thus, a person's entire pattern of social activity ultimately derives from past experiences of reward and punishment. Of course, the complexity and sophistication of contemporary *reinforcement, stimulus–response,* or *behaviorist* theories, as we see in subsequent discussions, are light years beyond this elementary statement (Berger & Lambert, 1968).

All motivational theories in social psychology assume *tension reduction* and are variously disguised forms of hedonism (Allport, 1968-1969). The basic paradigm views a person as recurrently experiencing specific *drives, needs,* or *forces,* originating either internally or from the external environment, which generate a state of tension in the person. Because tension is assumed to be unpleasant, social behavior occurs in an effort to reestablish the person's presumed tension-free equilibrium. These "deficit" theories of motivation have been criticized on the basis of research findings (Hunt, 1965), but they and their hedonistic model of human nature still are predominant in contemporary social psychology.

Dissonance theory (Festinger, 1957) has been one of the most influential doctrines of its era. Although astoundingly simple, it was a fecund source of ingenious research hypotheses for a generation of busy experimental social psychologists. It stated that *cognitive dissonance* arises in a person who has two ideas, beliefs, "facts," attitudes, or other thoughts, one of which implies the opposite of the other. The thesis is similar to Heider's (1958) *balance theory*, foreshadowed in his earlier articles and the circulation of informal copies of his manuscript. Both theories and research derived from them are discussed in a later chapter. Clearly, dissonance theory is similar to tension-reduction thinking in its hedonistic postulate that persons act to avoid or escape unpleasantness; except that the "tension" is cognitive rather than motivational. The two elements of Epicurean philosophy are repeated here: abnegation of desire and mental serenity.

Hedonism has had many adherents and has taken many forms throughout intellectual history, from the ancient Greeks, to Freud and his "pleasure-principle," to contemporary social psychologists. Without specification of a model of human nature and a theoretical context it becomes a truism. An example is the recent pervasives use of *stress* as an explanatory construct in social psychology (McGrath, 1970). It assumes quite different theoretical significance depending on the motivational modality and its implicit model of a person: *cognitive* (a thinking, rational being); *conative* (a striving, reactive being); or *affective* (an emotional, irrational being).

A Person as a Copying Machine: Suggestion and Imitation

Of all the attempted unitary explanations of human social behavior, *suggestion* and *imitation* are the most direct classical ancestors of contemporary social psychology. Like most major ideas, they can be traced back to ancient Greece; but they were potent influences at the threshold of the modern scientific discipline and the issues persist in today's theories and research. Both terms refer to a process of influence of one person by another: *suggestion* of a person's ideas or thinking, *imitation* of a person's activity. However, the distinction between them has not always been clear nor maintained, for example, Tarde (1901/1903) and his followers used the term *suggestion-imitation*.

Suggestion and Suggestibility. Theories of "suggestion" and "suggestibility" had two distinct paths into social psychology. One led from medieval mysticsm and faith healing, "animal magnetism," and hypnosis to French clinical psychiatry; and resulted in the wedding of social and "abnormal" psychology, a match which lasted until relatively recent times. The other derived originally from Aristotle's thinking about the "association of ideas," and then from St. Augustine, but was developed fully by the 19th century British associationists. It helped to shape the first behaviorist theory of social psychology (Allport, 1924).

The belief that a person could intentionally influence another person's thinking and actions by means of some type of emanation was current in 18th century Europe. Boring (1929) traced it back to Paracelsus, a 15th century mystic and physician. The therapy of "laying on of hands," part of general folklore, was practiced by famous magical healers all through that era (as it still is today in many parts of the world, including America). Mesmer (1779/1948), a Viennese physician, at first thought the phenomenon was due to physical magnetism, but later explained it by "animal magnetism." Although his theories were credulous and his practices bizarre, his demonstrations, complete with magnetized wand, seances and trances, were most convincing. His system was widely adopted in that period. Surgeons used mesmerism as an anesthetic, against virulent opposition of the medical establishment (Boring, 1929).

Braid (1843/1889), a conservative British physician, rejected Mesmer's explanations and modified his technique. He brought mesmerism into scientific respectability under the name *hypnosis* (originally *neurypnology*), and provided a physiological basis for the phenomenon, explaining it as a "nervous sleep" induced by sensory fixation. Gradually, he shifted to a more psychological theory involving the fixation of attention, and recognized a process of *suggestion* (Boring, 1929).

The practice of hypnotism by French psychiatrists, by Liébault at the Nancy and by Charcot at the Salpêtrière clinics, marked its legitimation by the medical profession. There was still dispute, however, regarding the underlying process. The Nancy school viewed it as a normal psychological phenomenon, essentially accepting Braid's theory that *suggestion* was responsible. Charcot disagreed, and considered hypnosis to be an hysterical phenomenon symptomatic of an abnormal state. The process involved was the dissociation of consciousness, a "splitting of the personality." His view prevailed in the early social psychology. It directly stimulated Gustave Le Bon (1895/1896), considered by some to be the father of the modern era. His contribution is discussed here. The acceptance of the linkage between social and abnormal behavior was marked by Morton Prince, Charcot's American student, who enlarged the *Journal of Abnormal Psychology* to become the *Journal of Abnormal and Social Psychology* in 1922. Not until 1965 did it become the present *Journal of Personality and Social Psychology*.

Suggestion also had a "cooler" or more cognitive tradition. It was related to the "association of ideas" a conception that went back as far as Aristotle, who wrote of one thing or idea suggesting another. In various forms, this doctrine was central to the thinking of the British 19th century associationists. Thomas Brown (1820) wrote of the "Primary Laws of Suggestion," by which he meant the laws of association. Sir William Hamilton (1861), introduced the "Law of Redintegration" or "Totality." He believed that all ideas originally were whole and that one idea suggested another because they were reassuming their original unity. He discovered this conception in the writings of St. Augustine.

Although Hamilton's conception sounds like an anticipation of the Gestalt psychology emphasis upon wholeness and good form (*prägnanz*), he based the process on conditions of similarity or contiguity, a formulation more acceptable to learning theorists. Allport (1968–1969) saw the association-of-ideas theory of suggestion as a direct antecedent of the *conditioned response*, used extensively in Floyd Allport's (1924) systematic presentation of social psychology within a physiological, experimental, and behaviorist framework.

Imitation. As a significant theory of social behavior *imitation* has fewer ancient roots than *suggestion*, although Allport (1954) did attribute it ultimately to Plato. He related the "simple and sovereign theories," Sympathy, Suggestion, and Imitation, to Plato's three psychological functions, the *affective*, or feeling, the *cognitive*, or thinking, and the *conative*, or acting.

Not until the 19th century, however, did *imitation* attain prominence, in the work of Walter Bagehot (1875), an English economist and Social Darwinist, who believed that societies, like biological organisms, progressed through evolutionary stages and could be classified as more or less civilized or culturally advanced. Like so many of his generation who opposed the democratic trend of the times (Carlyle had published his anti-populist *French Revolution* in 1837), Bagehot was concerned about *conformity* and its possible excesses. He blamed it on *imitation*, the central driving force behind social behavior. He observed that people had a universal tendency to copy others, to conform to the customs, conventions, and fashions all around them. Unconscious imitation, he proclaimed, was the most powerful force in the evolution of society. Although admittedly it served a conservative function, Bagehot bemoaned its larger consequences. He glorified the true builders of the nation, those strong-minded, inventive individuals who could resist mass-mindedness.

After Darwin's (1859) epochal work on evolution, many social thinkers embraced instinctual theories of human motivation (see chapter 2). *Imitation*, as a universal tendency to reproduce others' acts, appeared on many lists of instincts. Even William James (1890), the most influential psychologist of his era, said that imitation was an "instinct in the fullest sense." He also put his stamp of approval on the theory of *ideomotor response*, that an idea inevitably generates an action. Braid had used it as an explanation of hypnosis, and in the thinking of that period it was related to the imitative instinct. In the next section we follow the path of ideomotor theory, or *dynamogenesis*, into contemporary social psychology.

The most influential proponent of imitation as the basis of all social behavior undoubtedly was Gabriel Tarde (1901/1903). He proclaimed that "society is imitation." He and Gustave Le Bon (1895/1896), who viewed suggestion as the central process in social life, stood at the threshold of modern social psychology. They influenced all who came after them. It is appropriate to discuss their contributions in the next section, in a review of the impact of suggestion and imitation on contemporary social psychology. First, however, let us consider briefly some of the broader implications of these theories for the nature of persons and society.

Suggestion, Imitation, and Human Nature. In contrast to the "sovereign" theories discussed previousy, egoism, hedonism, and sympathy, neither imitation nor suggestion explicitly asserted a model of human nature. Does this mean that they were free of assumptions about the nature of a person and of society? It is true that according to these doctrines people were neither selfish nor unselfish, gregarious nor misanthropic. They reproduced whatever ideas or behavior they were exposed to.

Both suggestion and imitation emerged as full-blown theories of social behavior under the influence of French (Comtean) positivism and British empiricism. The founder of positivism, August Comte (1830/1853), said that all knowledge passed through three stages, the *theological, metaphysical,* and *positive.* In the positive stage, observation takes precedence over imagination and argument. John Stuart Mill (1806–1873), who provided the most complete exposition of empiricism (Höffding, 1955), proclaimed that only observation and experience could provide new truths. Thus, both systems attempted to avoid preconceptions, to observe objectively "what was out there."

What emerged to help shape the inchoate "scientific" social psychology was an implicit model of a person as a type of mechanical device, a copying machine, lacking self-direction or even the biological processes of, for example, homeostasis or regeneration. This "machine model" of a person has been influential in contemporary social psychology and is discusssed more fully in chapter 5.

What model of society is implied by such assumptions about human nature? At one extreme, one can speculate, if people were dominated by random forces of suggestion and imitation, society would be unplanned, accidental and chaotic, vulnerable to the catastrophies of chance: for example, as in the widely publicized mass-suicide of James Jones' sect in Guiana. At the other extreme might be a highly organized, regimented regime with legions of "happy" denizens, mindlessly following a blueprint to a "brave new world." A contemporary example is Skinner's (1948) novelistic proposal to construct a society according to principles of radical behaviorism. Noteworthy in his and other engineered utopian societies, as in the famous satirical novels of Aldous Huxley (1932) and George Orwell (1949), is that not all persons can be suggestible nor imitators: An elite cadre of intelligent, goal-oriented persons must be assumed, to create and to monitor the blueprint. Such a planned society with its castes is not unlike Plato's model, or, as Orwell intended, contemporary totalitarian regimes.

Suggestion and Imitation in Modern Social Psychology. Social psychology began to emerge into the modern era and to attack the problems of becoming a legitimate science around the end of the 19th and beginning of the 20th centuries. There is a direct line of development from that period to the contemporary discipline. The dominant pioneers were two French sociologists, Gustave Le Bon

(1895/1896) and Gabriel Tarde (1901/1903), whose primary concern was understanding society by means of the study of social behavior.

Le Bon applied Charcot's theory of hypnotic suggestion and dissociation to collective behavior—crowds, groups, social institutions, even parliaments. He believed that in such social phenomena the rational individual mind was displaced. His "group mind" theory is discussed more fully in Chapter 3, where we follow the great controversies and their resolution.

Although Freud spent a year with Charcot exploring hypnosis, he did not accept his explanation of suggestion as an abnormal process with dissociation of consciousness, but preferred his own general sexual instinct theory involving parental identification. He criticized Le Bon's work extensively and formulated a group psychology in terms of his own general theory (Freud, 1922). Freud's and his followers' contributions to contemporary social psychology are reviewed in chapter 2.

Tarde's systematic "laws of imitation" reflected his training as a criminologist, jurist, and statistician, and his debt to Comte, the great French systematizer and positivist. His theory attempted to explain all collective phenomena in terms of either *imitation* or *invention*, surely an exhaustive classification. Society was imitation, and imitation a dream-state, a kind of unconscious sleepwalking. Tarde described a social psychological process that combined sympathy, suggestion, and imitation. He did not analyze "suggestion-imitation" further, because he was more concerned with its effects and conditions, although he did distinguish between two types, spontaneous and reflective. Previously we have mentioned the same two categories of sympathy. This historical distinction between two aspects of observed social behavior contributed to early theoretical debates between *behaviorist* and *cognitive-Gestaltist* investigators of the social influence process, discussed here. Tarde's thinking departed from the tradition of unitary explanations or "sovereign theories" and was the forerunner of contemporary multiprocess social influence theories.

The first social psychology textbooks, by Edward Ross (1908), and William McDougall (1908), both were indebted to the French social psychologists, especially to Tarde's theory of imitation. This was noteworthy in Ross' treatment, essentially a systematic sociological treatment of social and collective behavior in terms of imitation. McDougall (1926) was a "bio- evolutionary" psychologist whose "An Introduction to Social Psychology" aimed to contribute to "a psychology that will at last furnish the much needed basis of the social sciences and of the comprehensive science of sociology" (p. 17). He criticized sociologists such as Comte and Durkheim who ignored or paid only lip-service to psychology, but quoted Tarde's theory extensively, and Fouillée, discussed here.

Closely related to suggestion and imitation was *ideo-motor theory*, mentioned previously as Braid's physiological explanation of hypnosis. The theory was generalized to explain all of society by Fouillée (1908), a French Social Darwinist, with his concept of *idée-forces*. He theorized that the dominating force in any social group was its central image or idea, which inevitably generated corresponding social activity. He explained this in terms of the psychological process of ideomotor action. Le Bon also called upon ideo-motor theory to account for crowd behavior. Émile Durkheim, another great French progenitor of contemporary social psychology, had argued against this "reductionist" thesis, and for the autonomy of social phenomena. His contribution to social psychology is discussed in chapter 2.

Ideo-motor theory, or *dynamogenesis*, provided the problems for Triplett's (1897) laboratory experiment on the effect of others' physical presence on a person's performance, usually considered to be the first experimental research in social psychology. This "alone-together" problem was investigated systematically by F.H. Allport (1924). His research on *social facilitation*, his term for the enhancement of performance due to others' physical presence, was a model for the first wave of experimental research in social psychology. The problem eventually wore itself out, due partially to an accumulation of contradictory results, until revived in contemporary social psychology by Zajonc's (1965) theoretical synthesis.

Early experimental social psychologists also were engaged in a theoretical debate about the suggestion-imitation process, which had implications for the underlying model of a person, and ultimately, of society. Early demonstrations that persons changed their opinions when exposed to those of higher status persons (Moore, 1921, Sherif, 1935) were explained in terms of *prestige-suggestion* based on principles of association. Gestalt psychologists, who assumed that persons were rational "information-processors" who behaved in terms of total patterns of phenomena rather than fragmentary bits of information, inveighed against the nonrationality and fragmentation of social events implied by the behaviorist theoretical explanation (Asch, Block, & Hertzman, 1938; Lorge, 1936). Their thesis was supported in a famous experiment on forming impressions of personality (Asch, 1946) in which single adjectives, such as "warm" or "cold," inserted into a long list of descriptive terms, changed the *Gestalt* (whole, or pattern) and its effects. Asch (1948) also wrote a systematic critique of imitation and suggestion theorizing and research in social psychology. The debate and the many research problems generated have continued into contemporary social psychology (Berger & Lambert, 1968; Zajonc, 1968–1969).

The stream of contemporary social psychology flows and branches endlessly from these early beginnings. The problem of social influence—its agents and targets, how and under what conditions it occurs—is pervasive throughout the field; in fact, it has been proposed that social psychology is the study of social influence. Certainly one finds it appearing under many topical headings in any current text: for example, in *Interpersonal Communication, Affiliation, Attraction, and Love, Aggression and Violence, Social Influence and Personal Control,*

Leadership, and *Attitudes, Prejudice, and Discrimination* (Deaux & Wrightsman, 1984). It will be important for students of the field to be aware of its early formulations, some discarded, some possibly neglected, in approaching contemporary problems, concepts, and theories. We must constantly inquire: To what degree are they new, or old wine in new bottles?

We continue our explorations of social psychology's historical antecedents in the next chapter by examining important sources of influence from the recent past. Some of the persons and issues mentioned briefly in this first chapter reappear, as they do, too, in chapter 3, where we review the periods during which social psychology's great, persistent controversies were "resolved," and its scientific status was established.

Chapter 2
Influences From the Recent Past

Modern social psychology's roots can be traced back to antiquity and classical social thought but it emerged as a scientific discipline only in recent times. August Comte (1830) often is nominated as its founder, since he conceived of a "true final science,"*la morale*, that would combine biological and sociological perspectives in its model of the individual person (Allport, 1954). His status as the only "father of social psychology" is arbitrary, however. One also could select Plato, Aristotle, Triplett, Ross, or McDougall, or others whose contributions were discussed in chapter 1 (Sahakian, 1974).

For our purpose, it may be more profitable to leave such questions to the historians and to focus on discernible influences from the recent past on contemporary social psychology. We can assume that the earlier philosophical and theoretical traditions must flow through those channels.

THE IMPACT OF DARWIN

The influence of Charles Darwin on western thought is acknowledged by scholars to be massive and pervasive. Even in social psychology it would require a volume to trace all of the varied effects of his doctrine of natural selection, survival, and evolution of species (1859), and his theory of emotional expression and recognition (1872).

Instinct Theory in Social Psychology

Darwin's theory and research demonstrated that the human species was the final product of an age-old evolutionary process that encompassed all biological organisms. Its major impact on social psychology was to legitimate instinctual theories. Even James (1890) and Dewey (1917) succumbed to the Darwinian instinct hypothesis, although only temporarily. Another giant of the intellectual world, Sigmund Freud, also was powerfully affected by evolutionary theory. William McDougall (1908) attempted to construct a complete theory of social behavior from instinct building blocks. The trio, Darwin, Freud, and McDougall, were credited with assuring the ascendancy of irrational theories in social psychology until recent time (Allport, 1954). The contributions to social psychology of James, Dewey, and Freud are reviewed later in this chapter.

Instinct theory itself gradually yielded to the American pragmatic tradition with its egalitarian ethos and distrust of nativistic theories. If all men were created equal, how could some inherit characteristics that were superior to others' genetic birthright? The rising theory of behaviorism, with its implications that anyone could learn to do anything, was much more congenial to the American temperament.

Knight Dunlap (1919) and his followers contributed to the demise of instinct theory with their varied and devastating attacks. For example, they pointed to the lack of factual proof of the existence of instincts, and the impossibility of distinguishing between primary (instinctual) and secondary (derived) motives in human behavior. Instinct theory departed but left many Trojan horses remaining within social psychology's walls. McDougall himself changed his terminology from *instinct to propensity*. Others have evaded the contentious issue of innateness by adopting such noncommittal terms as *wishes, desires, needs,* and *motives*.

The Issue of Animal Mentality

The theory of evolution asserted continuity between human and nonhuman species. Because mind was an unchallenged attribute of humans, the theory required that subhuman species possess mind in some form or degree. The resolution of the dilemma of subhuman mental activity, and the question of where on the phylogenetic scale mind appeared, brought comparative psychology to the fore in the late 19th and early 20th centuries.

Although the issue was central to the new science of psychology, the controversy was carried on mostly by biologists and physiologists. All agreed that humans had minds—without defining that mysterious attribution—but they varied in their willingness to locate the beginnings of mentality higher or lower on the evolutionary scale. At one extreme, Jennings (1904, 1906) argued that the reactions of protozoa, the lowest form of creature, were too variable and modifiable to permit a completely physicalist explanation. At the other, it was proposed that all psychological terms such as *sensation, memory*, and *learning* be discarded, and only "objective" terms be used to describe animal behavior (Boring, 1929). The problem brought experiments with animals into psychological laboratories.

The most influential research was conducted by E. L. Thorndike (1898) who enclosed cats, dogs, or chicks in boxes and pens with a release mechanism that operated in a specific manner. He observed their efforts to learn how to escape. From these studies he concluded that these animals did not possess "mind," in the human sense of imagery and rational thought. They learned by forming associations, by what Morgan (1890) later called "trial-and-error." Thorndike explained the retention of chance correct associations and the disappearance of incorrect ones by his *Law of Effect*, that pleasurable responses retroactively "stamp in" the immediately preceding associations.

Behaviorism

J. B. Watson was the second PhD in the new department of psychology at the University of Chicago. His thesis, on the maze learning of the white rat, concluded that only kinesthetic sensations were required for rat learning: That is, no higher mental processes need be assumed. He constructed a system of psychology in terms of objectively observable behavior, which avoided all mentalistic concepts. With the advent and success of Watson's theory of *behaviorism* (Watson, 1913, 1919), comparative psychology changed from "animal psychology" to a general physiological psychology. The distinction between animal and human behavior essentially disappeared. Behaviorism changed the face of all psychology and has had extensive influence in almost every aspect of social psychology.

Underlying the question of animal mentality just discussed was the dread of any taint of indeterminacy by those dedicated to science. "Mental" activity implies greater variability of response, more options and choice, less determinate relations between stimuli and behavior. The ghost of free will had walked through the laboratories and raised cold sweat on scientific brows. Watson's radical behaviorism was one answer to the problem: He dispensed with mentality, consciousness, imagery and thought, by relegating them to physiological and neurological activity.

But Watson's behaviorism was not the only answer. It should be noted that one of his professors was George Herbert Mead, who taught the course in animal behavior. Because Mead was preoccupied with the "mind-body problem," animal mind was one of his central concerns. He provided his own solution in his *social behaviorism*: Influenced by Darwin, he said that mind was not a separate type of "stuff" but an activity of the organism in its efforts to survive (Mead, 1903). But he was not widely read nor understood. Watson (1930, p. 274) confessed in his autobiography: "I took courses and seminars with Mead. I didn't understand him in the classroom, but for years Mead took a great interest in my animal experimentation, and many a Sunday he and I spent in the laboratory watching my rats and monkeys. On these comradely exhibitions and at his home I understood him." Mead's theory has been influential thoroughout social psychology, although often misinterpreted. We discuss it later in this chapter.

Even though behaviorists were adamantly opposed to instinctual theories, they were strongly influenced by Darwin. The evolutionary assumption that behavior develops as an adaptation to the environment in the struggle for survival is a central pillar of behaviorist theories (Berkowitz, 1969). That keystone of learning theory, the *Law of Effect*, has been recognized as "a special case of Darwin's *Law of Natural Selection*, applied to habits (social or otherwise)" (Berger & Lambert, 1968).

Social Darwinism

The amorphous field of social psychology always has been concerned with social entities and processes more comprehensive than the individual person: With groups, collectivities, culture, and social change. Evolutionary theory was the impetus for the rise of *Social Darwinism* in many countries: The biological theory was applied to social groups instead of to organisms. Theorists disagreed on the nature of groups and on the individual's relation to society but they all assumed essentially the same evolutionary process in social change (Sahakian 1974). Central to their credo was Darwin's idea of the survival of the fittest, applied to societies. This provided a rationale for ordering nations and ethnic groups in terms of their power and eminence, which they believed was positively correlated with their degree of advancement on the presumed evolutionary scale. Thus, some people were the most civilized and culturally advanced, and others were retarded and undeveloped.

William Graham Sumner (1906) was a social Darwinist whose concepts *folkways* and *mores* were precursors of the contemporary study of norms and normative processes. He proclaimed that patterns of social behavior that survive from experience must thereby be the fittest—consistent with his laissez-faire ideology. The massive pioneering studies of *Folk Psychology* (Lazarus & Steinthal, 1860–1890; Wundt 1916), an anthropological–historical perspective on the development of custom, myth, ritual, and language in human societies, reflected evolutionary theory in many places. It had a powerful but indirect influence on the emerging social psychology.

Interpersonal Perception

Darwin's (1872) second great work, on the expression and recognition of emotions, stimulated a number of eminent psychologists to begin research on that topic. It has persisted as a problem in contemporary social psychology. He and Heider (1944, 1958) are primarily responsible for what have now become the studies of *interpersonal perception* and *attribution theory*, areas of research concerned with one of social psychology's central questions: How does one person understand another person's psychological qualities and states (Tagiuri, 1969)? The cognitive theoretical orientation that is predominant in these areas joins the behaviorist, psychodynamic, and sociocultural perspectives in reflecting Darwin's pervasive influence.

PHYSIOLOGICAL AND EXPERIMENTAL PSYCHOLOGY

The founder of modern scientific psychology was Wilhelm Wundt (1862), who used the interchangeable terms *physiological psychology* to describe its contents and *experimental psychology* to describe its methods. Many had prepared the ground, of course: Johnannes Müller, the world-famous experimental physiologist, was Wundt's professor. The great Helmholtz, who measured the rate of transmission of the nervous impulse in 1850, was a senior colleague. Herbart (1776–1841), a philosopher, had written the most influential systematic psychology of the time in 1825. He had insisted that psychology be a separate science, empirical—although not experimental—with mathematical laws. Even the discredited pseudoscience of *phrenology*, which held public sway for a century, contributed to the knowledge of the central nervous system through the works of Gall (1758–1828), and led to research on the physiology of the brain (Boring, 1929).

Experimental Social Psychology

In the third century B.C., two Greek astronomers, Aristarchus and Eratosthenes, carried out the first scientific experiments (Boring, 1929). They measured the distance between the earth, moon, and sun, and the size of the earth. After Roger Bacon in the 13th century, the experiment had been recognized as the basic method of science. Physical science, that is, astronomy and physics, provided the model, methods, and some of the problems for physiology and the new science, *physiological and experimental psychology*.

Quite early in the development of psychology, the distinction between Wundt and his experimentalists and the nonexperimental but empirical Brentano and his school was crucial in distingishing "true scientists" from those tainted with philosophy. Although American psychology rejected Wundt's parochial definition of experimental psychology, it embraced the experimental tradition as intrinsic to science.

The large majority of social psychologists are trained in psychology, identify professionally with that subculture and share its values. From the beginning of modern social psychology, the experimental tradition has been supreme. As previously mentioned, Wundt's 10-volume *Folk Psychology*, a non-experimental "natural history of man" had little direct influence upon the developing discipline. Early publications by William McDougall (1908) and Floyd Allport (1924), as well as influential handbooks of experimental social psychology (Murphy & Murphy, 1931; Murphy, Murphy, & Newcomb, 1937) reflected the dominant experimental tradtion.

Many of social psychology's renowned accomplishments undoubtedly have resulted from ingenious experimentation. But critics, from Brentano to the present day, including the revered William James, have protested that an overemphasis on method would sacrifice important research problems. The veneration of the experimental method as the supreme criterion of scientific respectability has had its costs as well as its rewards. As we see later in this chapter, social psychology's roots were spread more widely than just the soil of psycholgy: in that of sociology and anthropology, especially. Relations between "establishment" social psychology and the other, primarily nonexperimental social sciences have suffered: for example, the rather cool co-existence with "sociological" social psychology. This question recurs later in chapter 5, in the discussion of the "crisis in social psychology."

Psychophysics: Measurement and Scaling Theory

Contemporary social psychologists are taught methods of "mental measurement," including theories and techniques of "attitude scaling," the construction of questionnaires for measuring the magnitude and direction of attitudes. This body of knowledge originated in the study of *psychophysics*, or "mind–body relations," whose methods and problems occupied the attention of all 19th century experimental psychologists.

Gustave Fechner (1860), a German physician, physicist, and mathematician by training and a philosopher by avocation, created experimental psychophysics in his efforts to correct Herbart's dominant psychology of the day. He disagreed with Herbart's inclusion of *metaphysics*, the philosophical inquiry into first principles such as the nature of reality or knowlege, as a component of scientific psychology, and his rejection of the experimental method. Fechner set out to prove experimentally that "mind" and "body" were one, by describing their precise relations of functional dependence. His experiments involved comparing objective *stimuli* with subjects' *sensations*, inferred from reports of their experience. He asked: When I objectively increase or decrease the magnitude of a weight, light, or sound, at what point does a person experience the difference? He created systematic techniques for making these comparisons, utilizing Herbart's idea of the *limen*, or threshold of consciousness, which he called the *j.n.d.*, or "just noticeable difference."

Fechner succeeded in producing a general mathematical formula. When he realized that a physiologist, E. H. Weber, had obtained the same experimental results earlier, he named the relationship Weber's Law. History has changed it to the Weber–Fechner Law.

Although Fechner's theories of mind–body relations have not survived, he was the first to achieve precise "mental measurement," the beginning of quantitative experimental psychology. Modern psychologists recognize that his formula describes the relationship between two different methods of measuring the same construct (Ferguson, 1966). But his psychophysical methods persist and have been developed and extended in contemporary social psychology.

An American psychologist, L. L. Thurstone (1927), adopted psychophysical methods, for example, having subjects judge the similarity of pairs of attitudinal statements rather than lifted weights or other physical stimuli, and demonstrated that attitudes could be measured. His standardized Thurstone–Chave (1929) attitude scales toward many social objects, such as members of a minority group or religion, have been used extensively in social psychological research.

Rensis Likert (1932) simplified the laborious Thurstone scaling procedures and demonstrated he could obtain similar results. Rather than use judges to evaluate items and to locate them upon a scale, he presented attitudinal statements directly to subjects and asked them to respond in one of five categories, from strongly approve to strongly disapprove. He popularized the Likert scale, making it available for large scale attitude surveys. Louis Guttman's (1941) mathematical developments produced criteria for assessing the degree of unidimensionality, or purity, of a scale. Clyde Coombs (1950, 1964) extended the use of psychophysical methods to generate scales with different degrees of quantitative power and corresponding amounts of information.

Mental measurement and attitude scaling were not the only contributions of experimental psychophysics to social psychology. Studies of lifted weights "established the effect of a temporarily operative frame of reference not manifest in the S's experience" (Scheerer, 1954, p. 109). The concept *frame of reference*, now standard, perhaps overemployed, in social psychological explanations, was introduced by Wever and Zener (1928) in their analysis of psychophysical research. It was adopted by Sherif (1935, 1936) in his classical study of social norms and his later work on social judgments (Sherif & Hovland, 1953, 1961).

Cognitive Social Psychology

In the latter half of the 20th century, the *cognitive theoretical orientation* increasingly has become the dominant persective in social psychology. Although a stream of thought invariably has many sources and tributaries, this orientation can be traced to important developments in and around experimental and physiological psychology of the 19th century.

Wundt had restricted experimental psychology to the analysis of sensations, a systematic introspection of the contents of consciousness. He excluded the study of the "higher mental processes" because it did not fit his experimental procedures. But Brentano and his disciples, for whom psychic processes rather than contents were the central focus, succeeded in bringing "thought" into the laboratory. From their Wurzburg school came the study of *imageless thought* and Ach's concept of the *determining tendency*: the experience of perceiving potentialities without having any sensations or imagery. "So far as consciousness goes, one does one's thinking before one knows what he is to think about" (Boring, 1929, p. 397). This was similar to Helmholtz' doctrine of *unconscious inference*, "that perception may contain many experiential data that are not immediately represented in the stimulus" (Boring, 1929. p. 300). Helmholtz said that the process was analogous to conscious inference, but that a person did not have to engage in a rational thought process to perceive these meanings.

These ideas are reflected in many similar concepts in what has become *cognitive social psychology*: for example, Bartlett's (1932) use of *schema* in his classical study of social memory; Bruner's (1951) *hypothesis*; and Kuethe's (1962) *schemata*. A relatively new development in social psychology called *expectation theory* derives from the same roots. Scheerer (1954) broadened the Gestalt concept *silent organization* to refer to all such concepts: "This construct would cover the formation of frames of reference and mental sets, the development of both generalizations and concepts in their preverbal form, and the carrying over of implicit organizing principles from one problem-solving situation to another" (p. 110).

Brentano's students and followers created some revolutionary changes in psychology that made a major difference in contemporary social psychology. The catalyst was the great intellectual exodus from Hitler's pre-war Europe to America. In the next section we discuss some of the fruits of that fortuitous harvest, the influence of *Gestalt psychology*, Lewin's *field theory*, and Heider's *social phenomenology*.

GESTALT PSYCHOLOGY AND PHENOMENOLOGY

Gestalt psychology was a revolutionary movement of the early 20th century in Germany, aimed at overthrowing establishd psychology and reconstituting its basic assumptions and methods. It succeeded more broadly than its founders could have foreseen, especially in its pervasive and lasting influence upon social psychology. Its essential thrust was against Wundt's insistence upon analytical introspection of the contents of consciousness as the only legitimate path to psychological knowledge. Gestalt eschewed analysis and insisted on the validity of a holistic phenomenological description of conscious experience. It made its impact by a combination of ingenious experimental demonstrations, ruthless theoretical critiques of the prevailing experimental psychology, and bold, sustained polemical writings.

Like all new intellectual movements, many aspects of Gestalt psychology were not entirely original; nor could it have arisen until others had created a receptive *Zeitgeist* (Boring, 1929). Its emphasis on "wholeness of the mind" and form rather than substance could be traced back to Aristotle. More immediately, it developed out of Husserl's *phenomenology* and Brentano's *act psychology*; and the doctrine of *Gestaltqualität*, or *form-quality*. This school, at Graz, Austria, was an earlier reaction against Wundt's "chemical view of perception" as composed of a bundle of sensations. It originated in Mach's (1886) recognition of form as a new type of "sensation," and essentially was a merging of Wundt's content and Brentano's act psychologies.

Gestalt Psychology

Gestalt psychology began in Germany with an ingenious experiment on the perception of movement by three former students of Stumpf, a disciple of Brentano. Wertheimer (1912) and his assistants, Köhler and Koffka, used the *phi phenomenon*, now so familiar to us in motion pictures, to demonstrate that by arranging a particular temporal pattern of stimuli, perception of movement could be produced in the absence of any "real" movement. They realized that the implications of their research spread far beyond the actual findings: Psychological experience did not have a one-to-one correspondence to objective, external, unitary stimuli. They began an active program to extend, develop, and systematize Gestalt psychology. In addition to their experimental research on perceptual phenomena, extensive critical analysis, and virulent attacks on the established psychology, Koffka (1924) produced a systematic Gestalt treatise on mental development, showing how it could be viewed in terms of successive stages of cognitive reorganization. Köhler (1917) introduced the concept *insight* in his landmark study, *The Mentality of Apes*, and undermined the accepted incremental, trial-and-error learning theory of the day. Wertheimer (1945) produced an experimentally supported Gestalt theory of productive thinking.

The new theory differed from the established psychology in specific ways: It insisted on the priority of immediate and whole experience, rather than its analysis into "artificial" elements; it denied that there was any one-to-one relationship between stimuli and phenomenal experience; it asserted that meaning was provided directly by the dynamic structure of "wholes" (Gestalten) rather than from the fortuitous temporal contiguity and association of elements; and it rejected "explanatory" concepts that did not explain, such as *attention* and *attitude*. Gestaltists emphasized that unitary structures were more than just the sum of the components, but had dynamic principles that influenced perception and thought. A change in any part resulted in a new whole. Some of their laws of dynamic structure were: *prägnanz*, the tendency of "natural form" to be emphasized in structures; *closure*, the tendency for incomplete structures to gravitate towards completion, or "perfect form"; and *figure-ground*, the tendency in visual perception to perceive an object with contours against a less distinct background, with interchangeability of figure and ground, and the capacity of each to modify the other.

Gestalt Influence Upon Social Psychology

The originators of Gestalt psychology did not contribute directly to social psychology. Their work was introduced to America and interpreted for social psychologists by Robert MacLeod, the great humanist and statesman of social psychology. As a graduate student he had "discovered" the Swedish David Katz' Gestalt-inspired research on color perception and translated his *The World of Color* into English (Katz, 1935).

MacLeod himself did little research, having been called successively to the chairs of the Swarthmore, McGill, and Cornell psychology departments. He wrote, taught social psychology from a Gestalt, phenomenological, and field-theoretical perspective, and stimulated and encouraged others' research and publication. For example, his two junior colleagues at Swarthmore, Krech and Crutchfield (1948), wrote that he should have been a co-author of their influential ground-breaking text that presented social psychology from a systematic holistic phenomenological position. MacLeod also acted directly to assist the relocation of the Gestalt psychologists, including Lewin and Heider, in American universities before World War II and the Nazi holocaust.

Of the many social psychologists who helped to assimilate and to extend Gestalt psychology in America, the best-known is Solomon Asch, a student of Wertheimer. In a study of a person's first impressions of others (Asch, 1946), he demonstrated that a key adjective, such as "warm" or "cold," added to a list of descriptive words, could reorganize the meaning of the entire list and the evaluation of the person described. Consistent with Gestalt theory, the list was not just a collection of elements of content in association but a dynamic structure of meaning.

His research also challenged the nonrational implications of the ancient doctrines of imitation and prestige-suggestion as they had been reformulated in social psychology by behaviorists (Asch, 1948; Miller & Dollard, 1941). His experiments attacked the common assumption that the prestige of an author "rubbed off" on statements that then were accepted uncritically. He attached the labels *Jefferson* or *Lenin* to statements with either pro- or antidemocratic content and effected the anticipated change in evaluations of the material. But his interviews with the subjects demonstrated to him that a change in the attributed author had created a new Gestalt, a cognitive reorganization that resulted in a different interpretation of a statement's meaning: The process was a rational judgment, not an uncritical evaluation influenced by the author's reputation. He summarized his own and others' research in his systematic Gestalt treatment of social psychology (Asch, 1952). Naturally, his interpretations did not go unchallenged by the behaviorists.

Asch's (1956) best-known research, on independence and conformity, was designed in reaction against Sherif's (1935) classical studies of norm-formation. Sherif had used the well-known *autokinetic phenomenon*—a stationary, isolated light in a dark room appears to be moving—in a series of ingenious well-controlled social psychological experiments. He had demonstrated that subjects tend to replace their own judgments of the direction and amount of movement with those of their fellows; and that with repetition, a convergence of judgments occurred, interpreted by him, and widely accepted in social psychology, as the genesis of a *social norm*.

Asch inveighed against the implications of Sherif's interpretation, that people were irrationally suggestible. His own experiments were designed to demonstrate that under different conditions, when confronted with a familiar and well-structured set of stimuli rather than a highly unstructured and ambiguous one, persons would act rationally rather than fall prey to the emotions of the herd. He discovered, however, that most subjects conformed at least some of the time when the other members of their group were unanimous in their publicly announced incorrect judgments. When interviewed, however, they confessed that most indeed had perceived the stimuli correctly but had submitted to social pressure and responded incorrectly.

Asch systematically discovered the conditions under which persons either would conform or remain independent. In a series of publications, he strove to interpret the total set of results within a Gestalt framework; but his model of "rational person" had not remained unscathed. His research really had demonstrated the limitations of the "rational–irrational" dichotomy. Ironically, in an era when conformity had become a critical social problem and when social psychologists were becoming more enamored of ingenious experimental techniques than of systematic theoretical issues, his research had become famous for its dramatic demonstration of people's tendency to be influenced by group pressure against their own better judgment, and for his surreptitious employment of collaborative "subjects."

Two other members of the group of "immigrants" who have enriched American social psychology were Kurt Lewin and Fritz Heider. Each participated in and contributed to the Gestalt psychology movement in Europe; yet each developed his own distinctive theoretical system. Together they have transformed contemporary social psychology.

Lewin's *field theory*, analogous to field theory in physics (Deutsch, 1968), probably has made its greatest impact on the study of groups. His founding of the Research Center for Group Dynamics with a coterie of brilliant students, his conception of *ecological psychology*, pioneered and developed by his disciples Roger Barker and Herbert Wright (1955), and a host of other conceptual and research contributions, direct and indirect, are discussed in appropriate chapters. Even more recently has Heider's (1958) phenomenological theory of interpersonal perception become a major and growing influence upon social psychology. His contributions to *balance theory* and *attribution theory* in cognitive social psychology also are discussed in other chapters in this volume.

THE FREUDIAN REVOLUTION

Sigmund Freud's psychoanalytic theory of personality and human behavior is part of a literate person's intellectual heritage. Many of his ideas have passed into popular thought and usage; if indeed they were not there in some form at least since Shakespeare's day. It can be assumed that our readers are sufficiently familiar with the essentials of his theory.

Many social psychologists have paid tribute to Freud's major impact on their discipline, classing him with Darwin and Lewin. Yet reviewers have been unable to discover either influential theories or systematic research developments—with a few notable exceptions, and those from an earlier era— that derive directly from psychoanalytic theory (Hall & Lindzey, 1954, 1968–1969; Murphy, 1956).

Freud's influence upon social psychology has been "cultural": general, diffuse, and indirect. It has not led to cumulative, systematic theory and research. If anything, it appears that it has been waning with the current hegemony of cognitive social psychology. His concepts have become prevalent in social psychological usage, but either redefined within a different systematic framework, or divorced from any theory, used as after-the-fact "explanations." Yet his general assumptions regarding the dynamic, emotional–motivational nature of a person persist in theories and research that we refer to from time to time as the *psychodynamic theoretical orientation*.

Many factors appear to be involved in Freud's lack of systematic, persistent, and cumulative influence upon social psychology: his instinctual assumptions; his parochial 19th century Vienese middle-class viewpoint, especially regarding gender; his clinical, nonexperimental methods; his colorful terminology derived from Greek mythology; his broad-ranging speculations that rest on inadequate empirical support; the difficulty of testing his equivocal "flip–flop" theory; and the only partial success of those controlled studies that have attempted to test his theoretical hypotheses.

In spite of the foregoing, there have been major research contributions to social psychology that derived from Freudian theory and that, at the time, had substantial impact. It may contribute to a more balanced evaluation of Freud's historical influence to review them briefly.

The recognition by Freud that frustration can lead to aggression "because the damming up of energy causes an increase in tension" (Hall & Lindzey, 1954, p. 147) has generated a stream of research on the *frustration–aggression hypothesis*. But little of it has retained any semblance of psychoanalytic theory. The classical research by Yale behaviorists proclaimed that every instance of frustration instigates aggression, and every aggressive act can be traced back to some experience of frustration (Dollard, Doob, Miller, Mowrer, & Sears, 1939). But accumulated research, although supporting the general validity of the hypothesis, has demonstrated that the linkage between frustration and aggression is weaker than originally assumed (Berkowitz, 1962, 1969).

Many of the psychoanalytic concepts appealed to the Lewinians' orientation toward dynamics, stimulating attempts to redefine them within field theory, for example, Barker, Dembo, and Lewin (1941). Freud's (1922) theory of social groups also aroused considerable interest and was responsible for a number of developments in group dynamics. Bion's (1948–1951) "dynamic theory of group functioning", and its extension in Stock and Thelen (1958), distinguished between unstated, "unconscious" assumptions of a "group mentality" and individual members' thoughts and behavior. Group phenomena could be attributed to three basic assumptions of groups, *pairing* (all relations between pairs of members are sexual in nature), *fight or flight* (the group can preserve itself only by one of these procedures), or *dependency* (the group can only be secure by depending on one individual, such as a leader or therapist). A group capable of work has emancipated itself from these assumptions and is relatively realistic and free of emotions.

Perhaps the most dramatic research directly generated by psychoanalytic theory was the classical study of anti-Semitism and the roots of prejudice that appeared shortly after World War II (Adorno et al., 1950). Although the thesis was inherently pessimistic, that bigotry was the product of very early defective socialization and passsed from generation to generation, the research was timely, massive, and innovative in both conception and methods. It stimulated a flood of further research and critical discussion. Its effects have been assimilated and dissipated but have left many residues in social psychology.

Social psychology is often coupled with personality theory, as in the major publication, *The Journal of Personality and Social Psychology*. This *psychodynamic theoretical orientation* to the problems and topics of social psychology—the conception of social behavior as primarily a product of a person's emotional-motivational system in a particular situation—is one of the viable perspectives which continues to transmit Freud's influence. His direct stimulation also was apparent in the writings of the "revisionists" and neo-Freudians, and in the research of cultural anthropologists, considered in the next sections.

The Revisionists and Neo-Freudians

Social pschologists have been more receptive to Freud's thinking when revised or modified in the writings of psychoanalysts who were his students or followers, such as Jung, Adler, Horney, Sullivan, and Fromm. Each of these developed an individual approach and fresh concepts. Collectively, they moved psychoanalytic theory away from its biological and instinctual foundations toward an increased emphasis upon rationality and a recognition of the influence of society and culure in the development of personality and social behavior: a "socialization" of Freudian theory (Bronfenbrenner, 1963). In doing so, they made psychoanalytic theory an "open system" and abandoned any predictive power of the original. Their impact was not in the stimulation of serious and sustained research but rather in the propagation of a point of view and suggestive ideas embodied in attractive new concepts.

The "revisionists," Jung and Adler, were students and associates of Freud who broke with him on key issues. Carl Jung (1953) has had little impact on social psychology except for the occasional use of his Hegelian concept *racial unconscious* that postulated a uniform collective unconscious mind derived from prehistoric cultural themes or *archetypes*. He also anticipated contemporary developments in role and identity theory by proposing that individuals must protect themselves against a malevolent society by wearing a mask, or *persona*.

Alfred Adler (1924) was much more of a social psychologist in spirit. He asserted that persons were inherently social in motives, interests, and values. Adler's concepts *inferiority complex, overcompensation*, and *masculine protest* described social behavior and personal attributes that served people's need to find validation of their social worth. He pointed out the significance for personality and social behavior of a person's family position, whether a first-born, middle, or youngest child, a problem that has been actively pursued in contemporary social psychology. Many of his suggestive ideas anticipated current research developments although it is difficult to trace direct lines of influence.

The neo-Freudians, Horney, Fromm, and Sullivan, comprise a later generation of psychoanalytic psychiatrists who have transmitted Freudian influence, although radically modified, to the social sciences. To this group should be added Abraham Kardiner and Erik Erikson. The former is considered here, because his principal contribution has been to anthropological research in the *culture-and-personality* tradition. The latter, whose work was more recent, is mentioned where relevant in susequent chapters.

Like her fellow psychiatrists, Karen Horney's (1937, 1945) theoretical insights derived from her clinical relationships with disturbed patients. She concluded that personality disturbances originated in cultural conditions and unconscious conflicts in adulthood rather than in infantile Oedipal conflicts, as Freud had maintained. She generalized from her experiences that people felt alone and alienated from a society that failed to meet their emotional needs. Very early in life they had to develop a survival strategy to cope with their anxiety: either *moving toward, moving against*, or *moving away from* others. Horney believed that these social attitudes persisted, characterized individuals, and accounted for much of their social behavior.

Horney's ideas are referred to frequently in social psychological writings and often anticipated contemporary developments. For example, in research on interpersonal influence, investigators have attempted to discover persons who are typically *compliant* (moving toward), *nonconformers* (moving against) or *independent* (moving away from) (Hollander, 1975).

Another neo-Freudian, Erich Fromm (1941) rejected Freud's assumptions about instincts and psychosexual development yet retained much of his psychoanalytic theory. His horrified reaction to events in Nazi Europe led him to extensive theoretical analyses of a person's relation to society. He used the term *social character* for the ideal character structure "required" by a particular form of social structure. Fromm identified particular polar types of social character suggestive of variations in social environnment, such as *humanistic* versus *authoritarian*, or *receptive* versus *marketing*. His thinking was consonant with research on "modal personality" or "national character" (Inkeles & Levinson, 1969). It also anticipated contemporary investigations of *role stress* in relation to organizational structure (Kahn, Wolfe, Quinn, Snoek, & Rosenthal, 1964). His ideas, with Freud's, were directly influential in the research on authoritarian personality discussed previousy.

Although usually included with the neo-Freudians, Harry Stack Sullivan's (1947, 1953) thinking and influence were sufficiently distinctive to stand apart. He contributed an innovative and systematic interpersonal theory of psychiatry that retained few traces of his Freudian antecedents. He defined psychiatry as the study of interpersonal processes, essentially social psychology. Social psychology for Sullivan dealt with processes *between* people rather than *within* them. He initiated and stimulated the movement toward *social psychiatry*, which involved a recognition of the effects of the socio-cultural milieu on a person's emotional and intellectual processes. He contributed to significant changes in thinking about institutional treatment of the "mentally ill," and stimulated research on the organizational environment of mental hospitals, beginning with Stanton and Schwartz' (1954) classical study.

Familiarity with the communication difficulties of persons with schizophrenia and with Sapir's (1929) writings on comparative linguistics led Sullivan to recognize the centrality of communication processes in a person's development. His knowledge of American sociology was reflected in his theory of the development of the *self-system*, which owed more to Cooley and Mead than to Freud. He said that it arose from a child's attempts to avoid anxiety generated by *significant others*, especially its mother. Although he retained the Freudian conception of repression of threatening experience into the unconscious, the conscious part of the self was similar to Cooley's (1902) *reflected appraisals*. He assumed that *consensual validation* by significant others was the key process in confirming not only the presented self, but any reality.

Sullivan directly influenced "sociological" social psychology more than "psychological." He anticipated many contemporary developments, such as *situated identity theory*: He said that personality manifests itself only in interpersonal situations and that "every human being has as many personalities as he has interpersonal relations" (Sullivan 1950, p. 329). His thinking also can be seen in many of Goffman's (1959, 1961a, 1963) theoretical proposals, for example, that persons construct their performances and present selves to meet others' situated expectations. Some of his theory is consonant with an apparently developing integration of social psychology that we call the *integrative* theoretical orientation, discussed in chapter 7.

CULTURAL ANTHROPOLOGY

Contemporary social psychology possibly is as much indebted to cultural anthropology for its theoretical assumptions, concepts, and methods as to any other single source. Hardly any area within social psychology has remained untouched by comparative ethnological evidence from observations of human behavior and customs throughout the world. As we have seen, in an earlier era folk psychology's massive attempts to systematize ethnological materials and assimilate them within a psychological framework had little impact on social psychology. But it did prepare the ground for social psychology's love affair with cultural anthropology in the 1930s.

The "Psychologizing" of Cultural Anthropology

Before cultural anthropology could influence social psychology it had to undergo a major change itself. Its emphasis had to shift from the comparative content and structure of norms and customs in different societies, with a presumption of within-group homogeneity of behavior (Inkeles & Levinson, 1968–1969), to an increased focus on the dynamics of individual personality development and acculturation. This "psychologizing" of cultural anthropology was fostered by the Cambridge Anthropological Expedition to the Torres Straits in 1898, which included trained experimental psychologists Rivers, McDougall, and Myers.

In America, the movement was headed by Franz Boas (1911), whose studies in Mexico, Puerto Rico, and North American Indian tribes began in 1886. His psychological approach to anthropology, which he called "the dynamics of life," dominated American anthropology for over four decades. His students, Ruth Benedict and Margaret Mead, perpetuated and expanded his influence.

At Chicago University the great linguist Edward Sapir also contributed to the trend. He advised all psychologists and social scientists to examine their data from both individual and social points of view (Allport, 1954). The major force in altering cultural psychology's perspective, however—although in a backhand way—was Sigmund Freud.

The Freudian Infiltration

Freud's initial and major impact on cultural anthropology was to stimulate field research aimed at repudiating his biological assumptions and claims to universality. A series of important studies appeared, demonstrating the almost unlimited malleability of temperament and personality, depending upon social structure and cultural milieu (Benedict, 1934; Malinowski, 1927; Mead, 1928, 1930, 1935, 1937).

However, psychoanalytic theory proved to be a Trojan horse in the cultural anthopologists' camp. They admired many of its elegant thoretical contrivances but scorned its misuse of ethnological data. Kroeber (1939) referred to Freud's (1913) *Totem and Taboo* as "an irridescent fantasy" that was unreal, yet deserved a more delicate touch than he had accorded it in his 1920 review.

Ironically, scholarly criticism requires *taking the role of the other* (G. H. Mead's famous concept, discussed in chapter 7), so that critics often are changed in the process. In order to conduct research and to generate data relevant to Freud's hypotheses, anthropological investigators had to familiarize themselves with psychoanalytic theory. Its interpretive focus on underlying processes and its array of explanatory concepts proved to be congenial to a cultural anthropology that lacked any theory of individual motivation (Allport, 1954). Although Freud did not conquer the field, he made many inroads and converts among cultural anthropologists. His ideas became familiar features of their writings.

The Impact on Social Psychology

As cultural anthropology became increasingly relevant to psychological theories, an awareness of the significance of its research spread throughout psychology. Ethnological evidence tended to fill the vacuum created by the collapse of the instinct movement (Murphy, 1954). *Cultural relativism* was in the air, and psychologists raised questions about the generalizability of both their clinical observations and experimental findings.

Collaborative field research between psychologists—both psychoanalytic and behaviorist—and cultural anthropologists produced cross-cultural tests and expansions of psychological hypotheses from the clinic and the laboratory. The effect of field testing these questions in other societies placed them in a broader sociocultural context, so that findings became more pertinent and useful to the understanding of social psychological processes.

During the early decades of the 20th century, the impact of cultural anthropology on social psychology was extensive and lasting. It created the potential for an independent scientific discipline. This was a period when "social" frequently was prefixed to individual psychological processes—*social perception, social motivation, social learning*—in recognition that findings from highly controlled laboratory experiments were not always adequate to explain social behavior in more complex settings. It still was assumed, however, that the psychological laws were valid, if only one could control the host of "other variables."

Systematic studies of social perception may have been initiated by Franz Boas in 1883 when he first investigated the cultural determination of color perception (Herskovits, 1953, p.9). The accumulated anthropological evidence led Sherif (1936) to conclude that perceptual processes varied extensively, depending on the group and cultural context. Bartlett's (1932) landmark research demonstrated that remembering and forgetting were social processes powerfully influenced by cultural values. Research on social learning and imitation (Miller & Dollard, 1941) integrated anthropological concepts with stimulus-response learning theory.

The modern theory of linguistics was influenced strongly by Boas' (1911) studies of American Indian languages. It was developed further by Sapir (1929) who enunciated the insight that still reverberates in contemporary social psychology, that "language is a guide to social reality," that it shapes and constrains the thinking of people who live in different societies so that they really inhabit different worlds (Kluckhohn, 1954).

Ethnological research had an especially important impact on the study of socialization and its effect on personality development, because that field is both catholic and eclectic, and thus receptive to material from a diversity of disciplines and perspectives. Benedict's and Mead's systematic observations in different societies highlighted the variability in socialization. Some of its uniformities were analyzed in Whiting's (1941) study of the Kwoma.

Cultural anthropology borrowed many concepts and methods from psychology. But it repaid its debts lavishly with an array of new concepts that have remained essential parts of social pschology's conceptual resources: for example, *culture, institution, status,* and *role.* As might be anticipated when an idea is borrowed by one group from another, it does not invariably retain its original meaning. For example, when defining *culture,* anthropologists typically emphasize abstract forms, but social psychologists often define it more concretely, in terms of observed patterns of behavior. Unfortunately, the term also too frequently is employed merely as a residual, catch-all to acknowledge and refer to all of the nonimmediate but not identified "forces" that influence a person's behavior.

The concept *institution,* as much sociological as anthropological, attained special significance in the collaborative research by Kardiner (1939, 1945), a psychoanalyst, and Linton (1945), a cultural anthropologist. Linton said that the personality of adults in a given society could be predicted from its child rearing techniques: There was a close relationship between the modal personality structure of a society and its institutional patterns. Kardiner wrote of *primary* institutions, the aspects of child rearing emphasized by psychoanalysis such as breast feeding or toilet training, and *secondary institutions,* such as religion and folklore. The primary institutions developed lasting personality needs and tensions; the secondary institutions arose to satisfy the typical person's emotional requirements. Thus, in a stable society personality and culture mutually sustained and perpetuated each other (Sahakian, 1974).

In his influential *The Study of Man,* Linton (1936) popularized the concept *status* among social psychologists. Initially, he referred to it as *position* to emphasize its function as an analytical tool for describing location in social structure. But social psychologists frequently use the concept in its popular, invidious sense, as in "high" or "low" status in an hierarchy.

The *role* concept or family of concepts—*role expectations, role strain, role conflict,* and many others (Jackson, 1966; Sarbin, 1954; Sarbin & Allen, 1968–1969)— also have become familiar to all social psychologists, although variably defined and imprecisely measured, if at all. Cultural anthropologists, especially Linton, Benedict, and Margaret Mead, first made social psychologists aware of their explanatory usefulness. Benedict's (1938) discussion of continuities and discontinuities in female role expectations and the resultant ambiguities and role conflict pioneered what today is a vital area of social psychology.

"SOCIOLOGICAL" SOCIOLOGY

To outsiders, a group appears to be more homogeneous and cohesive than it does to informed participants. Most psychologists are unaware of the deep schisms that fractionate sociology, some of which have a long history. In attempting to describe briefly the influence of sociology upon the development of contemporary social psychology, it is useful to distinguish between "sociological" and "psychological" sociology. The distinction might also be termed *structural* and *process* sociology. Even though the classification might be difficult to sustain in specific cases, it does represent in general an historical schism between sociologists who followed Durkheim and those who were influenced by psychologists, especially by James, Dewey, and G. H. Mead.

In many respects, an intellectual discipline is like a nation: It must have clear boundaries, citizens, a self-image or identity, and an ideology that maintains and justifies its independent existence. More than any other thinker, Durkheim has been the symbol of a "sociological" sociology that differentiates itself from psychology. His thesis that *social facts* must be explained in terms of other *social facts*, rather than being reduced to psychological or even neurological processes, has remained a rallying cry for many sociologists.

Although Durkheim wrote of *social mind* and *collective representations*, his theory was not an excursion into Hegelian metaphyics that argued for the transcendental reality of a *Folk Mind* of which individual minds partake, but simply a recognition of separate levels of analysis, each with its own reality. Such a position is quite acceptable in modern science. Psychologists do not feel required to explain psychological phenomena by reducing them to atoms and molecules. (But see the discussion in chapter 3 of *reductionism* and of the *group mind*, among the great controversies in a developing social psychology.)

Durkheim maintained that social facts were external to individuals, yet constrained and influenced their experience and behavior. His contemporary, Wundt (1916) took a similar position with regard to the influence of language. Durkheim's (1912) favorite example was religion, not reducible to individual psychological processes. Even suicide—or more correctly, suicide rates—needed to be understood in terms of societal disruption and consequent *anomie*, the lack of social rules and regulation (Durkheim, 1897).

Two of Durkhem's compatriots were influenced by his ideas. Le Bon (1895/1896) adopted the concept of *collective mind* in his theory of crowd behavior. Piaget (1932) accepted the view of social reality in his theory and research on the development of moral judgment. In his research on social influences in memory processes, Bartlett (1932) showed "a Durkheimian respect for the reality of the social" (Allport, 1954).

But the "sociological" sociologists have had little direct and traceable influence upon contemporary social psychology. In one sense, this is not surprising because of their anti-psychological orientation: Rejection inevitably becomes a reciprocal process.

It can be assumed that, like all major thinkers, Durkheim has wielded indirect influence by contributing to the general intellectual heritage. But such influence is difficult to demonstrate conclusively. The history of science has many examples of multiple origination or independent rediscovery of ideas. In recent times, social psychologists have become more familiar with "sociological" sociology through Parsons' and his Harvard associates' interdisciplinary efforts (Parsons & Shils, 1951), although it is unlikely that their terminological morass will produce many converts.

AMERICAN PRAGMATISM AND "PSYCHOLOGICAL" SOCIOLOGY

The pragmatic philosophers attempted to create a philosophy in the spirit of evolution and modern science. Like physical scientists, they assumed a "real" world prior to subjective experience and justified their assumption by its practical consequences. The American pragmatists, William James, John Dewey, and George Mead, have been a major influence on the development of contemporary social psychology. They also have had a substantial indirect effect by their influence upon both socially oriented psychologists and "psychological" sociologists.

William James and John Dewey

James (1890), the dean of American thinkers, could leave no intellectual stone unturned. It is difficult to distinguish many of his contributions from those of his associates, because he influenced everyone who had any relationship with him. With his students, and colleagues such as Baldwin, Hall, and Angell, he led American psychology away from a sterile Wundtian analytical introspectionism toward an emphasis on holistic behavior and social life. He and Dewey, and to a lesser degree, Mead, were involved actively in many facets of society and movements toward social progress. Their concern with education, religion, and the ethical consequences of conduct contributed to the appeal of their psychology to the value-oriented psychologists and sociologists of that era. By the same token, their ideas were less attractive to their "hard-nosed" experimental colleagues.

James' classic system of psychology has led in an unbroken line to many conceptions of contemporary social psychology (Sarbin, 1954). For example, it dealt with the *social self*, defined as a person's recognition obtained from others: "A man has as many social selves as there are individuals who recognize him" (James, 1892). His doctrine of the inseparability of the individual and society, shared with Baldwin (1895), has persisted through the influence of Cooley's (1902, 1909, 1918) social psychology. In the famous James–Lange theory of emotion— a person runs before an awareness of fear, not because of it—he illustrated a general thesis that behavior is prior to consciousness and thought. This assumption reappears in Mead and his pragmatic theory of meaning, discussed here, and is echoed by contemporary social psychologists such as Bem (1967) and Zajonc (1980).

At the end of the 19th century, John Dewey became the head of the philosophy department at the new University of Chicago and the leading figure in the famous Chicago School, which perpetuated and further developed the Jamesian perspective. The appellation has been used variously to describe the philosophic approach of Dewey, Mead, and their associates, the renowned group of sociologists and their research, and the distinctive school of functional psychology that developed at Chicago during that period. The functional psychologists studied mental processes as they mediated between the environment and the needs of an organism (Angell, 1907), in contrast to Wundt and Titchener's structural emphasis on the elements of consciousness. The influence and contributions of Dewey and Mead spread throughout the departments of philosophy, sociology, psychology, and education. They provided the roots of the modern movement in sociology and social psychology called *symbolic interactionism* (Lauer & Handel, 1977; Manis & Meltzer, 1978; Stryker & Statham, 1985).

Strongly influenced by evolutionary thought, Dewey emphasized the reciprocal interaction and dynamic equilibrium between an organism and its environment. Extending this thesis to human behavior, he distinguished between *conduct*, which "is always shared," and mere physiological processes. He was among the first psychologists to recognize that most human behavior was indeed social, both in origin and consequences, and to argue the need for a social psychology (Dewey, 1917). Although in their early thinking both he and James, in the spirit of the times, made instinct the basis of social conduct, they soon switched to a broad, social conception of *habit* as "the flywheel of society" (James, 1890). According to Dewey (1922), "every manifestation of a habit is altered by other people who are concerned in the act" (Allport 1954, p. 42).

In addition to his profound influence upon Mead, functional psychology, and the "psychological" sociologists, some of Dewey's direct contributions can be recognized in contemporary social psychology. His analysis of individual problem-solving processes (Dewey, 1910) became the basis for studies of group problem solving and research on group processes. His espousal of progressive eduction for enhanced group and community participation was a powerful influence upon the invention of the *T-group* and *sensitivity training* at Bethel, the National Training Laboratory for Group Development (NTL) by his disciples Kenneth Benne, Leland Bradford, and Ronald Lippitt (1975). His emphasis on democratic problem solving affected Lippitt's training in group work at Springfield

College and stimulated the classical Lewin– Lippitt–White research on group atmospheres, described in chapter 3.

George H. Mead and Charles H. Cooley

Contemporary social psychologists in crediting the source of their thinking, especially in regard to the social self, frequently couple G. H. Mead and Cooley. Although they shared some ideas, stemming from James and Dewey, they actually had contrasting views of the nature of persons and of society. Mead was not a sociologist, but like James and Dewey, a philosopher highly involved in struggling with solutions to the central problems of psychology of that era. He was active and influential in the development of a functional psychology that would be true to the traditions of natural science yet that would serve to contribute to problems of social living.

Today, we might describe Cooley as a social phenomenologist. His ideas are cited by cognitive social psychologists who fail to distinguish them from Mead's. However, G. H. Mead (1930) criticized Cooley severely for his solipsist, value-oriented approach which he said militated against a realistic involvement in activity toward improving society. He said that society and its problems had a reality independent of a person's perceptions and feelings. Mead believed that his own *social behaviorism* could contribute both to a scientific social psychology and also to social progress. We discuss his theoretical ideas more completely in chapter 7, because they are involved in a developing integration of social psychological theory.

Cooley's own conceptual contributions to social psychology have been substantial. His *looking-glass self* has been an influential idea. It has three components: the imagination of a person's appearance to others, of others' judgment of that appearance, and a consequent self-feeling such as pride or mortification. Another major influential contribution was his concept of the *primary group*, a face-to-face group such as a family or playgroup, which he saw as the unit of social structure and principal agent of socialization to an "organic" society. He described the affective bonds that tied a group together as *we-feeling*, a concept that subsequently reappeared in Festinger's (1950b) *group cohesiveness*, measured by questioning participants about their feelings of attraction to other persons in the group.

W. I. Thomas and The Polish Peasant

Another notable sociologist of the Chicago School, W. L. Thomas, held a broad, interdisciplinary conception of social psychology. His article, "The Province of Social Psychology," was published in two parts, the first in *The Psychological Bul-*

letin and the second in *The American Journal of Sociology* (Thomas, 1904, 1905). He also made significant contributions in the field of social anthropology.

Many of Thomas' distinctive theoretical and methodological contributions to social psychology had their origin in his classical 10-year study of Polish peasantry (Thomas & Znaniecki, 1918–1920). The central concept of the Polish peasant study was *attitude*, which the investigators succeeded in making a basic, lasting feature of "psychological" sociology. They were among the first to define social psychology as *the scientific study of attitudes*, a popular but no longer adequate designation. Their work led directly to Bogardus' (1928, 1933) scale of *social distance* for measuring interracial or ethnic attitudes, using Park's (1924) concept, and to Thurstone's (1927) attitude scales.

One of the central tenets of Thomas and Znaniecki was that the cause of individual social behavior could not be found solely in either an individual or a social phenomenon, but always in a combination of both individual and social. Their generalization was strikingly similar to Lewin's well-known formula, $B = f(P.E.)$ that *behavior (B)* is a combined *function (f)* of forces both from within a *person (P)* and from the external *environment (E)*.

Another of Thomas' contributions was in the area of social motivation and personality. His "four wishes"—*desire for new experience, security, response*, and *recognition*—became well-known and provided social psychology a socioculturally derived substitute for instinctual conceptions of motivation (Thomas, 1928). They also led to a proposal for three related personality types: *philistine, bohemian*, and *creative man*. Each type represented for Thomas a way of adapting to one's social milieu, an "attitudinal life- organization," what today might be termed a *lifestyle*, or a *situated identity* (see chapter 7).

Thomas' works also anticipated other areas of contemporary social psychology, such as the social psychology of sex and of intergroup relations. His contributions have had a lasting influence, especially on what has become "sociological" social psychology.

In this chapter we have reviewed some of the major influences that have shaped the newly developing field of social psychology. We have seen how diverse are social psychology's antecedents, and how inevitable it was that a long period of conceptual confusion and theoretical disarray would ensue before any consolidation of a scientific discipline might appear. Some great controversial issues had been inherited from philosophy, but could not be dismissed readily, because they arose whenever theoretical or methodological choices had to be made. In the next chapter, we describe these "great controversies" and how social psychology attempted to resolve them. We also review the decades prior to World War II, during which social psychology demonstrated that it indeed could become a viable scientific enterprise.

Chapter 3
The Formative Years of Scientific Social Psychology

At the fourth annual meeting of the American Psychological Asssociation at the University of Pennsylvania in December 1895, "The question of the formation of a philosophical society or a philosophical section within the present association was ... referred to the Council with full power to act." At the fifth annual meeting in 1896, the Council presented a plan for the formation of an American Philosophical or Metaphysical Association, as an affiliate organization...." A motion also was made by the 45 members attending, the largest gathering yet, that Council be recommended to select only papers and contributions to annual meetings "as are psychological in subject matter." A further motion recommended that the names of new members must be publicly displayed in written form or on a blackboard at an opening session with a statement of contribution to psychology, "in virtue of which the persons named are eligible to membership." (Notes in *The Psychological Review*, 1896, *3*(2), 121-122, and 1897, *4*(1), 109)

By the end of the 19th century the fledgling psychological association was cleansing itself of impurities, like philosophers and sociologists. It was a period when the achievements of the physical and biological scientists were widely recognized and acclaimed. The miracle of science promised unlimited further miraculous progress. Psychologists and most social psychologists were swept up in the trend toward empiricism and an abnegation of speculative thought.

Social psychology was struggling to become a scientific discipline, to develop methods of objective research, controlled experimentation, more rigorous measurement techniques and a body of scientific theory. Yet the ghosts of the past seemed to continue to haunt it. Philosophical issues refused to remain banished and reappeared to harass each new development in theory or research. In spite of the insistent intrusions of these "great controversies" and the attention given to them, social psychology made progress in the four decades prior to World War II in demonstrating to the world and to itself that it had indeed arrived as a scientific endeavor.

RESOLUTION OF THE GREAT CONTROVERSIES

The early years of social psychology formed a period of transition from social philosophy to the beginnings of a scientific discipline. The change was gradual and uneven: Empirical and experimental research increased; theoretical formulations became more rigorous and systematic; concepts were defined with an increased concern for the possibilities of data collection. Throughout this developmental period, however—roughly from Darwin to the decade preceding World War II—both theorizing and research were dominated largely by the "great controversies," universal issues inherited from antiquity and classical philosophy: *nature–nurture, the group mind, the nature of a person, of society*, and *of their relationship*. We have seen these issues intrude repeatedly in our discussion of the various sources of influence upon the emerging discipline. Before real progress could be made in a scientific social psychology there had to be some resolution of these ubiquitous dilemmas.

The Nature-Nurture Controversy

Was human social behavior the product of biological heredity or of environmental experience? To what degree could social life be attributed to each? Where did one look for explanations, within a person's past living situations and present environment, or in an individual's "character" or "personality" that carried the traits of preceding generations? Such questions are not unfamiliar to contemporary social psychologists although today most knowledgeable persons have general agreement—except on specific questions, such as the sources of aggression, benevolence, gregariousness, or intelligence. On each of these topics one can find serious proponents of a genetic explanation of the behavior. Although presented in the trappings of scientific debate, the issue has never fully escaped the passions of theological and ideological conviction (Baumgardner, 1977).

As mentioned previously, Darwin's epochal theory of natural selection and evolution, and Freud's shocking theories of subterranean emotional–motivational dynamics with their instinctual origins, temporarily tipped the scales in psychology and social psychology toward a nativistic emphasis. Prestigeful theorists, such as James, Dewey, McDougall, Thorndike, and Woodworth busily compiled long, and different, lists of instinctually based motives.

McDougall (1926) felt that Darwin's lead had not been followed adequately. He aimed at a social psychology based on "the innate tendencies to thought and action that constitute the native basis of the mind" (p. 441). He wrote that "the instinct problem . . . stands at the parting of the ways in psychology" and placed himself on the side of the *vitalists*, as against the *mechanists* who explained social behavior entirely in terms of the physical sciences and "left no room for belief in the reality and effectiveness of our efforts, our striving toward goals and ideals" (pp. 441-442). Yet he saw the question as a scientific one to be decided by objective rather than metaphysical evidence.

McDougall's (1908) influential theory of social psychology attempted to build a systematic account of social life on a foundation of specific instincts and their corresponding emotions, such as *flight* and *fear*, *repulsion* and *disgust*, *curiosity* and *wonder*, and *pugnacity* and *anger*, and some non-specific "innate tendencies." From these, he constructed his *purposive* theory of social conduct, identifying complex "social" instincts such as "the reproductive and the parental instincts," instincts of "gregariousness," "acquisition," and those related to "religious conceptions."

However, the reaction against instinct theory mounted by Dunlap (1919), Bernard (1921, 1924) and others prevailed. The pendulum of psychological opinion swung back toward environmentalism, aided by the strenuous arguments of an emerging behaviorism, which stressed learning and environmental control of behavior, and by the accumulating evidence of cultural anthropology. Instinct concepts were modified to more neutral motivational concepts: *habit, propensity, wish, desire, need,* or *motive*. Social psychologists assumed a noncommital "middle position" (Allport 1954), both heredity and environment as multiple determinants of social behavior in some unspecified mix (Kluckhohn, 1954).

Although there were many empirical arguments against nativism in social psychology, they were not definitive. But the American temperament and ethos demanded a more optimistic, "progressive" theory with implications for social improvement (Allport, 1954); and psychologists refused to recognize the bases for self-determination that McDougall insisted were fundamental to his own theorizing.

The controversy was not resolved. It continually re-emerges, for example in the recent flurries of excitement caused by ethological reports, and by the issue of racial versus sociocultural influence in the testing of intelligence. Presently, it is undergoing a reformulation under the impact of scientific advances such as those in the fields of genetics, genetic engineering, neurophysiological effects of experience, and organ transplants. During its formative period, fortunately, social psychology was able eventually to sidestep the controversy and move on to empirical research.

The Group Mind Controversy

Another great scientific debate with both ideological roots and implications can be traced through the years of a developing social psychology. The *group mind controversy* emerged in modern times from Hegel's (1770–1831) idealistic metaphysics which adulated the State and its social morality as against individual thinking. It was stimulated by German nationalism with its idea of a "folk soul," partially transformed in *folk psychology*, and almost entirely in Durkheim's *collective representations* and the anthropological concept of *culture*.

For some, the issue was a fatal threat to the entire modern social psychological enterprise and to their own identities as scientists. "Group mind" concepts took them back to the days of metaphysical speculation and theological fancies. *Mind*, if it was to be accepted at all within a scientific discipline—and the behaviorists, of course, had outlawed it—was a property only of an individual organism, its brain and central nervous system. Otherwise, one cast off from an anchored moorage into a sea of phantasms, and all the years of stubbornly constructing a scientific social psychology based on objective evidence would be wasted.

The controversy also was never far removed from ideological and political convictions and frequently was carried on with the intemperance common in those arenas. Le Bon's (1895/1896) *crowd mind* and his theory of crowd behavior undoubtedly was stimulated by a reaction against the excesses of the French revolution and the crude, populist "democracy" of that period. He and McDougall (1920), who rather naively adopted the *group mind* concept without realizing the passions its metaphysical and political connotations would generate, were pilloried in some circles as enemies of democracy; although they probably were no more supportive of the status quo than most bourgeois intellectuals.

The introduction of sociological writings into the psychological literature had brought the issue home to psychologists quite early, when Tufts reviewed books by Small and Vincent, Simmel, Tarde, and Durkheim in *The Psychological Review*, 1895. He quoted J.S. Mills' statements to express the sentiments of most psychologists: "men are not, when brought together, converted into another kind of substance ... human beings in society have no properties but those which are derived from and may be resolved into the laws of the nature of individual man" (p. 307). He agreed that there existed no "knowledge or feeling ... not in the medium of individual consciousness" (p. 308). But he also said that "individual mind" was an abstraction divorced from the constant influence of social relations.

Tufts concluded that "neither psychologists nor sociologists can ignore the work of the other" (p. 308).

A form of the controversy that was more closely related to empirical evidence developed around the question of the "reality of the group." Research on groups had begun in the psychological laboratories, stimulated by Triplett's (1897) ground-breaking experiment, discussed here, on such questions as whether individual performance was affected by an audience, co-workers, rivalry, social encouragement and discouragement, group discussion, or the size and prestige of a group. It had been concluded that under specified conditions "group thinking" was superior to "individual thinking" (Britt, 1941; Murphy, Murphy, & Newcomb, 1937). But Floyd Allport (1924, 1933), who conducted the classic *alone–together* experiments, also discussed here, argued vehemently that only the individual had any reality and that all so-called group phenomena could be accounted for in terms of the laws of individual behavior.

Kurt Lewin (1948, 1951) responded that the "reality" of anything hinged upon its consequences. Groups were real to the degree that they had unique effects. He and his associates buttressed that argument with experimental demonstrations of the effects of an induced "group atmosphere" and the differences produced by "organized" compared to "unorganized" groups (discussed later in this chapter).

Confronted by the evidence of these and other studies, social psychologists lost interest in the "group mind controversy" and embarked upon a fruitful period of research on social behavior in group contexts.

The issue is still alive in contemporary social psychology, however, for example, between reductionists like Homans (1961, 1964), a sociologist who attempted to account for group phenomena in terms of Skinner's (1953) principles of individual behavior, and those who accept multiple levels of analysis. An increased sophistication with regard to the nature of science and scientific concepts (Kaplan, 1964; Kuhn, 1962, 1970) has led to an acceptance in social psychology of supra-individual concepts such as *culture, social structure, group, norm*, and *role*. As discussed previously, this has not occurred without some discomfort among individually oriented social psychologists with a traditional suspicion of Hegelian metaphysics.

It would be a mistake to exaggerate the receptivity of "psychological" social psychologists to concepts from sociology. Few of them have been able to completely escape the reductionist bias of their training. For example, when Cartwright (1959) recognized that *power* had been "a neglected variable in social psychology," he did not define it objectively, as a relationship in social structure, the definition traditionally accepted by sociologists and political scientists. He defined it subjectively or "psychologically," as *perceived power*, one's own and others'. It thus became a characteristic of an individual person. Similarly, when Christie and Geis (1970) studied *Machiavellianism*, they avoided the issue of the individual's relation to society, central in that classical work, and explained the manipulative and exploitative processes described there in terms of an individual's personality.

Although the group mind controversy has been transformed into the question of the appropriate units of analysis for a science of social psychology, the issue certainly has not been resolved. Social psychologists generally accept Cooley's (1922) injunction "that 'society' and 'individuals' do not denote separable phenomena but are simply collective and distributive aspects of the same thing" (p. 37). Although they freely utilize supra-individual concepts in their research and writings, and even sometimes manage to escape their individualistic predilections, there has been no successful theoretical integration of individual and collective concepts. The problem is discussed further in chapter 7 on the developing integration of the discipline.

Nature of a Person and Society

For Plato and Aristotle the nature of society and of a person constituted a single indissoluble issue. In classical philosophy the two questions were interrelated. The various unitary conceptions of human nature discussed in chapter 1—*hedonism, egoism, sympathy, imitation*, and *suggestion*—were answers with implications for the forms and possibilities of society.

These models of a person, reformulated in terms of theoretical orientations, mini-theories, and operational concepts, still can be found in contemporary social psychology. During the decades before World War II, the *behaviorist, psychodynamic, cognitive*, and *sociocultural* theoretical orientations to social psychology all were developed into more complete systems with bodies of supportive empirical findings. It was an era of system building. The quest in psychology and its related social psychology was for the one "true" theory. Much research was devoted to demonstrating that a particular conception of human nature was correct and competing theories invalid. Not suprisingly, however, a single theoretical orientation did not emerge as superior. Rather, social psychologists wearied of the intradisciplinary strife and constraints of systems and turned toward an eclectic empiricism.

Little attention was diverted to the broader, societal implications of their theoretical orientations. At times, however, the model of society implied by a particular psychological theory was made explicit, for example by Freud, the neo-Freudians Horney and Fromm, and the behaviorist, Skinner.

In *Civilization and Its Discontents*, Freud (1957), not unlike Hobbes, presented a view of human nature as hostile, aggressive and cruel. Society and its culture evolved to "erect barriers against the aggressive instincts of men" (p. 86). It accomplished this aim by restrictions on unbridled aggression and sexual activity, and by religious ideals such as the command to "love one's neighbour as oneself .. . justified by the fact that nothing is so completely at variance with original human nature" (p. 87). Society is pictured by Freud as a system of inhibitions of a person's instinctual nature, accomplished by building in a pervasive sense of guilt.

Karen Horney's (1937) modified psychoanalytic theory also assumed a close relationship between human nature and society, with repression of hostility the basic process underlying social behavior. Her neurotic patients all exhibited *basic anxiety*, "a feeling of being small, helpless, deserted, endangered in a world that is out to abuse, cheat, attack, humiliate, betray, envy" (Newcomb, 1950, p. 380). But Horney was familiar with the new findings of cultural anthropologists who reported the great variation in societies and their cultures and corresponding social behavior. She also had observed significant differences between her European and American patients. She differed with Freud in recognizing that hostility was not instinctual, but developed from the interpersonal relations of a particular society.

In chapter 2 we described Erich Fromm's (1941) theory of *social character* and the requirements of different forms of society for the development of appropriate character structure and patterns of social behavior.

In *Walden Two*, B. F. Skinner (1948), a radical behaviorist, followed Plato in designing a model society in fictional form which embodied his theory of human nature. By utilizing a behavioral technology based on *operant conditioning* principles, socially desirable patterns of behavior were developed from birth and undesirable behavior eliminated. Also eliminated were many aspects of contemporary culture, its institutions and its values, as unnecessary and useless artifacts. To outraged critics Skinner replied that society is already engaged in the same process of conditioning individuals by rewarding them for desired behavior; except that its present forms are inefficient and produce flawed consequences.

In spite of these and other attempts to emphasize the close interrelationship between human nature and society, at the end of the prewar era of development social psychology still was essentially an individually oriented field, the study of individual behavior in a social context. Because most of the research occurred in the experimental laboratory and used college undergraduates as subjects, the findings did not really warrant generalizations either about human nature or society; even though, naturally, such generalizations were made. This subsequently became one of the many critical issues debated in the "crisis in social psychology," discussed in chapter 5.

Another perspective, long active in sociology, *the sociology of knowledge* (Mannheim, 1936; Marx & Engels, 1846/1937), recently has appeared in writings critical of the accepted history of social psychology (Baumgardner, 1976; Samelson, 1974). Its central theme assumes an intimate relationship between theorists' view of society and their conception of human nature. Its thesis is that the prevailing ideology of a society or its ruling class, constructed to protect vested interests, strongly influences the conception and direction of the production of knowledge. Allport (1954) recognized this process and cited Dewey's (1899) discussion of its influence upon the development of social psychology. It also is implicit in Kuhn's

(1962, 1970) influential exposition of the way "legitimate" research is defined in science. This perspective is also one of those discussed further in chapter 5.

DEMONSTRATING THAT SOCIAL PSYCHOLOGY WAS SCIENTIFIC

Social psychology became a science, in the eyes of many, when it demonstrated that it could experiment on social phenomena in the laboratory. The first experiments in social psychology were conducted at the end of the 19th century and led to a growing flood of laboratory experiments, at first still under the influence of the "great controversies" but gradually extending the questions investigated.

The decades of the 1920s and 1930s also saw the development of more precise measurement techniques. We have referred previously to the introduction of *attitude* as an empirical concept by Thomas and Znaniecki (1918–1920) leading to Bogardus' (1928) *scale of social distance* for measuring attitudes toward different racial or ethnic groups. We also have discussed briefly the origin of "mental measurement" in psychophysics, Thurstone's (1927; Thurstone & Chave, 1929) adaptation of psychophysical techniques to attitude scaling, and Likert's (1932) simplified attitude scale. These more rigorous methods, as they became familiar to social psychologists, were adopted in the field studies and laboratory experiments of the period. They provided more precise descriptions of data and facilitated statistical evaluation of the findings.

During the decades just prior to World War II, there were research developments in psychology, sociology, anthropology, child development, and industrial management that contributed to a developing science of social behavior. The foundations of a scientific social psychology were being laid; although the lack of extensive communication among the academic disciplines prevented attempts to integrate these diverse contributions to social psychology into a single structure. These awaited the catalytic effects of the social scientists' cooperative war effort, discussed in chapter 4.

During this fruitful prewar period, however, all of the constituents were developed that made possible the successful contributions of social psychologists to the war against fascism and to the development of their own discipline. The conceptual domain of social psychology was expanded and appropriate methods of measurement were developed. New techniques were employed in field studies for systematic research on naturally occurring social structures and processes; and in the laboratory for experimental investigation of holistic conceptions such as *norms, group membership, leadership,* and *social climate.* The confidence of social psychologists in their ability to tackle complex social questions as scientists increased. The boundaries of social psychology seemed to extend outwards without visible limit. We review briefly some of the more significant developments of this generative period.

Beginnings of Experimental Social Psychology

A pioneering experiment by Triplett (1897) has become known as the first experimental study in social psychology. He compared children's performance on simple tasks in the laboratory when working alone or when other children were present. When working *together* 50% of the children exceeded their performance *alone*; although 25% of the subjects performed less well under group conditions. Triplett concluded that the presence of others will normally enhance a person's energy output and achievement.

He explained and published his results in terms of *dynamogenesis*, or the theory of ideo-motor response, described in chapter 1 in our discussion of various explanations of *imitation*. As Allport (1954) pointed out, however, he failed to distinguish between possible competitive feelings and stimulation by the sight and sound of other workers.

An extensive program of research on the same problem, quite independent of Triplett, was conducted by Moede (1920) in Germany beginning in 1913. His plan was to replicate all of the standard psychological experiments under "social" conditions, that is, with subjects working in each others' presence rather than alone. Unfortunately, his work was not translated and had little influence upon American social psychology, with one important exception: It prompted Münsterberg at Harvard to induce his student, F. H. Allport to begin research on the topic (Allport, 1954).

Allport (1924) distinguished between situations in which subjects worked independently of one another but in each others' presence and those in which competition or other relations existed. He called the former *co-acting groups* and said that the latter belonged to a different category, *face-to-face groups*, in which persons directly influenced each other by interaction or by implicit or explicit feelings such as rivalry and competition. He introduced the term *social facilitation* to describe the enhancement of effort or performance in the co-acting situation. Social facilitation became a popular problem in social psychology for a generation. It spawned an extensive and heterogeneous literature but its studies often were incomparable and its results contradictory and inconclusive. Interest in the problem waned until resurrected by Zajonc (1965) with his unifying theory.

During the prewar years, Floyd Allport's systematic program of research on the *alone-together* problem really established the laboratory experiment as social psychology's basic method of research. His work was extended by other investigators in many different directions. A large number of elaborations and variations introduced new variables such as *expert* and *majority opinion* (Moore, 1921), and *competition* (Whittemore, 1924). Moore's experiments also introduced conditions that have become standard techniques in experimental social psychology, *the imagined presence of others* instead of their actual presence and *the reported opinion of a fictitious majority.*

Initially, research topics were derived from historical problems in individual psychology. Gradually, however, social psychologists moved away from this dependence and began to experiment on newly conceived group and interpersonal processes.

Early Field Studies

Parallel to the development of experimental social psychology during the pre- war decades, a number of brilliant field studies were conducted. Each has become a classic in social psychology, its methods and insights still referred to by contemporary social psychologists. Thomas and Znaniecki's (1918–1920) landmark study of the Polish peasant and the outstanding early research by cultural anthropologists, discussed previously, provided the models from which these pioneering studies were developed; but each of the investigators contributed fresh approaches and new techniques. Collectively, they established field research as complementary to the experimental laboratory in social psychology's tested and approved methods.

The Chicago Monographs. During the first decades of the 20th century, Chicago was a raw, heterogeneous, burgeoning metropolis into which had poured emigrants from all over the country and many foreign lands. It was an ideal laboratory for the social scientist. A series of descriptive and analytic field studies by University of Chicago sociologists made full use of this research opportunity.

The *Chicago Monographs* (Shaw, 1930; Thrasher, 1927; Wirth, 1928; Zorbaugh, 1929) employed a positivist or "nonevaluative" approach to document systematically many areas of the diverse urban social life such as the slums, the "ghetto," and the "Gold Coast," a wealthy strip along the shore of Lake Michigan populated by an affluent elite. They also were concerned with making their data relevant to social problems and related it to delinquency, crime, and mental "illness." They furnished detailed evidence of the relationships between objective environment, life circumstances, and social behavior and personality.

A study of boys' gangs in the Chicago slums (Thrasher, 1927) made detailed observations of the "spontaneous efforts of boys to create a society for themselves where none adequate to their needs exists". The study provided bases for Newcomb's (1950) generalization that "it is not the boys but the norms which are 'abnormal' from the point of view of the larger community" (p. 526).

The formation of informal groups was not unique to deprived areas of the city. Zorbaugh (1929) described the exclusive clubs of the "Gold Coast," and those that hung around the pool halls in the slums. He found asssociations that satisfied members' needs, no matter how diverse, in every neighborhood of Chicago. The great variation in patterns of social behavior and how intimately they were related to belonging to particular informal groups was clear from his report.

The significance of the environment for "delinquent" social behavior emerged from an 8-year study of the metropolis (Shaw, 1930). The research analyzed data from 100,000 individuals in the files of schools, courts, police, and probation agencies. Investigators also obtained detailed life histories of some of their subjects. By plotting delinquency rates geographically, they identified *delinquency areas*. The central area of Chicago had accepted successive waves of immigration during the 80 years prior to the study: German, Irish, Scandinavian, Polish, and southern Negro. In addition, new citizens poured in from all over the world. Yet Shaw and his associates found no relationship between delinquency rates and ethnic or racial origin, a finding that contradicted popular beliefs.

High delinquency rates were strikingly associated with particular areas of the city, however, and these delinquency areas persisted in spite of changes in the ethnic composition of the inhabitants. It appeared that psychological, social, and economic factors contributed to delinquency, which could be understood only in terms of patterns of social life. The *ecological* approach of the study was systematized and extended by Wirth, Park, Mackenzie, and Dawson and became characteristic of many Chicago studies. It was a significant forerunner of the ecological emphasis in contemporary social psychology.

Middletown. Studies by Lynd and Lynd (1929, 1937) also provided encyclopaedic details of a "typical" American community. They revealed how group membership and social pressures affected every mundane aspect of contemporary social life, even though unrecognized by participants. Although their books were very popular, the investigators employed highly evaluative and interpretive methods and analysis—more characteristic, at that time, of the Columbia University than the Chicago approach—which did not please their more positivist and conservative colleagues. On one occasion, for example, the author witnessed Carl Dawson, a devout product of Chicago ecological training, order a student to remove a copy of *Middletown* from a McGill University classroom on the grounds that it was a biased and unscientific work.

The Hawthorne Studies. Beginning in the mid-1920s, another series of ground-breaking studies was conducted in the Hawthorne Works of the Western Electric Company by investigators from the Harvard School of Business Administration. These Hawthorne Studies (Mayo, 1933; Roethlisberger, 1941; Roethlisberger & Dickson, 1939) demonstrated the possibilities of observing and experimenting upon small groups of workers under "natural" conditions.

The initial study had not been focused on social psychological factors but on aspects of the physical working environment. Investigators asked whether productivity could be increased by greater illumination in the work place. They found a marked improvement in production when lighting was increased. Production grew with each step-wise increase in illumination. As an experimental control, experimenters then began to decrease the illumination. To their astonishment, production continued to grow. Each time the lighting was lowered, production improved, until the illumination was less than the original conditions. These dramatic and unforeseen results came to be known throughout social science as the *Hawthorne Effect*, the principle that experimenting upon workers or just paying special attention to them tends to be an additional source of motivation.

The research program then veered toward an exploration of the social relationships within and between industrial working groups. Investigators began to recognize that the informal social organization of the workers was more significant in understanding employees' behavior than the formal organization in management's blue print. Among a variety of studies and approaches conducted over a 20-year period, the *Bank Wiring Observation Room*, the culminating project, had the greatest impact on social psychology.

The researchers initiated an experimental work group separate from the others to carry on, under continuous observation, the customary job of wiring and soldering banks of terminals. Fourteen men including their supervisors were involved. Over a 6-month period a massive collection of data provided detailed insights into the attitudes, feelings, motives, relationships, and social behavior of the participants. Concepts such as *group membership, social structure, leadership, authority*, and *social norms* emerged out of dusty library shelves and came alive before the fascinated observers.

The classic Hawthorne studies were highly influential not because they were without shortcomings. They did not result in any body of systematic theory nor confirmed hypotheses (Shils, 1948) and their methods became the target of increasing and stringent criticism. Hindsight is always so wise. But they forced a dramatic realization among social psychologists of the possibilities of the future.

Yankee City Series. During the prewar period, sociologists from Yale University also conducted an important series of theoretically oriented studies of American communities. This Yankee City Series (Warner & Lunt, 1941) used both interviewing and systematic observation methods to focus on social stratification. It provided clear evidence that respondents could locate and report their own and others' position within a highly consensual class structure, from *upper upper* to *lower lower*. These positions also were highly related to objective criteria such as occupation, education, income, and the type and location of residence. The research was conducted in a New England, Midwest, and Southern community (Davis, Gardner, & Gardner, 1941) and the methods adapted to reveal the status system within an industrial organization (Warner & Low, 1947).

Not only did these studies strike at the popular myth that American society was egalitarian and classless, but they showed how it was possible to relate social attitudes and relationships to readily observable census-type data. The research achieved a new level of precise measurement and sophisticated analysis of data and influenced the subsequent development of opinion polling and survey research.

Street-Corner Society. One of the most influential field studies of the period was conducted by a young sociologist, W. F. Whyte (1943). He observed a street-corner gang in the slums of Boston for 3 1/2 years after gaining acceptance and participating in many of its activities. He was able to achieve a mutually trusting relationship wthout concealing his identity or purpose.

Whyte provided a systematic analysis of the group's dynamic structure in its various types of relationships over time. He also was able to describe the social psychological processes of influence that produced and changed the structure. His detailed account of the powerful normative processes by which leadership was exerted and accepted showed how members' behavior was regulated according to their relative positions in the group.

Street-Corner Society has become one of social psychology's modern classics. It provided concepts and theoretical insights for the study of group processes and products, interpersonal influence and power, and the processes of role performance and identity validation, all vital areas of contemporary social psychology.

The Bennington Study. During the late 1930s a unique longitudinal study was conducted by Newcomb (1943) at Bennington, a small college for women in Vermont. Over a 4-year period, he measured the attitudes of the 250 students toward current public issues. He also conducted intensive interviews. His exhaustive data analyses revealed relationships between changes in students' attitudes and their ties to their affluent, conservative families and home communities, and also to the more liberal campus community.

Newcomb's initial interpretation of his data stressed the relationship between personality processes and attitude change, although he also recognized that powerful influence processes emanated from the campus, family, and community groups to which students belonged. His theoretical position gradually shifted to place greater emphasis on multiple reference processes and different ways of playing the role of student. Newcomb's and Whyte's studies are precursors of the contemporary integrative theoretical orientation discussed in chapter 7.

Sociometry

A major contribution of the same period, without apparent antecedents in either psychology or sociology, was Moreno's (1934) *sociometry*, a method for determining patterns of attraction and repulsion among members of a group. For example, children in a classroom were asked to indicate, usually on a paper- and-pencil test, those whom they would "like to sit next to." Many other criteria also were used, such as "liking or disliking," or "spending leisure time with." The resultant "group structure" was then depicted graphically in a *sociogram*, a network of points to represent persons and connecting lines to represent relationships. The sociogram could identify *leaders, isolates*, and *cliques* or subgroups. Such a structure is recognized by contemporary social psychologists as a mathematical *graph* (Harary & Norman, 1953; Harary, Norman, & Cartwright, 1965).

Moreno was a Vienna-trained psychiatrist with a highly original view of social life and relationships. He translated it into measurement techniques, training procedures, and clinical practices. He called his original contributions to group psychotherapy *psychodrama* and *sociodrama*, specified precise techniques and operations for each of his inventions, and insisted on an orthodoxy. You either performed sociometry, psychodrama, and sociodrama exactly as he had specified or else it was only "quasi-." For him all of his approaches derived from his worldview and systematic theory. Those who claimed to understand him became devout disciples and almost formed a cult within the social sciences. His influential journal *Sociometry* at first was devoted to publishing his own and his followers' contributions. It gradually broadened to become more representative of the field of social psychology, especially after Moreno's death, when he willed it to the American Sociological Association. Subsequently, its title was changed to *Social Psychology Quarterly*.

Moreno's measurement techniques and graphic representations found immediate favor among social psychologists and were adapted to many research problems: for example, in the study of leadership (Jennings, 1937, 1943); for research on community structure in a Vermont village (Lundberg & Steele, 1938) and in the South and Southwest (Loomis & Davidson, 1939); and in anthropological-type studies of interaction patterns (Chapple & Arensberg, 1940). Whyte (1943) was able to depict the structure of the Norton Street gang in a sociogram; and Newcomb used sociometric techniques to explore the structure of the Bennington student community. Sociometry or "quasi- sociometry" have been assimilated into social psychology's methods as have the many conceptual and theoretical insights provided by Moreno's inventiveness.

Sherif's Autokinetic Experiment

Experimental methods in social psychology made a quantum leap forward in the 1930s, largely due to Sherif's (1935, 1936) famous autokinetic experiment under Gardner Murphy's leadership at Columbia University, and to the brilliant innovations of Lewin and his associates at the Iowa Child Research Station (Barker, Dembo, & Lewin, 1941; Festinger, 1942; Lewin, Dembo, Festinger, & Sears, 1944; Lewin, Lippitt, & Escalona, 1940; Wright, 1943).

Muzafer Sherif, a Turkish scholar who completed his doctoral degree in psychology under Murphy at Harvard, was broadly familiar with the sociological concept *norm* used by Durkheim, and Thrasher's (1927) and Shaw's (1930) reports of the emergence of norms in groups (Sahakian, 1974). From his training in experimental psychology he also knew of the *autokinetic effect*: On a dark night a bright star appears to move; a stationary point of light in a totally dark room "moves" erratically as seen by different observers. Using this phenomenon he carefully designed an elegant experiment to explore the conditions and factors that led to the formation and persistence of social norms.

Sherif told his subjects that they would see a moving light and asked them to report the amount of movement. He exposed the stationary light momentarily 100 times in different parts of the room. Persons who judged alone gradually established a typical judgment with a characteristic amount of variation, although individuals had quite different "reference points" and "ranges." Persons who judged in groups of three or four heard each others' judgments, which gradually converged to a common standard within a range. A similar convergence occurred when the persons who had established their individual standards and ranges in the "alone" condition were tested again in a "together" or "group" condition. They formed a new, shared standard and range of variation. Subsequently, when the same subjects again were asked to make judgments alone, they had abandoned their original reference points and ranges in favor of the shared ones.

Sherif (1936, pp. 105–106) interpreted his research as demonstrating "the basic psychological process involved in the establishment of social norms." Persons had a tendency to structure their cognitive experience, to create "anchors" and "scales." When they became habituated to these psychological scales, these norms became endowed with a "rightness and desirability." Sherif distinguished between routine, everyday situations and ambiguous ones. Norms were generated in unclear, problem situations. Although his original experiment involved only 19 subjects in the individual condition and 40 in the group condition, the results have been repeated many times. Under the same conditions they are reliable, although recently their interpretation has been challenged. There is no doubt, however, that his classic experiment succeeded in bringing norms and normative processes into modern social psychology.

Lewin's Field Theory

Kurt Lewin's *field theory* derived from the Gestalt psychology of his University of Berlin background and his sophisticated knowledge of contemporary physical science (Deutsch, 1968; Lewin, 1935, 1936). It led directly to the experimental programs at the Iowa Child Research Station on *level of aspiration*, or goal setting, and on frustration in small children. These and other early experiments essentially employed the experimental "state- of-the-art" of that period. For example, the level of aspiration research was preceded by Volkmann's research at Harvard on *anchoring* (Chapman & Volkmann, 1939; Volkmann, 1936), itself influenced by Sherif's experiments. What distinguished the Lewinian approach, however, was the translation of his *life-space* concept and the energy gradients of his *force-field analysis* into experimental operations and the interpretation of the data within the same holistic framework.

The earlier experiments reflected Lewin's motivational and personality psychology. The breakthrough toward a truly social psychological experimental program and the beginning of *group dynamics* came in the renowned *autocratic–democratic leadership* studies (Lewin, Lippitt, & White 1939; Lippitt, 1940; White, 1938; White & Lippitt, 1960). The impetus for the research derived from Lippitt's group-work background and Lewin's (1948) increasing awareness of supra-individual social forces, catalyzed by his experiences as a refugee from Hitler's Europe and the necessity to adapt to a new culture; plus his conviction that anything that had "real" effects could be investigated experimentally.

The researchers trained leaders of boys' hobby clubs, which met regularly, in divergent styles of leadership: *autocratic, democratic,* and *laissez-faire* (a subclass of the "democratic" style initially created for the experiment). Leaders were rotated systematically among the three leadership patterns to control for personality differences so that the behavior of the boys, which was observed and recorded, could be attributed only to the differences in *group atmosphere* generated by the different leadership styles.

Dramatic differences in productivity, aggression levels, and amount of scapegoating, for example, were found in the different experimental conditions, all "favoring" the democratic style of leadership. The findings of the experiments were widely reported and had a tremendous impact because of their ideological implications at a time when America was preparing for war against totalitarian systems. The demonstration that systematic and controlled experiments could be conducted on "real" groups also impressed social psychologists. The research had combined the advantages of longitudinal field studies, like Whyte's and Newcomb's, with the power of experimental variation and controls, and was reported and interpreted within a coherent theoretical system.

Lewin's field theory and Lippitt's "total behavior technique" also were employed by French (1941) in the prototype laboratory experiment in group dynamics. He had been with Lewin at Iowa but conducted his doctoral research at the Harvard psychological laboratory.

His experiment compared six-man *organized* and *unorganized* groups under conditions of either fear or frustration. The organized groups were either members of athletic teams from upperclass Harvard houses or athletic clubs from the Italian section of Boston. The unorganized groups were formed from Harvard undergraduates with no previous acquaintance. Each group was given 45 minutes to solve three different problems—which were unsolvable—as rapidly as possible. Data were obtained by observers, questionnaires, and recordings of samples of verbal behavior.

French found many marked differences between the two experimental conditions, for example, the organized groups showed higher levels of aggressive behavior but also much greater tolerance of frustration. The investigator explained these differences in terms of Lewin's topological diagrams that depicted forces of disruption and cohesion, treating a "group space" as if it were an individual's life space.

These two pioneering experiments on groups by Lippitt and French, just before World War II, developed techniques for laboratory research on groups that have persisted with relatively little modification to the present time.

At the beginning of the 20th century, social psychology had not yet attained maturity. It was still plagued by adolescent fears of excessive dependence and parental influence. It was unproven as a scientific discipline and faced with the task of entering a world of mature, sophisticated sciences that had acknowledged accomplishments and universal prestige. Social psychology had to discover a distinctive identity and ways of playing its role in the scientific and larger world of affairs, and had to establish a record of accomplishment that would be acknowledged and respected outside the discipline. During its formative years, social psychology substantially accomplished most of those objectives, to the surprise of most of its own members and, increasingly, other scientists and knowledgeable people.

By the outbreak of World War II, social psychologists were well prepared and eager to contribute their knowlege of social behavior and their research expertise to the general war effort. In chapter 4 we describe their diversified and significant contributions, the enhanced confidence and status of social psychology by the war's successful conclusion, the postwar periods of great accomplishment and of excessive optimism and disillusionment.

Chapter 4
Contemporary Social Psychology :
The Early Decades

The history of social psychology, like William James' *stream of consciousness*, has no real "present": By the time one is aware of the present, it is past. Contemporary social psychology is a "specious present," a construction that combines the past, present, and future. Yet the early decades, from the end of World War II to the mid-1960s, can be viewed for analytical purposes as a single *moment*, using Lewin's term, a period during which the structure of the field underwent relatively little change (Clark, 1965).

In this chapter we describe some of the catalytic effects of the war and the continuation of prewar and wartime developments after the end of hostilities during the tremendous postwar expansion of social psychology. The era of golden optimism in the 1950s was succeeded by the pessimism of the late 1960s, which culminated in the *crisis in social psychology*, reviewed in chapter 5. As we see later, a growing dissatisfaction with the state of social psychology and its lack of progress finally burst through all restraints and temporarily took center stage. Yet, in terms of sheer volume of notable achievements, new theories, ingenious research, more powerful methods, and distinguished publications, the first two postwar decades also can be viewed as a period of immense progress by social psychology.

SOCIAL PSYCHOLOGY AND THE SECOND WORLD WAR

In spite of all its tragedy and horror, the war proved to be a uniquely stimulating and unforgettable professional and social experience for those American social psychologists who participated in its cooperative social scientific activities (Cartwright, 1945, 1948, 1979; Smith, 1983). For the first time, an overriding collective purpose reduced the barriers between members of different disciplines and enlisted their joint effors in projects designed to further the Allied war effort. In his famous Robbers' Cave experiment, Sherif and his associates (Sherif, Harvey, White, Hood, & Sherif, 1961) were to reproduce this intergroup phenomenon.

The range of these activities was great: It included studies of civilian morale and propaganda (Berelson, 1954; Watson, 1942), the sale of war bonds (Cartwright, 1949a), administration of occupied territories (Leighton, 1945), selection of operatives for covert activities (O.S.S. Assessment Staff, 1948), and attitude surveys of the effects of mass bombing (Krech & Crutchfield, 1948; U.S. Strategic Bombing Survey, 1946). It was during the war that the attitude and opinion survey techniques came to maturity and won acceptance as a prime tool of large-scale administration and policy formation. Among all of the intriguing applications of the social scientists' lore, the program of "action research" by Lewin (1947, 1948) and his associates was the most dramatic in attracting public attention to and support for social psychology.

Previously we have compared an intellectual discipline to a nation, in their common need for clear boundaries, criteria for membership, and validated identities. Before the war, the different social sciences had been maintained as cohesive and viable groups by their distinctive histories, traditions, languages, bonds of association and "we-feeling" among members. Group memberships also had perpetuated ingroup-outgroup social distances among the disciplines. The war generated powerful new forces which submerged previous differences among subgroups for the duration: patriotism with its increased consciousness of belonging to a single group with shared heritage and values, and collective purposes directed against common enemies and their loathed ideology.

Smith (1983) described his own experience of this novel blurring of disciplinary identities. Even before Pearl Harbor, as a graduate student in psychology, he did research for a government office headed by a historian under the supervision of a psychoanalyst. Subsequently, his close association with sociologists under field conditions led to new understandings, for example, of Chicago sociology and Myrdal's (1944) classic research on the Black experience in America. The collaborative efforts of psychologists, sociologists, anthropologists, and other specialists on actual projects involved daily interaction and the necessity to learn each others' meanings and ways of thinking. The consequences far exceeded the prewar interdisciplinary influences: Participants developed shared meanings and accomplishments, and newfound reciprocal respect and affection.

Wartime also provided ideal conditions for the development of the sample survey of attitudes and opinions as a mature tool for social psychological research: novel problems of personnel administration, both military and civilian; the availability of resources; concentrations of specialists with intense commitment; opportunities to explore new procedures where no precedents existed; unlimited pools of potential respondents with known demographic and psychometric characteristics; and ready acceptance of findings by harassed officials confronted by massive decisions with few guidelines.

The preceding decade had prepared the ground, with advances in interviewing procedures (Cantril, 1940; Katz, 1942; Lazarsfeld, 1935), content analysis (Bruner, 1941; Lasswell, 1938), the measurement of opinion (Lazarsfeld & Fiske, 1938; Murphy & Likert, 1938) and the study of voting behavior. The first large-scale election study had been conducted during the 1940 presidential campaign (Lazarsfeld, Berelson, & Gaudet, 1944).

The methods of the sample survey were perfected during the war in two major programs. One was composed mostly of psychologists and sociologists under Rensis Likert and Angus Campbell in the Bureau of Program Surveys of the Department of Agriculture. The other included sociologists guided by Paul Lazarsfeld in Stouffer's Information and Education Division of the Army. The scope of problems tackled was limited only by time and resources. For example, surveys were conducted in many parts of the world to determine the satisfaction of military personnel with combat assignments, promotion rates, and demobilization procedures (Stouffer et al., 1949, 1950); to provide information to help decrease the rates of absenteeism, and of venereal disease; to assess the reaction of the local populace to D-day landings (Riley, 1947); and to determine the relationship betweeen enemy morale and saturation bombing (U. S. Strategic Bombing Survey, 1946).

Although the luxury of explicit theories and methodological formalization had to await the postwar era (Campbell, 1946; Stouffer et al., 1949, 1950), both programs contributed a greatly expanded body of techniques and masses of data for subsequent analysis.

In a program designed to improve wartime nutrition, Margaret Mead's Food Habits Committee of the National Research Council enlisted Kurt Lewin and his band of researchers at the Iowa Child Research Station. They conducted a series of innovative field experiments comparing traditional methods of persuasion, such as lectures or individual instruction, with small-group guided discussion followed by group decision. They demonstrated the superiority of the group participation techniques in convincing housewives to serve previously despised but highly nutritious intestinal meats, such as beef hearts, kidneys, and sweet breads; to increase home consumption of milk; and to feed orange juice or cod liver oil to newborn infants (Lewin, 1943).

Although the experiments did not permit the scientifically cautious Lewin (1947) to draw "definite conclusions," his brilliant theoretical analyses elucidated the problem of "overcoming resistance to change," and of "unfreezing" *quasi-stationary equililbria.* These studies initiated the famous "action research" tradition of group dynamics.

Cartwright's (1949b) field research on the sale of U.S. war bonds participated in and extended the same tradition. He demonstrated the superiority of utilizing powerful group forces generated by a well-established group's commitment to a goal over traditional techniques of "salesmanship," such as solicitation of individual members. His results were compatible with Lewin's theoretical analysis of the dynamics of groups; and can be seen frequently demonstrated in contemporary charitable drives at the community level.

INTERDISCIPLINARY OPTIMISM

At the end of World War II, victorious America was swept by a tide of euphoria and optimism. A "one-world" movement, symbolized by the United Nations, envisioned worldwide citizenship and universal democracy. The spirit of the times was mirrored in social psychology. Successful wartime cooperation among disciplines had bred many advocates of "one-world" in social psychology, dedicated to the development of an integrated discipline that would combine the psychological and sociological subdisciplines (Newcomb, 1950, 1951). Shortly before his death, Lewin (1947) wrote of "the attempt to integrate cultural anthropology, psychology, and sociology into one social science" (p. 330). The article was included in a comprehensive book of readings in social psychology, planned by a research team on a project in Germany in 1945 (Newcomb & Hartley, 1947). The volume's editorial committee was a virtual Who's Who of social science, including psychologists, sociologists, anthropologists, and social psychiatrists. It envisioned social psychologists "having a discipline of their own."

The approach commonly advocated was via interdisciplinary research. Projects should be designed to relate to both "levels" and with multi-disciplinary staffs who would overcome the language barrier of divergent concepts and definitions (Murray, 1949; Newcomb, 1951; Sherif, 1948). A unified social psychology also must be worldwide, argued Sherif (1951), with conclusions based on data obtained in many different situations.

Just as in the larger society, however, there also were "nationalists" who opposed "worldism" (Lentz, 1950). They advocated unification of social psychology with psychology alone rather than with the other social sciences (Krech, 1951; Krech & Crutchfield, 1948).

The immediate postwar period also saw the establishment of a number of permanent organizations for research in social psychology, associated with graduate training programs at major universities. They provided professional staff, research facilities for faculty and students, and continuity for large-scale programs.

To some commentators this institutionalization seemed symptomatic of a new stage in the evolution of social psychology as a scientific discipline (Dennis, 1948).

Only two of the training programs were explicitly interdisciplinary, the Department of Social Relations at Harvard headed by Talcott Parsons and the Doctoral Program in Social Psychology at the University of Michigan led by Newcomb. Each had psychologists, sociologists, and anthropologists on its faculty. Only the Michigan program, however, accepted graduate students with a master's degree in either psychology or sociology and awarded a PhD in social psychology.

Many of the research institutes had their genesis in wartime activities because the leading social psychologists had been so heavily involved. The Bureau of Program Surveys at the Department of Agriculture became the Survey Research Center in 1946, headed by Likert and Campbell. It was joined at the University of Michigan by the Research Center for Group Dynamics in 1948, headed by Cartwright after Lewin's death. The two centers became the Institute for Social Research. Although it subscribed to interdisciplinary research there was only a scattering of sociologists, economists, and political scientists on its professional staff. The overwhelming majority were trained and identified themselves as psychologists, providing Michigan with the largest collection of "psychological" social psychologists in captivity (Smith, 1983). Elsewhere, although the prevailing ethos was interdisciplinary, the new research and training programs were staffed either by psychologists, for example, Hovland's program on communication at Yale, or by sociologists as at Lazarsfeld's and Merton's Columbia Bureau of Applied Social Research.

As always, when large and increasing amounts of money become available, people were not always in agreement about their allocation and use. Agreement on overall values had been assumed rather than explicitly discussed. "Interdisciplinary" had become a catchword that was little questioned although variously defined. Underlying tensions existed although they did not emerge far enough to disturb the calm surface of harmony and optimism.

The military and governmental departments, and the foundations, had assumed that the social or behavioral sciences, fresh from wartime achievements, were prepared to deliver up solutions or at least valuable assistance with myriad complex problems of postwar human management. All that would be required was a sufficient infusion of resources. Social psychologists encouraged this belief, especially when applying for funds. The agencies pressed for unification since their pragmatic objectives might be threatened by disciplinary schisms (Darley, 1951). They also wielded the power of the purse. Some basic scientists felt they had to compromise their standards of "pure" research to accommodate their sponsors' applied aims (Cartwright, 1949a).

Divergent purposes and standards also existed among different agencies. The National Science Foundation expressed the conservative viewpoint of the scientific establishment. Its spokesman expressed caution about the meaning of "behavioral science" and the possible threat to scientific research that "social engineering" and the relaxation of scientific rigor might imply; although, naturally, subscribing to "interdisciplinary" activity (Wilson, 1954). International agencies such as UNESCO had programs of applied social science dedicated to broad humanistic goals: international understanding, improvement of human rights, racial equality, and "action" programs; and the social implications of changing technology. They were impatient with the plodding progress of "pure science" (Klineberg, 1956).

The era was one of frenetic activity. It seemed that hardly a month went by without another conference to review progress and to exchange programmatic papers charting the future (Dennis, 1948; Guetzkow, 1951; Merton, 1949; Patton, 1954; Rohrer & Sherif, 1951; Sherif & Wilson, 1957).

Members of the various disciplines made strenuous attempts to recognize and understand concepts from the other fields and to extend their own conceptual framework. In anthropology, for example, Murdock (1949) tried to synthesize ideas from cultural anthropology, sociology, behaviorist psychology, and psychoanalysis to arrive at universal generalizations about kinship and family based on cross-cultural data from a sample of 250 societies. Sociologists attempted to incorporate the facts of learning and motivation into their traditional thinking about social interaction and the social self (Young, 1956).

Psychologists struggled to incorporate alien concepts such as *group, role*, and *institution* into their predominantly individualist framework. The Lewinian group at the Research Center for Group Dynamics made great progress in experimenting on group processes and products (Lippitt, 1948). But sociological concepts typically were redefined psychologically, changing their traditional meanings and theoretical context. For example, Sargent's (1951) definition of *role* in terms of subjective perception and personality traits effectively deleted the concept's interpersonal significance. Or else operationally defined neologisms were invented, such as *group syntality* (Cattell, 1951), *group standards* (Festinger, Schachter, & Back, 1950), and *group belongingness* (Festinger, 1950a).

Sociologists were quick to point out that their contributions and experience of 50 years were being ignored. "Action research" was what they had been calling the fields of *social problems* and *social conflict*; and "group dynamics" was another term for *social process*. Regardless of the validity of these complaints, the feelings were real and had lasting effects on the relations between the two subdisciplines of social psychology.

In a massive handbook of social psychology (Lindzey, 1954), Allport noted the increase in "combination points of view" but concluded that "the master chart is not yet available" and that students of social psychology still must learn many different maps. The psychological–sociological schism persisted (Ancona, 1954; Karpf, 1952). There had been a zealous overproduction of data but a critical shortage of integrative theory (Bruner, 1950).

The participants in the recurrent interdisciplinary conferences typically presented papers that epitomized their own distinctive theoretical or methodological positions. The published reports provided a potpourri of concepts and perspectives but no integration (Dennis, 1948; Hulett & Stagner, 1952). The same "conjunctive" principle characterized the avowedly interdisciplinary texts that included concepts and research from a variety of discipines (Bonner, 1953; Newcomb, 1950; Sherif, 1948). Because a concept derives its theoretical meaning from its position in a systematic theory or else merely expresses an observation or intuition (Northrop, 1949), it is not surprising that the assorted concepts of American social psychology seemed ill-defined and difficult to understand, especially to foreign observers (Gurmund, 1955; Souief, 1954).

There were a number of reasons why the postwar interdisciplinary optimism and zealous activity made little headway toward an integrated discipline of social psychology. Neither the practitioners nor their sponsors fully understood the difficulties of the task and were too impatient for the final solution. "Interdisciplinary" had many different meanings: In addition to the conjunctive procedure of simply adding together an assortment of diverse ideas or approaches, it often meant the Procrustean assimilation of others' concepts and theory to one's own disciplinary perspective. For example, Frenkel-Brunswik (1952) acknowledged the growing interest in *how different individuals experience* social structure and processes—psychologizing those traditional sociological concepts. One of the leading advocates of integration insisted, ironically, that a unified social psychology must be derived entirely from the principles of general psychology (Sherif, 1951).

Approaches toward an integrated system of social psychology took many forms. One involved a recognition of different "levels" of social organization, using the analogy of biologic evolution (Schneirla, 1951). Another employed Lewin's popular field theory model, again only by analogy, to include both personality, situation, and their interaction (Sargent, 1952). The speculative writings of Fromm were seen as a possible basis (Murphy, 1954). An experimental paradigm of *independent, intervening*, and *dependent* variables in psychological and sociological research yielded a typology of interdisciplinary "theoretical" problems (Tolman, 1952). Sociologists, psychologists, and anthropologists at Harvard demonstrated that they had some interaction by contributing to a grandiose compendium presenting a "grand theory" which few readers could understand (Parsons & Shils, 1951).

It became increasingly clear that to achieve true collaboration in research and to make progress towards a unified science, social psychologists had to acquire adequate backgrounds in the theories and methods of the "parent disciplines" of psychology, sociology and cultural anthropology (Stagner, 1952; Xydias, 1955). This, of course, is what the interdisciplinary training programs at Harvard and Michigan were meant to accomplish: to produce a new breed of social psychologist that would construct the unified discipline. This dream faced a number of disruptive realities. Graduate students were forced to ingest a massive, heterogeneous aggregate of information from diverse sources and then to disgorge it, with no necessary digestion. In the absence of integrative theory or much agreement among their instructors the burden of integration was left to the students themselves.

The greatest obstacle and the paramount reality was the central question of professional identity. Career opportunities for social psychologists existed primarily in the academic world whose professional, economic, and social forces were channeled through a firmly established departmental structure. Students had to acquire professional identities as psychologists, sociologists, or anthropologists even though their "specialty" was social psychology. They had to select appropriate role models from among their instructors, each of whom identified with a particular discipline.

Graduate students soon learned tht the "real" professional world was still structured by separate disciplines, each with its technical journals and books, professional societies, "old boy" networks that effectively controlled appointments, and claims on a fair share of available resources such as governmental and foundation support. To identify with a particular discipline meant to adopt a way of thinking, a sufficient acceptance of its traditional values and conformity to its norms in exchange for the right to participate in its interaction networks and allocation of rewards, and to have one's professional identity validated by reference others.

INTERDISCIPLINARY DISILLUSIONMENT

By the mid-1950s, the postwar euphoria in social psychology had begun to cool (Cartwright, 1961). The interdisciplinary pendulum was swinging away from excessive optimism toward disillusionment. As in the world at large, confronted by the insuperable obstacles to achieving "one world," the idealists gradually were overpowered by superior forces of realism, nationalism, or even chauvinism.

A retreat to the parent disciplines began, with many indications. The much-abused term *interdisciplinary* appeared less frequently in publications. There were fewer conferences to stimulate what someone had called "interdisciplinary cross-sterilization." Anthropologists abandoned the "culture and personality" movement and reasserted their traditional disciplinary identity (Levinson, 1964). The "identity anxiety" also was evident among psychologists and sociologists in the tone of their publications and re-emphasis of their unique conceptual and methodological frameworks. At several universities the collaboration ended between departments of psychology and sociology that jointly had offered the introductory course in social psychology. Each resumed teaching its own course, often under the same title. The culmination of this pullback was the abandonment of the interdisciplinary graduate programs at both Harvard and Michigan, events that shocked and angered many participants.

In addition to the events discussed previously, the tremendous growth and public acceptance of psychology seemed to make inevitable the failure of the postwar interdisciplinary movement. Integration or even true collaboration between unequal groups is a hazardous process, often evoking majority group-minority group feelings and stereotypes. In the 1950s psychologists had begun a movement to obtain certification by state legislatures to prevent the pre-emption of private practice by psychiatrists or unqualified practitioners. Sociologists who worked in the field of social psychology were threatened by this development and felt impelled to reassert their independent professional identity and defend their rights (American Sociological Society, 1958).

The retreat from unification in social psychology generated a range of feelings, explanations, and subsequent relationships between disciplines. One sociologist who had been associated with the Michigan program asserted that "the ideology of professional psychology ... is linked to the anti- philosophical, anti-historical, narrowly means-oriented and optimistic character of much American thought and culture" (Janowitz 1954, p. 528).

But there also were more temperate and optimistic social psychologists who adhered to the interdisciplinary ideal. Levinson (1964) pointed to considerable progress, especially in areas of social problems, and wrote of "the early stages of a genuine convergence ... a new social psychology" (p.77) that transcended traditional disciplinary lines.

Although he acknowledged that social psychology had retreated from some of its initial aims and problems, Back (1963) maintained that it still required "full-range theories" that could account for both experimental situations and historical patterns. It was clear, however, that in the immediate future there would be no more than coexistence between psychological and sociological social psychologies, and with the other social sciences.

SOCIAL PSYCHOLOGY'S EARLY ACCOMPLISHMENTS

Expansion of the Field

In spite of the failure of the interdisciplinary movement, social psychology in the first two postwar decades had become a well-established, productive scientific field by almost all criteria. The number of well-trained PhDs who identified themselves as social psychologists had increased greatly, a "population explosion" (Cartwright, 1979). Graduate training, research facilities, professional societies, technical journals and books, and public support and acceptance all had multiplied.

In 1954, a two-volume handbook had appeared (Lindzey, 1954). The update (Lindzey & Aronson, 1968–1969) required five massive volumes to accommodate the voluminous theoretical, research, and applied literature. A stream of varied undergraduate and graduate texts were being made available. By 1965, about 100 textbooks had appeared, two thirds written by psychologists and one third by sociologists (Allport, 1968). In three texts reviewed by Smith (1966) over one half of the references dated from 1955 or later.

Social psychology had not yet achieved the maturity of an integrated theoretical framework or consensus among its diverse practitioners on a host of important issues. In terms of both quantitative and qualitative standards, however, and especially in the assurance of the majority of its members, it appeared to be a healthy and successful enterprise.

There seemed to be solid grounds for social psychologists' professional confidence. A torrent of research had provided advancements in most of the established areas of the field. There were many notable contributions by distinguished social psychologists. Innovative and insightful developments also were stimulating new directions for research and theorizing. In the limited space available, we mention some of these early accomplishments.

Advances in Established Areas

Methods of Research. The 800-page second volume of the 1968–1969 *Handbook of Social Psychology* was devoted to discussion and evaluation of the many significant advances in research methods. It included chapters on attitude measurement, experimentation, simulation of social situations, data analysis, observation, interviewing, and content analysis. Especially prominent was the newly achieved mastery of experimental techniques, evident in "virtually every chapter" of the five volumes (Aronson & Carlsmith, 1968). Technical journals were crammed with the often surprising results of laboratory experiments with innovative, ingenious designs. The development and availability of computers wedded to advances in mathematical-statistical theory conferred upon researchers undreamed of power to analyze and manipulate their data. A variety of creative methods for measuring attitudes and opinions transformed that traditional area (Scott, 1968). Scaling theory was extended to nonmetrical and partially metrical data and then generalized by Coombs (1950, 1964) in an enlightening "theory of data" that pointed to the costs that inevitably accompanied increased power of measurement and analysis.

Indeed, for some social psychologists who did not unequivocally admire or welcome these tremendous strides in technical research proficiency, the costs may have outweighed the benefits. They raised questions: Did the more powerful methods contribute to increased knowledge or only to a vast accumulation of narrow, localized "facts" that were nonadditive because of the great variation in methods, experimental designs and analysis procedures? Could almost any desired results be attained by powerful manipulative experimental designs and analysis techniques in the hands of brilliant and determined investigators? Did the preoccupation with method block the development of general, integrative theories in social psychology? These issues are discussed later in this section.

Group Structure and Processes. The Lewinians had pioneered the experimental study of groups and their utilization as vehicles of social engineering and social change. They continued to lead the way in these directions. Festinger and his associates at Michigan demonstrated that in the laboratory they could manipulate dimensions of groups, such as *cohesiveness* and *hiearchical structure*, and achieve hypothesized effects on communication and conformity (Cartwright & Zander, 1960). Lippitt and his colleagues at the Research Center for Group Dynamics, together with Bradford, Benne, and other leading educators, founded the National Training Laboratory for Group Development at Bethel College, Maine. They introduced and experimented with *T- Groups, sensitivity training*, A-Groups (skill training groups), and new leadership and large-group techniques (Bradford, Gibb, & Benne, 1964). These brilliant innovations were adopted widely; sometimes, unfortunately, without regard to their intellectual antecedents, which led to a wave of somewhat unsavory "encounter group" applications or exploitations (Ruitenbeek, 1970). In Britain, the Tavistock Institute continued its clinical application of group techniques in industry (Jaques, 1951; Sofer, 1961). Maxwell Jones (1953) pioneered his *therapeutic community* approach to mental hospitals, which led to widespread recognition of the significance of group processes in the treatment of persons with emotional, intellectual, or behavioral impairment.

These exciting developments in research and application stimulated a surge of corresponding activity that spread in all directions. The resultant mountains of data—experimental findings, clinical reports, "mini-theories" that did not extend much beyond the findings on which they were based— demanded codification, separation of the genuine findings from the sludge. Many attempts were made, using various schema. Two integrative theories, by Thibaut and Kelley (1959) and Homans (1961) both adopted a reinforcement, cost- reward, "exchange" perspective wedded to normative theory from classical sociology. Each systematized a segment of the literature within its conceptual scheme and stimulated extensive research and discussion. As Steiner (1964) reported, however, "the field (of groups) covers an unruly assortment of theory and research which has so far defied integration" (p. 421). Olmsted (1969) compared it to "Stephen Leacock's famous horseman riding off in all directions at once" (p. 616).

Attitudes and Opinions. The study of attitudes was temporarily eclipsed during the interdisciplinary flirtation of the first postwar decade. It reassumed its traditional central position in social psychology during the second, with an increased focus on attitude structure and change (McGuire, 1966). Social psychology long had outgrown its early appellation as "the science of attitudes" but research on attitudes still defied any clear boundaries and often included many of the established topics such as social influence, persuasion, and conformity (McGuire, 1966). It constituted a vast, amorphous area with little unity. Many of the solid empirical studies were clustered around one of the isolated mini-theories and its parochial problems. Measurement issues and attempts to contribute to pressing social questions also generated considerable research. As Moscovici (1963) concluded, "many remarkable achievements are short-lived because they lack continuity and orientation" (p. 236). There were, however, a number of more general distinguished contributions.

Attempts were being made to assimilate research findings within one or more of the traditional psychological theories. For example, the widely used *semantic differential* scales for delineating the dimensions of meaning in attitudes (Osgood, Suci, & Tannenbaum, 1957) had antecedents in both behaviorism (Hull, 1943) and in cognitive theory. A large volume of laboratory experiments on attitude change were generated by the *theory of cognitive dissonance* (Festinger, 1957), discussed later. The *functional theory of attitudes* (Katz, 1960) theorized that attitudes served the dynamic needs of the personality. Research and theory on *dogmatism* (Rokeach, 1960) attempted to bridge the gap between the psychodynamic theory of the authoritarian personality work and the Gestalt cognitive orientation. Newcomb's longitudinal follow-up of his classical Bennington study, to determine the relative stability of social attitudes initially generated on the campus, attempted to understand the processes using *role* and *reference group* concepts (Newcomb, Koenig, Flacks, & Warwick, 1967).

There were many other noteworthy attempts to integrate the attitude domain. However, McGuire's (1966) scholarly review had to conclude that no general theory of attitude change was supported by the voluminous evidence. The massive research findings still sought an integrative framework.

Person Perception. How one person obtains and processes information about another person's attributes, motivation, and activity has been one of social psychology's traditional problems, often called—somewhat unsatisfactorily—*person perception* (Tagiuri, 1969). In the postwar period, Asch's experiments on forming impressions of others, discussed previously, provided a cognitive (Gestalt) reformulation and created renewed interest in the area. A number of ingenious experiments and theoretical contributions identified relevant variables and fostered increased understanding of the problem's complexity.

Fritz Heider's (1944, 1946, 1958) scholarly articles and his distinguished volume on interpersonal perception were among the most influential contributions of the era. A student at Kansas once asked the gentle scholar when he had begun writing his book. The answer was: "Right after the first World War!" In that long-awaited work Heider brought together his academic antecedents as one of the early Gestalt psychologists and a lifetime of scholarship in a meticulous examination of interpersonal processes. Although his "theory" was not systematic in any formal sense, it contained a great many original theoretical insights and conceptual formulations. It provided the basis for both *balance theory*, which itself spawned a variety of related conceptions (Zajonc, 1968), and *attribution theory* (Jones et al., 1971). Together these two areas generated a sizable segment of the research and theorizing in early contemporary social psychology.

New Developments and Trends

Assimilation of Classical Contributions. Science progresses not only by creating conceptions and techniques that stimulate new trends in thinking and research but also by revising past contributions. The two postwar decades saw extensive efforts to review, analyze, replicate, modify, extend, and assimilate pioneering contributions. Among the classical studies whose findings were qualified and expanded within modified theoretical frameworks were the Hawthorne studies (Franke, 1979; Franke & Kaul, 1978; Wardwell, 1979), the American Soldier research (Merton & Lazarsfeld 1950), and the Authoritarian Personality project (Christie & Jahoda, 1954). Although Kurt Lewin's well-respected theories did not lead directly to much research, his *field theoretical* orientation became widely diffused in social psychological thought.

Socialization of Reinforcement Theories. The traditional psychological theories also underwent continuous expansion and revision as they were adapted to research on social psychological problems. The individually oriented behaviorist theories were revised to deal with multiperson interactional phenomena (Berger & Lambert, 1968). In the process the original theories lost a great deal of their rigor. They were not always recognizable in the *social learning theories* (Bandura, 1962; Bandura & Walters, 1963; Rotter, 1954); or in new, eclectic formulations that borrowed heavily from divergent orientations. For example, Hovland's highly productive research program on communication and social influence melded reinforcement thinking with both psychodynamic and cognitive ideas (Hovland 1957; Hovland, Janis, & Kelley, 1953). Thibaut and Kelley's (1959) interpersonal reinforcement or *exchange* theory incorporated both cognitive conceptions and normative, sociological ideas. Homans' (1961, 1964) similar theory was a wedding of Skinnerian reinforcement thinking to classical sociological thought.

These and many other eclectic "socializations" of reinforcement theories evoked mixed responses: Some analysts saw them as the possible basis for a general social psychological theory (Berger & Lambert, 1968). Others were less sanguine, believing that behaviorist theories with their roots in research on animals were inherently unsuitable for conceptualization of human behavior: They ignored central questions of human social psychology, such as what is rewarding to a particular person, and how persons respond to their own behavior (Deutsch & Krauss, 1965).

Rise of the Cognitive Orientation. The two postwar decades saw the cognitive orientation become the dominant approach in social psychology. The "mind" had returned to favor; and social psychologists were confronted with the age-old problem of "combining subjectivities" (Jackson, 1964, 1965) in order to avoid an entirely individualist psychological approach to social phenomena.

The move toward cognitive social psychology began with MacLeod's introduction of Gestalt psychology, Lewin's field theory, Krech and Crutchfield's phenomenological text, Asch's cognitive interpretation of imitation and suggestion, and Heider's scholarly articles and book, all mentioned previously. The catalyst was Festinger's *theory of cognitive dissonance*, with its simplistic thesis that a person experiences discomfort when "cognitive elements"—thoughts, attitudes, opinions, memories, perceptions—are contradictory, or "dissonant," and is motivated to make them more consonant by thought or action.

Festinger's imaginative derivations of hypotheses that contradicted "common sense" and his ingenious, dramatic but highly contrived experimental demonstrations attracted countless disciples. Other theorists made unique contributions to the same general problem, the dynamics of thought when confronted with divergent phenomena (Feather, 1964, 1965; Osgood, Suci, & Tannenbaum, 1957; Zajonc, 1960). The total volume of literature on cognitive dissonance and related theories was immense. It included considerable criticism, both positive and negative (Chapanis & Chapanis, 1964; McGuire, 1966). In an incisive review, Zajonc (1968–1969) remarked that "the conceptual bravado of dissonance psychologists has been accompanied by an appropriately cavalier attitude to experimentation" (p. 390). Dissonance theory undoubtedly had excited and activated a generation of researchers. Deutsch and Krauss (1965) pronounced that "Festinger would rather be stimulating than right" and found his attitude sensible, because "no one is 'right' for very long" (p. 76). But perhaps all theories should be "right" at their inception, before being replaced by those that have greater validity and generality.

Many other notable contributions had a cognitive or cognitive hybrid perspective, for example, the semantic differential and Rokeach's cognitive reformulation of Authoritarianism, mentioned previously. Zajonc's distinguished *Handbook* chapter reviewed the massive work on cognitive structure and dynamics and noted how completely the era's social psychology had been transformed.

Reappearance of the Self as an Empirical Problem. Social psychologists' confidence that anything conceivable could be measured led to the exodus of the "self" from its Watsonian limbo. A large volume of research was conducted with a seemingly endless stream of hastily defined concepts. In the absence of substantial systematic theories of the self, operational definitions often sufficed. Research procedures were guided by an investigator's preferred theoretical orientation. For example, cognitive theorists conducted research on the *self-concept, self-definition,* and *self-perception*; psychodynamic thinkers investigated *self-esteem, self-accep-*

tance, and *self-actualization*; behaviorists observed a person's *self-response, self-assertion* or *self-control*; and role theorists dealt with *self-role congruence, self-presentation*, and *social identity*. What emerged was a massive accumulation of data with assorted theoretical antecedents, often mixed, unrecognizable, or entirely missing. Heroic efforts were made to review and systematize the polyglot literature, understandably with less than complete success (Diggory, 1966; Gordon & Gergen, 1968; Stoodley, 1962; Wylie, 1961, 1968, 1969). Although solid accomplishments awaited future developments, an important step had been taken in recognizing that self-processes no longer could be ignored in a scientific social psychology.

Increased Recognition of Environmental Influence. Following Lewin's (1943, 1944) pioneering theoretical analyses, Roger Barker and Herbert Wright (Wright & Barker, 1950; Barker & Wright, 1955) developed *psychological ecology*, concepts and methods for systematically observing and measuring the milieu of social behavior. They began with a positivist, atheoretical approach, emulating natural scientists' studies of flora and fauna—somewhat reminiscent of the earlier ecological school of sociologists (Dawson & Gettys, 1948; Mukerjee, 1932; Park, 1936; Park & Burgess, 1925; Quinn, 1934).

Psychologists struggled with conceptualizing and measuring aspects of the *environment*. As with the *self*, they typically adopted their accustomed theoretical perspectives. Behaviorists focused on the stimulus properties of an environment and its structure of rewards. Cognitive theorists looked at the information provided and beliefs fostered by environments; and the process by which persons constructed meaningful environments. Psychodynamic theorists concentrated on whether or to what degree an environment was fulfilling, frustrating, or threatening. And role theorists attempted to identify and understand the environment's options and potentials for persons to engage in social acts, perform roles, and present social identities.

The recognition of environmental influence even forced its way into the experimental laboratory, where all situational influences traditionally had been sterilized as intrusive impurities. Rosenthal's (1963, 1966) brilliant work demonstrated that the experimental environment—and indeed the situational context of all research—invariably conditioned research findings.

Sociological thinking and research made a significant contribution to this increased recognition of environmental influence. Social psychologists were aware, for example, of studies by sociologists, often in collaboration with psychologists or psychiatrists, of the treatment environment of mental illness (Dunham & Weinberg, 1960; Greenblatt, Levinson, & Williams, 1957; Stanton & Schwartz, 1954), of the urban environment in deviant behavior (Cloward & Ohlin, 1960; Cohen, 1955, 1966; Sutherland & Cressey, 1966), of Goffman's (1959, 1961a) *dramaturgical* approach that emphasized the situational setting and its props, and of related work by the increasingly appreciated *symbolic interaction* school (Stone & Farberman, 1970). Recognizing this contribution to social psychology, Deutsch and Krauss (1965) remarked that empiricism was primarily an inheritance from psychology and environmentalism from sociology.

Problems of the Discipline

In spite of these and many other substantial contributions to theory, methods, and research, social psychology toward the end of the 1960s had important unresolved disciplinary problems. Were these only to be expected, endemic in any healthy, growing, adolescent science? Or were they, as some insisted, critical flaws in the discipline that required radical reform and new directions?

In any era, the large majority of members of a scientific field encompass in their research, often without awareness, the prevailing meta-theoretical and methodological assumptions of their discipline (Kuhn, 1962, 1970). They do "normal" science, without challenging the existing *paradigm*. Kuhn defined a paradigm as the set of conventions—models and assumptions—in a field that for the time define the "correct" way to formulate problems, conduct research and, in general, make acceptable contributions to scientific knowledge. Although social psychology had not yet evolved to the stage where one paradigm was dominant, only a small minority actively were striving to change the generally accepted way of "doing" social psychology.

In spite of this overall consensus among social psychologists, each did have an implicit or explicit position, usually well-grounded, on far-reaching issues such as the relative emphasis to be placed on *empiricism or social humanism, how to identify the significant problems of the discipline*, or *eclecticism versus general integrative theory*. In the following sections these and other issues are reviewed briefly and some of the advocates are quoted. Each clearly is expressing a position on the issue; it would have been equally possible to quote other distingished social psychologists with contrary positions. The author, too, has his position—as discussed in the Preface— reflected in his choice of materials and discussion, in spite of an effort to achieve a balanced presentation. In the final chapter the author's theoretical orientation, if not already evident, will become manifest in his attempt to distill from the current literature the direction of social psychology's future development.

Empiricism or Social Humanism? One of the dilemmas that divided social psychologists was their relative emphasis on empiricism or social humanism. Preoccupation with method, clever research designs or techniques, rigorous formal or mathematical models, and miniature theories all were deplored for stressing "form rather than substance." They failed to deal with "urgent social realities" (Clark,1965) or produce "socially useful knowledge" (Deutsch & Krauss, 1965). Gordon Allport (1968) complained that "some current investigations seem to end up in elegantly polished triviality—snippets of empiricism, but nothing more" (p. 68).

Yet even those who called for social amelioration rather than a sterile "scientism" valued empirical research. For example, Festinger's theory was prized even though incorrect because it stimulated such a great volume of experimental research. Even Merton's theoretical essays were welcomed because they led to empirical work. But Goffman's insightful analyses of social relations and situations were critized for failure to generate research: "Theories that rely on illustration are vulnerable to counterexamples "(Deutsch & Krauss, 1965, pp. 211). The question remained: Could Lewin's vision of a general theory that led to both experimental verification and progressive social action be realized?

How to Recognize the Significant Problems? Another unanswered question was: How does one recognize the significant problems of the discipline? Social psychologists were unwilling to accept everyday definitions of a "problem": A social problem such as alcoholism or vandalism required conceptualization before it could be investigated in scientific research. The analysis of such social concerns formerly had been derived from one of the traditional psychological or sociological theories, without notable success. Now social psychologists, imbued with empiricist fervor, adopted an inductive approach, sometimes disguised in one of the many mini-theories that were restatements and generalizations of research findings.

As mentioned earlier, topics or areas within social psychology proliferated and were either very general or idiosyncratic. Distinguished social psychologists attempted to impose structure and boundaries upon particular areas, in the *Handbook, Annual Review* chapters, books, and journal articles. These endeavors mostly ended in frustration. For example, Collins and Raven (1968–1969) in their review of the "psychological aspects of group structure" confessed that "we were unable to devise a theoretical system which would encompass even a small percentage of the studies. . . . Eventually, perhaps, an all-encompassing system of codification will be developed" (pp. 184, 185). Similarly, the literature on "person perception" was described as "a puzzling mosaic (which) fails to be amenable to systematic cumulation" (Tagiuri, 1968–1969, p. 434).

Eclecticism or General Theory? The dominant spirit of the times was *eclecticism*, a tolerance of ideas and concepts without regard to their pedigree, as long as they could be accommodated within the same research project or mini-theory. Deutsch and Krauss derided "the outdated and grandiose notion that there can be one general theory which will embrace all social psychological phenomena." They defended the "variety of conceptual frames and theories" as necessary "to embrace the richness of human behavior" (p. 215).

Many of the well-respected accomplishments in social psychology were essentially free-floating from any "well-established theoretical tradition" (Tagiuri, 1968–1969, p. 434). This applied in varying degrees, for example, to work on cooperation and trust (Deutsch, 1962), bargaining behavior (Fouraker & Siegel, 1963), coalition formation (Gamson, 1964), and emotional experience (Schachter, 1964). Fiedler's theory of leadership effectiveness is an especially good example of the genre. Beginning merely as a cluster of measuring instruments and the continually revised interpretation of systematic data from studies in many different situations, it gradually achieved theoretical status.

Eclecticism was not antitheoretical, but was based on a Baconian faith that truth will out and error correct itself. McGuire (1968–1969) epitomized this position: "Pursuing any theory with persistence is more likely to be enlightening than is engaging in unprogrammatic research involving one little experiment after another" (p. 272).

Arrayed against eclecticism in the 1968–1969 *Handbook* were social psychologists such as Gordon Allport, Tagiuri, Gibb, and Berkowitz who called for an integrative general theory. Some who bemoaned the anarchy and chaos of extreme eclecticism may have been nostalgic for the good old days of an overarching authoritative general theory, as their opponents claimed. But their position was a classical one in science. It seemed inherent in the principle of parsimony that unity be sought and integrative attempts be made: The alternative was not science, but a collection of unrelated "facts" or "theories."

But the position did not necessarily imply a dogmatic devotion to one particular theoretical creed. Quoting the august Edwin G. Boring that "eclecticism can be laziness," Berkowitz (1968–1969) advocated that the various general theories should compete for ascendancy in social psychology: "Controversy is productive . . . the rival claimants should sharpen their arguments—and let the best theory win" (p. 118).

In the publications of the era, many discussants formulated these issues as critical, all-or-none conflicts: The choice between extremes was imperative for the future health and survival of social psychology. But these controversies also could be viewed as normal disciplinary problems involving questions of the degree of emphasis, to be resolved in the course of the customary collective efforts of all social psychologists.

Fragmentation of Social Psychology

In his review of the *Handbook* (Lindzey & Aronson, 1968–1969), Volkart (1971) described social psychology as "a rather vast umbrella under which a number of different theorists and researchers huddle together for protective reasons; but few of them know how to talk to each other. They may all be 'social psychologists'; but they speak different languages, have different assumptions, and use quite different methods" (p. 899).

One of the major schisms was between social psychologists trained and identified as either psychologists or sociologists. There were two main branches of social psychology, a majority-group and a minority-group, with divergent perspectives and ways of defining the field, and separate texts, sourcebooks, and journals. The comprehensive Handbook omitted much relevant research by sociologists and only four of its authors belonged to that discipline (Stryker, 1971; Volkart, 1971). In attempting to account for this omission, Stryker proposed that it was partly due to recipocal negative attitudes and partly to unfamiliarity. It appeared that members of the two branches did not really understand each others' perspectives or activities.

We have proposed earlier that the schism between the two sub-disciplines of social psychology involved questions of identity and reference processes. An illustration of the potency of these forces comes from communist Hungary, where the official dialectical-materialist doctrine was used by psychologists to justify their Pavlovian physiological theory, but by sociologists to support a Marxist ideological interpretation of social and psychological phenomena, rejecting "psychologism" (Hunyady, 1966). The author reported a lack of cooperation between the two groups and suggested that social psychology might offer a common meeting ground!

Among social psychologists from the same parent discipline the amount of understanding and agreement was hardly better. In psychology, a half-dozen major "systematic" theoretical positions claimed adherents, each with its own distinctive assumptions, formulation of problems, conceptual levels of analysis and language, and technical literature (Deutsch & Krauss, 1965; Lindzey & Aronson, 1968–1969).

Sociology was split by acrimonious debates between traditionalists who accepted in some degree Parsons' *structural-functionalism* and critical sociologists influenced by Marxist theories of conflict (Gouldner, 1970)—a division not unrelated to the larger political situation in the country. Followers of Mead, Cooley and Blumer, called *symbolic interactionists*, also were tending toward forming a separate movement, even though they themselves embraced a wide variety of divergent perspectives (Kuhn, 1964). The defection of Homans (1961, 1964) to the ranks of psychological reductionism, when he embraced Skinner's radical behaviorism, added an additional dimension to the disorder.

Social psychologists also were divided by their preferred research methods, the "topics" in which they specialized, and by the pervasive distinction between "basic" and "applied" social pschology (Cartwright, 1949a; Lindzey & Aronson, 1968–1969).

A large number of mini-theories were formulated by "ambitious young 'social psychologists who sought to stake out new territory for themselves" (Smith, 1983, p. 175). Although each of these ingenious theoretical constructions enlisted temporarily the efforts of a coterie of eager researchers and exegesists, resulting in a stream of narrowly problem-oriented research, they supplanted efforts to make progress on the larger issues of integrative theory and on what Smith called the "socially and humanly important problems" (p. 175). Riecken (1965) said that "everyone is talking, but only about his own game" (p. 15). One of the pioneers of social psychology (Katz, 1967) pointed to the critical problem of "the continuing and growing fragmentation of the discipline" (p. 341).

In spite of these schisms, there were still some interdisciplinary voices and activities directed toward the solution of theoretical issues required by a unified scientific discipline. Although the tide had receded, Meltzer (1961) and Levinson (1964) continued to appeal for an integrated social psychology; and Boulding (1962) renewed his efforts to demonstrate the integrative possibilities of universal concepts such as "communication" or "conflict."

However, the state of the field permitted only the loosest of integrations (Smith, 1966). The two current interdisciplinary texts, co-authored by psychologists and sociologists, either concentrated on a review and assessment of the massive research literature, ignoring its disciplinary origins or problems of systematization (Secord & Backman, 1964); or presented a somewhat illusory picture of a unified field (Newcomb, Turner, & Converse, 1965).

A few scattered attempts were being made to solve historical problems, such as the dilemma of individual and group levels of phenomena: the "master problem of social psychology" (Allport, 1962), or the "problem of combining subjectivities" (Jackson, 1964, p. 225). But the Zeitgeist dictated little attention to or influence by these efforts. The spirit of the times seemed to welcome confrontation rather than the resolution of conflict.

Chapter 5
The Crisis in Social Psychology

Certain periods in history attain their own identity and label, such as the Renaissance or the Great Depression, although few agree as to their beginnings, duration, interpretation, or significance. On a microcosmic scale, of course, such a period during the late 1960s and the 1970s impressed itself on the consciousness of social psychologists and was tagged the "crisis in social psychology," when the forces of dissatisfaction and dissensus shattered the traditional norms and unleashed a torrent of self-criticism.

More than 100 articles and a number of major volumes appeared, attacking every conceivable aspect of social psychology: its theory, methods, assumptions and biases, scientific and social contributions, and prospects as a scientific discipline. Each criticism evoked one or more counterattacks from the ranks of the large majority of social psychologists still busily engaged in "normal science." The exchanges in the journals and symposia were searching and often intemperate.

What distinguished this period from the normal dialogues concerning metatheoretical and methodological issues, and the traditional criticism of specific contributions, legitimate and essential in all science, was the assault on the total enterprise, the volume, vehemence, variety, and duration of the critical exchanges, and the participation by many of the eminent members of the profession.

To be a social psychologist during this period meant to participate in the "crisis," even if not overtly. As a collective social act, however, it lacked any common definition. The participants played many different roles and presented diverse identities; they marched to the tunes of different drummers. The lack of agreement was almost total: in the targets of criticism, the perspectives, interests, and purposes of the critics, and in the interpretations of and responses to the crisis. It is problematic how much understanding was generated by this paroxysm of self-analysis.

Toward the end of the 1970s, the stormfront had passed through, only scattered flashes of criticism continued and even the "crisis" rubric had become "tedious" to some social psychologists. The immediate appearance of the field was little changed. The journals, monographs, and texts provided essentially the same image of gradual change within the continuity provided by a framework of shared assumptions. The theoretical problems and methods of research had not altered noticeably, nor had there been any upheaval in the prestige establishment of social psychology; although the crisis had provided some opportunities for professional mobility.

However, a new norm for social psychology legitimated more open discussion of basic theoretical and methodological assumptions and militated toward social psychology's definition as a pluralistic field. During and immediately after the crisis period, a number of major proposals were made for drastic reorientation that continued to generate discussion and influence.

In the preceding chapter we reviewed the fragmentation of social psychology and the tensions and forces growing beneath the surface, despite tremendous progress. In this chapter we analyze the diverse criticisms, critics, and responses to the crisis. Although most traditional social psychologists may have concluded that the "crisis in social psychology" was little more than a cathartic or catalytic period, it remains to be seen whether or not real change was generated or the same tensions and forces remain active in contemporary social psychology.

CRITICISM AND CONFUSION IN SOCIAL PSYCHOLOGY

Early Rumblings of Dissatisfaction

Volkert's metaphor of assorted social psychologists huddled together under their vast umbrella was apt, because the storm clouds were gathering. There was a growing malaise in American social psychology. The discomfort of foreign scientists with the vagueness of concepts (Gurmund, 1955; Souief, 1954) and the lack of theoretical integration (Ancona, 1954; Xydias, 1955), mentioned previously, had little impact because it was not available in English. Nor did the early criticism by Moreno (1948) that experiments in social psychology sacrificed substantive problems to fascination with methods. He always was such a strident advocate of his own approach and contributions; and his status in social psychology was marginal.

More central to the values and identities of social psychologists were continuing questions about the ethical propriety and scientific validity of their research methods. The "bugging" of a jury for research purposes had created public outrage, an investigation by the Senate Judiciary Committee, and considerable discussion of the conflicting social values of freedom of scientific inquiry versus the sanctity of the judicial process and the right of privacy (Amrine & Sanford, 1956; Gross, 1956).

In a major psychological journal, Kelman (1967) expressed the ambivalence of many colleagues toward the widespread use of deception in manipulating the thoughts and behavior of subjects in laboratory experiments. He discussed the scientific justification for such procedures, but also their ethical, methodological, and public relations disadvantages.

The problem of safeguarding human subjects from harm or infringement of their rights was not the same, however, as the question of the scientific validity of social psychologists' research methods—although the two sometimes were confounded. They represented cherished values of social psychologists that were not always compatible. Indeed, it was the quest for increased rigor, control, and validity in social psychological research that had led to the boundaries of ethical propriety. Some members of the field were willing to assign priority to one of the two social values; most sought to maximize compliance with both or to achieve a viable compromise.

The scientific validity of methods used by social psychologists also was being scrutinized and questioned, especially the "small group" laboratory experiment in the tradition of Sherif, Asch, and Festinger. Sociologically oriented critics deplored interpretation of an experimental situation as an analogue of a physical science experiment: This ignored its interpersonal system and social influence processes (Back, Hood, & Brehm, 1964; Ex, 1960). Psychologists were becoming aware of a "social psychology" of the laboratory experiment that introduced situational variables such as "demand characteristics" (Orne, 1959, 1962)—the implicit influences upon subjects' behavior of the experimental situation—or "experimenter effects" (Rosenthal, 1966)—the non-verbal transmission to subjects of experimenters' expectations or predictions. In a reversal of his interdisciplinary zeal, Boulding (1967) questioned the legitimacy of all of the social sciences, because investigators and their findings were parts of the systems being studied.

These early rumblings disturbed the atmosphere but did not penetrate the consciousness of social psychologists like Ring's (1967) thunderbolt published in experimental social psychologists' own journal. In a frontal attack he denounced the frivolous "fun-and-games" orientation, and accused social psychology of abandoning Lewin's vision of a discipline that would advance both scientific understanding and human welfare, in favor of one that was "exhibitionistic" and that "equates notoriety with achievement." He said that "social psychology today (is) . . . in a state of profound intellectual disarray" (p. 117).

The Storm Bursts: Torrents of Criticism

Although Ring's denunciation of the state of social psychology did not evoke immediate responses, except for McGuire's (1967) exculpatory rejoinder in the same issue, it became perceived as the "opening salvo" of the crisis literature (Smith, 1983). As the outpouring of self-criticism mounted, however, the most common theme was social psychology's lack of theoretical progress (Tajfel, 1972). It was castigated for "theoretical retardation" and "shallowness of analytical treatment" (Kruglanski, 1975, p. 491), for failure to develop the traditional criteria of a scientific discipline (Moscovici, 1972), and for neglecting its cumulative history and a coherent theory based on it that would generate fundamental problems and paths toward their solution (Silverman, 1977).

Among many social psychologists, the term *paradigm* (Kuhn, 1962, 1970) became a popular catchword to symbolize their dissatisfaction, their somewhat nostalgic longing for a "grand theory"; or at least consensual assumptions and authoritative research models that would provide the order and power to unify the discipline, dispel its hesitancies, and permit the confident resumption of scientific progress towards historic goals (Secord, 1977; Smith, 1973).

More fundamental than complaints about lack of theoretical progress were attacks on social psychology's basic assumptions: its models of science, human nature, and society. American social psychology had patterned itself after the successful late 19th century physical sciences and reflected its sociocultural context. It was pragmatic and antiphilosophical; and aimed to be objective and value-free. Now a flow of searching, well-documented analyses of its theories from both sides of the Atlantic concluded, with considerable moral fervor, that social psychology had violated its own ethos and reflected particular "stipulations" about human nature and society (Harre & Secord, 1972; Israel, 1972; Moscovici, 1972; Tajfel, 1972). Although these—and all of the critics—clearly had their own "stipulations," they succeeded in raising serious doubts about social psychology's value-free status and focused attention on its implicit assumptions.

Argyris (1969, 1975) proclaimed that social psychology's theories were incomplete: The model of a person assumed and then created in laboratory experiments probably reflected the "typical interpersonal world" of competitive, rational, gain-oriented, conforming, and untrusting social life. But there also were "atypical" persons who expressed their feelings more openly, were more individualistic and trusting, competed and conformed less, and took more risks. By restricting research to the typical social patterns and ignoring the possibilities for development of improved social functioning, social psychology supported the status quo of both human nature and society. The same theme, that social psychology could be "emancipatory" rather than merely positivistic, was elaborated in Rommetveit's (1976) scholarly philosophical essay.

The deluge of self-criticism did not spare social psychology's research methods or methodological assumptions. In this area, however, criticism was traditional and there were well-established procedures for reacting to it. The discovery of unsuspected "artifacts" in the research process by Orne, Rosenthal, and others (Rosenthal & Rosnow, 1969) evoked traditional responses. Techniques and designs were improved and experimental controls tightened to remove sources of error or adulteration of results.

An increasing awareness, however, that all psychological research generated experimenter–subject interpersonal processes (Miller, 1972) raised disturbing questions. Could these "intrusive variables" be controlled and neutralized, or were radically different interpretations required of all experiments? Were the effects endemic to the very methods? Should laboratory experiments be replaced by "nonintrusive" naturalistic field studies (Webb, Campbell, Schwartz, & Sechrest, 1966)? Sherif (1970), always in the lead, saw the definition of the social situation in research as its core problem and said that "in effect, the researcher stages his own scenario" (p. 146).

Broader questions inevitably were raised regarding the relations between theoretical assumptions about the nature of persons and social life, and the research methods employed (Argyris, 1975; Harre & Secord, 1972). It was unusual, in fact, for critics of social psychology's theoretical assumptions not to concurrently challenge its methods of research. Calls for a new theoretical orientation were coupled with demands for a reformed methodology: not just research methods, but assumptions about the research process.

In spite of these disagreements and dissatisfactions with theory and methods, defenders of social psychology's historical progress pointed with pride to its "vast storehouse of well-established empirical findings" (Cartwright, 1979, p. 87). Yet, many critics were less sanguine about the stability, generality, or practical usefulness of social psychology's accumulated data.

Every school child had been taught to replicate classical experiments in the physics and chemistry laboratories. Replication, the *sine qua non* of physical science, had been adopted by traditional psychology as its criterion of verified knowledge. Yet, social psychology's storehouse contained a great deal that never had been replicated. Some voices called for remedying this shortcoming (Smith, 1970). Others argued that replication of theoretical hypotheses was preferable to mere repetition of research designs; and that many of the former were published but unrecognized as replications (Hunt, 1975). Four different types of replication—*retest, internal, independent,* and *theoretical*—were formulated by La Sorte (1972) and illustrated by published examples. In 1973 the *Psychological Abstracts' Index* volumes initiated a section on "experimental replication" that included many social psychological studies. There did not seem any reason for traditional social psychologists to doubt that under identical conditions almost identical results would be obtained—except for the discovery of error, as in Goldstein's (1963) exact replication of Festinger's (1942) classical level of aspiration study.

The question remained, however: Was it possible in social psychological research to reproduce identical or even sufficiently similar conditions? Gergen's (1973, 1976) answer was that findings were not stable nor replicable because of historical change and the increased sophistication of subjects in an era of mass communication. We discuss his thesis that social psychology is an historical inquiry elsewhere in this chapter.

The specificity of the context of social psychological research became another major focus of criticism. Sherif (1970) attributed the contradictory findings in small group and attitude studies to the different social situations within which research was conducted. A leading methodologist in psychology asserted that its results—including those of social psychology—were not generalizable beyond either the experimental laboratory or the field situation because research occured in a "local context" that involved higher order interactions (Cronbach, 1975). The lack of generality of laboratory experiments was attributed by Tajfel (1972) to the social expectations of subjects in a specific social context. American social psychological research was described as "culture bound" (Moscovici, 1972); it took place within a cultural context that limited its generalization to other cultures (Smith, 1978; Triandis, 1976).

The betrayal of Lewin's vision of a social psychology that would both "further scientific understanding of man ... and ... also advance the cause of human welfare" (Ring, 1967, p. 119) became another reverberating alarm bell of the mid-seventies crisis. Helmreich (1975) lamented the "pernicious distinction ... between theoretical and applied social psychology" (p. 548). Respondents who both agreed and disagreed with him offered an assortment of diagnoses and prescriptions. Bickman (1976) asserted that there was a rapprochement rather than a conflict, pointing to journals, graduate programs, and increased governmental funding. Applied social psychologists were exhorted to evacuate their ivory tower and to increase their contact with everyday life and ordinary people (Ryckman, 1976). Social problems were too complex, enduring, and protected by vested interests for social psychologists to make any impact: They should teach people to reduce their expectations and to withstand frustration (Thorngate, 1976b). The problem was seen by Weissberg (1976) as disciplinary rather than methodological: Social psychologists did not define their discipline properly, they do not focus on the central phenomena, "human relationships in real social environments" (p. 121). There was no essential incompatibility, as Lewin had maintained, between theory and application.

Another torrid conflict regarding unethical research procedures—to what degree were they really unethical, and how justified were they?—arose during the crisis period, spawned by the historical dual allegiance of social psychologists to the advancement of scientific knowledge and to humanitarian values. Since World War II, in the interests of rigor and control, social psychology increasingly had relied on deception of human subjects in laboratory experiments as its primary method (Kelman, 1967; Ring, 1967; Smith, 1976; Tesch, 1977). In spite of some early warnings (Vinacke, 1954), the attendant possibilities of emotional or even physical harm to participants typically were dismissed as minimal.

Social psychologists had developed a subculture that rewarded ingenious methods for deceiving subjects and publicized these "creative" efforts. "Somehow the whole field got corrupted," commented one of its senior scholars (Smith, 1976, p. 452). But the *Zeitgeist* in America had shifted to an increased sensitivity to issues of privacy, individual freedom, and human rights. An extreme example of the genre but not necessarily the most offensive, Milgram's (1963, 1964, 1974) behavioral study of obedience in which subjects were ordered to administer increasingly severe electric shocks to persons in an adjoining room—both fictitious—was a catalyst to the revulsion that erupted both within the profession and in public and governmental circles.

Alarmed by the possibilities of harm to participants in all psychological research and of damage to its public relations, the American Psychological Association published a more stringent and detailed ethical code for research on human subjects (APA, 1973). The Department of Health, Education, and Welfare, a principal source of research funds, cognizant of much publicized abuses in both psychological and medical research, issued tough regulations for protection of human subjects requiring jury-like review panels in Washington and on every campus to evaluate research proposals for compliance. Many social psychologists felt, however, that these guidelines imposed unrealistic medical research standards upon their relatively innocuous, non-life-threatening experiments.

These measures made it impossible for researchers to remain complacent about ethical issues and exacerbated the potential conflict. It became apparent in the light of mounting evidence that debriefing, the standard safeguard (Aronson & Carlsmith, 1968), did not always undo psychological damage to subjects of experiments nor correct their misconceptions (Tesch, 1977). Although he had participated in formulating APA's new ethical standards, Smith (1976) concluded that the two major criteria of ethical research conduct, *informed consent* by participants and an *excess of benefit over harm*, involved incompatible philosophical assumptions and were replete with ambiguities and unknowns: It was impossible to define truly voluntary consent or when a subject was adequately informed; to determine whether or not harm or benefit to a participant had occurred; or to balance potential harm to a subject against potential benefit to society.

The voluminous literature that emerged to discuss and debate the proliferating disagreements hardly mentioned two latent issues: the benefits of conducting research to the careers of social psychologists in a "publish-or-perish" institutional environment; and the disparity in models of man and theoretical orientations that were assumed in designing research and in the treatment of subjects. Both of these made conflict inevitable.

Social psychology had aspired to be value-free and objective, as mentioned earlier, modeled on 19th century physical science. Another vortex in the storm of criticism revolved around denials that this ideal had been, could, or should be attained. The vociferous critics insisted that both cultural and sociopolitical biases were deeply ingrained in the social psychological enterprise. Although not new—see Dewey's (1899) similar thesis and Allport's (1954) recognition of it, referred to earlier—the climate now was receptive to a full-fledged assault from this direction.

There was no doubt that social psychology was "almost exclusively American"; its research problems derived from issues and perspectives in American society but failed to reflect European social experience and culture (Cartwright, 1979; Moscovici, 1972; Smith, 1978). In a "declaration of independence" by European social psychologists that spearheaded the attack, the cultural biases and latent value assumptions of American social psychology were analyzed with eloquent precision (Israel & Tajfel, 1972). Its positivist epistomology, assumed model of linear, unidirectional causality, and what Sampson (1977) later called "self-contained individualism" all were dissected and rejected as inappropriate foundations for a scientific social psychology.

It was no coincidence that the crisis in social psychology erupted at a time of social upheaval. In both Europe and America, barricades had been erected on streets and college campuses. The themes and choruses of Marxist critics of capitalist society were well-worn; but the ingenuity and fervor of the New Left found novel vehicles and targets for its critique. Social psychology was attacked ruthlessly for its sociopolitical biases and its conspiratorial function in justifying, by its value-free image of neutrality, a "particular distribution of power in industrial society" (Gross, 1974, p. 43). Even non-Marxist commentators agreed, however, that American social psychology was "one-political system specific" (Smith, 1978, p. 173), that its "intellectual content had been greatly influenced by the political ideology of American society" (Cartwright, 1979, pp. 85-86).

PERSPECTIVES AND POSITIONS

The Crisis: Mirror of Contemporary Social Psychology

The crisis in social psychology was not just a passing squall. The storm ripped off the flimsy fabric of assumed consensus under which social psychologists huddled and revealed a shocking disarray. There appeared to be disaagreement among them in basic assumptions, interests, and objectives. Every conceivable position could be found in the extensive literature, attacking and in defense of assumptions about the nature and definition of social psychology, its history, theory, and methods, its subject matter and significant problems, its institutional power structure and reward systems, and its role in society.

The crisis revealed considerable disparity in the explicit interests and objectives of social psychologists. The traditional goals of advancement of knowledge about social behavior and society, and the amelioration of social problems, were not only questioned but were derogated. Dedication to science, for some almost an end in itself, was ridiculed by others. The professional norm of generosity toward colleagues' motives, an assumption that they were at least as faultless as one's own, began to decay. It was an era of confrontation and conflict rather than consensus. Moscovici (1972, p. 19) had accused the American discipline of being a "social psychology of the nice person," created by nice persons. But the revealed social and professional discord generated a tendency toward rougher professional intercourse, more like the customary European unrestrained polemics.

Critics of Social Psychology

Individual contributors to the voluminous crisis literature varied greatly in their philosophical, theoretical, methodological, and ideological positions and perspectives. The combinations and permutations of these made each contribution unique. It was difficult to encompass, assimilate, and understand this massive intellectual outpouring about the state of social psychology. In an attempt to impose a little order, we briefly ennumerate major positions and perspectives; but are not so foolhardy as to categorize particular authors.

A substantial majority of social psychologists probably could be termed *traditional scientists*. They believed that positivist, value-free science and continuous improvement of their theories, methods, research, and applications would produce cumulative scientific knowledge and amelioration of social problems. Their theoretical models were disparate, but derived largely from traditional theories in general (individual) psychology or, to a lesser degree, in sociology.

Among the traditional social psychologists were the *methodologists* and *technocrats*, preoccupied with improvement of the techniques and procedures of research. They focused on the sins of error, omission, imprecision, narrowness, and bias. They variously believed that the road to salvation would be constructed on the mathematization of hypotheses, computer-simulations, large-scale field research, unobtrusive methods, or other advances in research designs or mathematical–statistical procedures. On the whole, they accepted traditional theoretical models; although a small number rejected current experimental and statistical procedures because they reflected inappropriate models of social behavior.

The *applied social psychologists* criticized the enterprise for its failure to yield useful products. Primarily traditional in their theoretical and methodological emphases, and pragmatic in their objectives, they found numerous rationales for social psychology's nonfulfilment of its (or their) promises to contribute to a golden age of well-being.

Humanists and *liberal activists* criticized social psychology for failing to share their vision and contribute to their aspiration for a more enlightened society and more creative, compassionate human beings. They said that social psychology's theories, methods, and research reflect and help perpetuate the status quo rather than actively exploring new possibilities and potentialities of social behavior. By melding scientific procedures with humanistic assumptions, research should be actively helping to establish new social models and priorities.

The *radicals* and *revolutionaries* applied Marxist-Leninist ideology or neo-Marxist critiques to a bourgeois social psychology that reflected a corrupt capitalist society. Their conspiratorial theories accused social psychology of actively preventing change by ignoring the real world of conflict and the struggle for liberation and emancipated identities; and of constructing theories that fostered error and prevented the recognition of true social relations. In their eyes, the power structure of the profession prevented the appearance of new ideas and preserved the status quo by controlling career advancement and the publication of new information; and by dominating faculty-student relations. Although many of their criticisms were echoed in part by others, these critics advocated a clean sweep of social psychology's theories, methods, and institutional structure.

A new perspective also began to appear among psychological critics of social psychology who had been influenced by a traditional sociological school of thought stemming from Marx, Mannheim, Durkheim, and Weber. These *sociologists of knowledge* questioned assumptions about the nature and development of social psychology: that it was or could be independent of the historical era and sociopolitical structure within which it was practiced. Critical reanalyses of the contributions of historical figures such as Comte and McDougall revealed extra-scientific influences upon the development of social psychology. An important influence, too, was Kuhn's epochal treatise on the paradigmatic development of science. It contradicted positivist assumptions that science was solely the product of a continuous accumulation of evidence from which self-correcting knowledge emerged.

Kuhn's (1962, 1970) analysis of the implicit presuppositions inherent in scientific research stimulated renewed activity in social psychology by *philosophers of science*. They scrutinized and evaluated every aspect of the enterprise: its assumptions about the nature of persons and of society, its conceptual structure and levels of analysis, and the legitimacy of its methodology and research methods. Awareness of the narrow philosophical basis of traditional social psychology and of alternative assumptive possibilities led to considerable dissatisfaction with the existing "paradigm."

RESPONSES TO THE CRISIS

Responses to the crisis in social psychology clearly derived from respondents' positions and perspectives. Sociological social psychologists, who had their own disciplinary problems, on the whole tactfully had refrained from intruding into their neighbors'—or rivals'—troubles; although occasional cues appeared that suggested subliminal feelings of pleased vindication. Most psychological social psychologists either denied the seriousness of the crisis or were optimistic that the illness was not chronic. Some major analysts, however, were more pessimistic in their prognoses: Their prescriptions and programs for recovery required major changes in social psychology's goals, theoretical orientation, or methods of research.

Sociological Social Psychology

The status of sociological social psychology since the abortive attempts at integration in the 1950s and 1960s was separate but unequal. Its adherents were a minority of the profession, it attracted less public acclaim or financial support, and its published products, at least in volume, were only a small proportion of the total literature of social psychology. The psychological majority had adopted and mistreated many of its venerable concepts, as reported earlier. The charisma and prestige of popular psychological theories, such as *dissonance* and *attribution*, and of laboratory experimentation, had seduced many promising young sociologists (Blank, 1978; Segal & Segal, 1972; Stryker, 1977). As in any minority group, the sheer power and confidence of the majority generated uncertainties, and anxiety that sociological social psychology with its distinctive intellectual heritage was in danger of "withering away" (Burgess, 1977) or being dissipated (Liska, 1977).

Responses to the crisis among sociologists were thoughtful and magnanimous. There was general agreement that the distinctive character of sociological social psychology—its emphasis upon reciprocal interaction processes and nonexperimental methods—must be maintained as a separate subdiscipline (Archibald, 1976), especially because many psychologists were demanding just such emphases in their own subfield. Rather than integration, the call was for equal status and a recognition that each branch of social psychology could benefit by greater interchange (House, 1977) and recognition of "mutual relevance" (Stryker, 1977).

Crisis of Confidence, Identity, or Paradigm?

Some psychologists in the field thought that the "crisis" was nothing new, because social psychology perpetually was in a critical state due to the inherent duality of its foci: on both the individual and the social, the general and the particular (Deutsch, 1976). Calls for a paradigmatic reorientation were scathingly rejected by Shaw (1974). He derogated the "process of self-flagellation" and "polemical" approach of Harré and Secord (1972). Rather than seeking to replace its existing philosophy of science, he asserted, social psychology should correct its faulty approaches and solutions to traditional problems. Although recognizing the lost enthusiasm, sense of direction, and faith in the future of many social psychologists, Elms (1975) concluded that the crisis was primarily one of confidence rather than theoretical or paradigmatic. Improved theories and methods, greater tolerance of pluralism, and tenacity in pressing on should lead to a revival of optimism (Kiesler & Lucke, 1976).

Many social psychologists accepted the criticisms of their field as valid and responded with proposals to improve the quality and power of theory and research. The phrase *new paradigm* frequently heralded such suggestions; although they really did not represent the revolutionary discontinuity from prevalent assumptions and models that Kuhn's concept had signified. For example, McGuire (1973) called for more "creative" hypotheses to be tested in naturalistic field settings and more complex computer and statistical models. For Triandis (1976), the solution to social psychology's problems was the formulation of more complex, precise theory that would account for the interaction of diverse peoples, settings, and behaviors, and the discovery of universal, dimensionalized variables in multi-method, cross-cultural research.

At an international conference of social psychologists in Ottawa, participants disparaged the prospects and desirability of an "integrative theory." Participants used the occasion to promote their own favorite solutions to the crisis, but mostly talked past one another (Kiesler & Lucke, 1976; Strickland, Aboud, & Gergen, 1976; Strickland, Aboud, Gergen, Jahoda, & Tajfel, 1976).

By 1976, there was a growing impatience among traditional social psychologists with the preoccupation with "the state of social psychology." They either questioned whether there ever had been a distinctive crisis, urging their colleagues to return to their appropriate pursuits, conducting research (Berkowitz & Walster, 1976; Deutsch, 1976) or they felt that the pendulum already had swung and greeted the sudden emergence of social psychology into the "postcrisis period," pointing to its adoption of many of the relevant suggestions for changes in theory, methods, and training (Guttentag, 1976). However, Smith (1976) pointed to the serious deficiencies in social psychology that still persisted and had not been overcome by adjustments in the traditional scientific models.

Some pessimistic analysts not only denied that the critical storm was passing but asserted that the problems of social psychology were insoluble. Thorngate (1975) said that local contexts determine social behavioral processes, which in general are variable and unpredictable; a conclusion similar to Cronbach's (1975), cited previously. A Heisenberg-like principle limits what can be learned because the more precision attempted the greater the interference by research methods. Even where massive efforts yield a little progress, the benefits achieved do not justify the costs incurred (Thorngate, 1976a). Discussions on the possibilities of achieving an integrated theory yielded similar pessimistic conclusions: that social psychology was attempting too much and that its aspirations were unattainable (Strickland et al., 1976). These lugubrious critics appeared to be accepting the traditional assumptive bases of contemporary social psychology, however, rather than conceiving the possibility of alternative models.

PROPOSALS FOR MAJOR CHANGES IN ORIENTATION

Less Ambitious Goals for Social Psychology

One of the most challenging proposals for change was Gergen's (1973, 1976) thesis that social psychology should abandon its goal of being a positivist science seeking general laws with predictive stability, and should become an historical inquiry, dedicated to increased social understanding of the temporal and cultural diversity in social behavior. He advanced two major reasons with supporting evidence and arguments to justify his position. First, he pointed to the rapid cultural changes with attendant shifts in social behavior and its evaluation. Second, he asserted that in an era of mass communication and concern with personal identity, the feedback of social psychologists' research findings to the general public changed the relationships in social phenomena that were being studied; so that any knowledge obtained was transient and had little predictive value.

The reactions from traditional social psychologists to this heretical thesis were prompt, voluminous, and almost entirely negative (Hendrick, 1974). Gergen's arguments that social science was distinctly different from natural science were "timeworn" topics of classical debates that had been rejected by philosophers of science (Schlenker, 1974). All science has difficulty in applying and proving its theories unequivocally (Manis, 1976); and in any case, scientific laws are never permanent but decay and are replaced (Greenwald, 1976). The temporal and cultural variability of social behavior does not deny the generality and stability of underlying social processes, said Manis (1975), using Lewin's terms *phenotypes* and *genotypes*. Gergen's "enlightenment effects" were overstated, because there was evidence that people did not behave rationally, in accordance with the information available to them; nor was it important for most people to demonstrate their freedom and uniqueness by contradicting the social scientists.

After a flurry of sometimes acrimonious debate, participants wearied of the game and began to call for empirical tests of Gergen's proposals that social behavior varies with sociocultural change and with feedback of social psychological information (Wolff, 1977).

One of the few who accepted Gergen's thesis, perhaps because it accorded with his own critical view, was Sampson (1975, 1977), who applied it to the dual principles of justice as *equity* or *equality* in social psychological research. He concluded that the ideas were not universal but were "historically located" principles of social behavior.

Proposals that social psychology's goals should be limited to the description and short-term control of local events (Cronbach, 1975; Thorngate, 1975, 1976a) were discussed previously. These suggestions did not imply any clear nor immediate actions and did not evoke much response.

Changing the Orientation

A recurrent critical theme had been that social psychological theories and research derived from biological, individual psychology: They dealt with "self-contained" individuals in relation to other individuals and neglected the essentially social nature of a person and the interdependence of social life (Moscovici, 1972; Partington, 1976; Pepitone, 1976; Sampson, 1977; Tajfel, 1972).

A number of major proposals conceived a reorientation of the field toward its proper study of interactional processes. Moscovici (1972) made the critical distinction between individual *cognitive* processes and inherently interactional *symbolic* processes that involve the generation of common and new meanings. This dialectical emphasis on "self-transforming interactive process" was seen by Smith (1977) as "highly appropriate to social psychology"; he traced the perspective in John Dewey to his Hegelian origins. The dialectical system of Hegel (1816), the great German philosopher, conceived of ideas developing in triads—*thesis, antithesis,* and *synthesis*—with each stage of the unification of opposites yielding an emergent, higher level truth. As applied to social psychology, it implies that interaction among persons produces ideas, concepts, or meanings that differ from those held initially by any of the individual participants.

Of course, this emphasis is most pronounced and developed in G. H. Mead's thinking, highly influenced by Dewey. Harré and Secord (1972) viewed their own detailed and somewhat formalized philosophical proposal as very similar to Mead and the symbolic interactionists, but attempting to progress beyond them.

Related to the criticism that social psychology was insufficiently social was the complaint that it failed to consider the "cultural, economic, and societal context" in which social behavior occurred (Gottlieb, 1977). The demands for increased contextual emphasis transcended Sherif's (1970) and others' analyses of the ubiquitous social situation in research; and did not heed Cronbach's (1975) strictures that overriding contextual effects must necessarily limit social psychology's aims. Proposals were made for a re-oriented social psychology that would accommodate diverse contextual influences. Secord (1976) agreed that theories and research had been "person-bound" rather than studying behavior in its "social context." He called for an "overall theoretical matrix" that would supply a taxonomy of situations across different historical periods and subcultures. Triandis (1978) continued to pursue the panacea of cross-cultural research and the discovery of "universals of social behavior"; but his approach had been criticized for ignoring the social system within which social behavior is constructed and interpreted (Jahoda, 1976).

Discouraged with the prospects for a reorientation of the discipline, some social psychologists self-consciously defined a new field, "environmental psychology," which would devote itself to the study of human behavior in its physical and—by extension—its social and cultural contexts (Proshansky, Ittelson, & Rivlin, 1970). Broadly multidisciplinary, its enthusiastic adherents soon experienced difficulties in agreeing on its definition, scope, or relationship, if any, to social psychology (Altman, 1976; Epstein, 1976; Krupat, 1977; Proshansky, 1976; Stokols, 1976).

A variety of critical contributions seemed to share common themes and to point in a similar direction. After many years in limbo, the *self* and *subjectivity* had emerged to reassume legitimacy in social psychology (Hewitt, 1976; Stryker, 1977). Although no conceptual consensus had yet emerged, these concepts were compatible with the mounting evidence in psychology that the assumption of total external determination of behavior no longer was tenable; and the growing conception of a more active, initiating, and self-regulating person

In preference to de Charms and Shea's (1976) "origin-mode of personal causality," too redolent of indeterminism, Partington (1976) proposed an "interdependent mode." The view prevalent in the 1950s, of a person as part of a larger interpersonal system or group, was described by Steiner (1974) as more appropriate for social psychology than the individualistic model of the 1960s.

A key component of the emerging model was the normative character of social behavior (Pepitone, 1976). Similarly, Harré (1972) had said that persons were "rule-following animals." The danger that a cultural determinism might supplant an environmental one—an "over-socialized conception of man" (Wrong, 1961)—was forestalled in Tajfel's, (1972) declaration that social conduct was greatly influenced by a person's evaluation of the appropriateness of prevailing norms and values to the immediate social situation. These various proposals were, in effect, summed up in Sherif's (1977) statement that the core of social psychology should be the topics of the human self, norms, and reference groups.

Although these proponents of a changed orientation in social psychology appeared to share similar critiques and ideas, they did not necessarily agree on their assumptions about the nature of a person, of society, or of the processes involved in the construction and modification of social behavior. These issues are pursued further in chapters 6 and 7.

Chapter 6
Current Trends in Social Psychology

THE CRISIS: TEN YEARS LATER

The crisis in social psychology ended because everything had been said, at least once. It began to foster ennui rather than excitement. It may be useful, however, to briefly evaluate that unique episode from the perspective of the late 1980s. How is the crisis perceived today—if at all—by social psychologists? Is the "malaise" still with us, or has it evaporated with the tensions and uncertainties of an earlier era, dissipated by the solid accomplishments of a decade? Was the storm of self-criticism merely a temporary loss of nerve, or an expression of the need of social psychologists for "self-flagellation" (Jones, 1985; Shaw, 1974)? Or were the issues and dilemmas so fervently discussed "real"—of substantive significance? If they were, have they been resolved, evaded, or are they still influencing current developments? An evaluation of the crisis is not just sterile historicism. It may contribute to our understanding of contemporary social psychology, its discernible trends, and their projection into the future.

Elms (1975) had provided the *leitmotif* for those who were eager to dismiss the crisis and return to business as usual: It was a "crisis of confidence." He generalized, somewhat incautiously, from Kuhn's (1962) influential work, a theory based on a study of the history of physical science, and declared that because social psychology had not yet achieved paradigmatic status, the crisis clearly could not be paradigmatic. He also had pointed to many possible external causes of the crisis—theoretical, methodological, ethical, institutional, and sociopolitical—and proferred advice for remedial action. But finally he succumbed to the prevailing personalistic bias and located the trouble within social psychologists who had unrealistic expectations and "weak egos." He prescribed therapy, preferably self-therapy, for those unfortunate dissidents.

Most social psychologists have accepted Elms' conclusion, at least in part. In the new *Handbook*, Jones (1985, pp. 98, 100) scolded those "restless, dissatisfied social psychologists" whose malaise may have damaged the discipline's institutional relationships. But some commentators are not entirely convinced that no paradigmatic shift is in the offing (Cartwright, 1979); some query whether psychology itself is not paradigmatic or multi-paradigmatic (Lachman & Lachman, 1979); or whether there are at least "paradigmatic preferences" in social psychology (Steiner, 1986). Some, like Gergen (1985b), view the crisis even more seriously: "not a matter of localized dyspepsia" (p. 545) but the beginning of an entire intellectual transformation of social psychology and psychology.

During the period of the crisis, hundreds of intelligent, well-trained, and serious scholars, geographically dispersed, contributed in technical journals, edited volumes, and books. In the preceding chapter it was evident they represented a diversity of perspectives, offered a variety of diagnoses of social psychology's ills, and prescribed many different treatments. A social psychological analysis of this event certainly would challenge our conceptual and theoretical resources: It is improbable that an individualistic explanatory framework in terms of *ego-strength, self-confidence*, or *masochistic need* would prove adequate. One might be tempted to recruit concepts from theories of collective behavior, such as *social influence* and *emergent norms* (Turner & Killian, 1972). What is more pertinent to our present inquiry, however, is the substantive status of the issues raised. If they were ephemeral, the product of temporarily impaired resolution in the unending competitive struggle to advance knowledge and careers, then surely they must have dissipated after a decade. If they are still evident and influential in contemporary social psychology, then more credence must be assigned the crisis as a significant historical event with implications for the course of the discipline.

The social and professional climate of the 1980s has shifted away from emotional confrontation. There is increased dedication to career development and accompanying commitment to solving social problems within established intellectual and sociopolitical frameworks. But the absence of the frenzied atmosphere of the crisis period does not signify that the critical voices in social psychology have been stilled. They are, however, with some exceptions, less strident, less ideological, and reason from more substantial philosopical and empirical bases.

A review of the preceding chapter yields four principle criticisms of social psychology that together just about exhaust the possibilities: (a) its theoretical development was inadequate; (b) its methods were inappropriate and improper; (c) its application to problems of human welfare was neither sustained nor significant; (d) The assumptions on which social psychology's theory and research were based—its "paradigm"—were outmoded and false. In spite of the resumption of normalcy in the discipline, it is more common today than before the crisis for influential social psychologists, recognized for their contributions, to raise these and related objections. Without necessarily accepting all of their arguments, one cannot ignore them because they recur in many different areas of social psychology.

Criticisms of Theoretical Development

Theory and research in contemporary social psychology are criticized frequently for not being *social* but individual, difficult to distinguish from general psychology. The focus is on "internal processes," typically perceptions, thoughts, and attitudes, but occasionally feelings or motives (Bar-Tal, 1984; Cartwright, 1979; McGrath & Kravitz, 1982; Pepitone, 1981; Sampson, 1981; Steiner, 1986). An individual is studied in isolation from ongoing events in social life (Manicas & Secord, 1983). Influential theories and their research, respected models for social psychologists, have been attacked as individualistic and essentially nonsocial in their orientation: Lewin's group dynamics, Festinger's cognitive dissonance, and Zajonc's social facilitation (Pepitone, 1981; Steiner, 1986).

The research problems derived from these nonsocial formulations are viewed by some critics as trivial and fortuitous, divorced from naturally occurring social events (Steiner, 1986). Social psychology is carved up into innumerable topical subdivisions, with individual investigators homesteading particular terrains as they play the game of research (Bronfenbrenner, Kessel, Kessen, & White 1986; Gergen, 1985a; Zander, 1979). Interest in particular topics ebbs and flows without sustained attacks and cumulative progress on significant scientific issues.

This fragmentation of the field also occurs within topical areas, for example, in theory and research on attitudes (Eagly & Himmelfarb, 1978), social motivation (Brody, 1980), attribution (Harvey & Weary, 1984), self (Gergen, 1985), and prosocial behavior (Clark, 1986). Within each area, mini-theories based on divergent assumptions and frequently employing idiosyncratic methods compete for adherents and resources.

The opinions expressed are undoubtedly those of a minority; otherwise criticism would not be apposite. But prestigeful voices are raised in a call for greater theoretical integration—across topics and disciplines—to provide coherent general theory and cumulative scientific progress in social psychology.

Criticisms of Methodology

Although it is agreed generally that progress has been achieved in the power and ingenuity of research methods, there is less enthusiasm about any concomitant increase in understanding of social phenomena (Abelson, 1982; Cartwright, 1979). Critics trace many of the theoretical deficiencies just discusssed to shortcomings in social psychology's research methods. Although in the ideal model of scientific practice, theory arises from naturalistic observation and then is tested in experiments, in social psychology the process more often is reversed. Experiments are initiated because models and techniques are available and convenient. Most theory is based on inductive generalizations from experimental findings rather than from observed naturally occurring social events. Thus, deficiencies of the experimental method are preserved in and restrict the formulation of theory.

For many critics of social psychology, the laboratory experiment has become the villain. It studies isolated individuals and their psychological processes under contrived, constrained and sometimes bizarre circumstances, in relation to strangers, for brief periods of time (Gergen, 1985a; Staub, Bar-Tal, Karylowski, & Reykowski, 1984). Many reviewers distrust the *ecological validity*—generalizability to the "real" world—of findings from laboratory experiments and call for confirmatory field studies (Brislin, 1983; Stephan, 1985). For example, McGrath and Kravitz (1982), usually friends and advocates of experimental research, commented that the field study by Clore, Bray, Itkin, & Murphy, (1978) "stands in pleasant contrast to the plethora of studies of artificial relationships, contrived conditions, and single and reactive measures" (p. 214).

Criticisms of Social Psychology's Metatheory

A generic critique of contemporary social psychology challenges its assumptions about the scientific process and human nature. We have discussed previously the dominant influence of 19th century physical and biological science upon social psychology's development. Critics now point out that modern physics, chemistry, and biology long ago abandoned the logical positivist philosophy of classical science. Kuhn's epochal work sensitized social psychologists to the new philosophy of science, but they have not yet revised their assumptions. Social psychology's metatheory is outmoded, for example, its assumption of a value-free, objective scientific process (Kroger, 1982; Rorer & Widiger, 1983). There is a "postpositive crisis in social science" (Haan, 1982, p. 1096).

Positivists believe that facts will emerge under appropriately designed and controlled experimental conditions, and that from the continuous accumulation of this knowledge general laws can be induced. This is the basis for assumptions of the universal validity of findings over time and place. Yet, most social psychological research lacks a temporal dimension (Cartwright, 1979); and extensive arguments have been advanced against transhistorical generality (Gergen, 1973, 1976, 1985a), even though they have not yet been widely accepted.

Assumptions of universal validity across situations, societies, and cultures also are under attack. Social psychologists undoubtedly agree that social behavior occurs in a cultural context, but most research ignores the significant, often crucial, conditions imposed by situational and cultural variables (Gibbs, 1979; Segall, 1986).

In spite of the multiplicity of theories, mini-theories, concepts, and isolated hypotheses in social psychology, critics argue that an incorrect model of human nature is implicit in most theorizing and research, which asssumes an individual person primarily passive and reactive to external stimuli. Social behavior occurs in response to prior attitudes, thoughts, feelings, desires, or behavior: The linear process can be traced from cause to effect. But many social psychologists believe that this model of a person corresponds to neither observable social phenomena nor to extensive empirical evidence in both psychology and social psychology. Persons are active and initiate behavior in their efforts to shape situations, selves, and others. Social behavior involves complex interactions, exchanges, bargaining, negotiation, ingratiation, presentation of self, and other inherently social processes: "psychologists have discovered reciprocity" (Tyler, 1981, p. 7). A simple linear process model inadequately represents the complexity of human social feedback processes (Petrinovich, 1979).

Some criticis believe that social psychology's "paradigm" is obsolete and call for a "Kuhnian revolution"—a new metatheory that assumes a more valid model of science, human nature, and social action (Kroger, 1982; Petrinovich, 1979).

A number of summary observations can be made from this brief review. The collective fervor of the crisis period has waned, but the issues persist. They have been expanded, deepened, and supported by empirical example and logical analysis. Many knowledgable social psychologists—although still a small minority—consider that these problems endanger or vitiate what has been achieved thus far. It appears, therefore, that the questions raised during the crisis period had substance: They introduced or focused attention on significant unresolved problems of social psychology.

In conclusion, it appears that the "crisis in social psychology" of a decade ago should not be dismissed as a temporary aberration. More likely, it was a collective expression of frustration and a concerted endeavor to redirect social psychologists' attention to ignored issues, crucial to the viability and survival of their discipline as a scientific enterprise capable of contributing to human welfare.

CURRENT TRENDS IN RESEARCH, THEORY, AND METATHEORY

Social Psychology in the 1980s

The preceding section's focus on the criticisms of contemporary social psychology resulted in a somewhat distorted and biased view of the discipline. We must emphasize again that only a minority view has been presented. To partially redress the balance, we attempt to describe the current state of social psychology as represented by the great majority of contributors. The field now is massive—almost unbounded—highly diversified and complex. Its literature is huge, international, and growing constantly. Any brief characterization runs the risk of banality; and clearly must be impressionistic and highly selective. A number of questions can be asked, however, and answers sought in the most authoritative current literature. What is the general direction of development? What theoretical or metatheoretical models are influencing activity? How are the substantive issues and problems changing?

Contemporary social psychology has continued to develop and to expand within its established framework. Most social psychologists subscribe to the traditional positivist model; or at least to "logical empiricism" that superceded classical positivism (McGuire, 1985). They believe that controlled observation or experimentation, as objective and value-free as possible, will lead via inductive generalization to general principles, at least within particular topical areas if not across all social phenomena (Stephan, 1985).

Increasingly powerful and ingenious research methods have produced massive bodies of data that frequently defy generalization. Considerable creative effort has been invested in *meta-analysis*, a systematic procedure for drawing general conclusions across all acceptable extant investigations of a problem (Rosenthal, 1978). Like most inductive approaches, however, and like the majority of studies cumulated, the method tends to be atheoretical (McGrath & Kravitz, 1982; Segall, 1986). Formal mathematical models also provide steely rigor, but some do so at the cost of divorcing their elegant postulates from the reality of natural social phenomena (Buss, 1986).

These and other objections do not go uncontested. Traditionalists vigorously defend the logical rationale and empirical validity of their procedures (Berkowitz & Donnerstein, 1982). They are confident that social psychology is on the right track and making steady progress. The traditional paradigm (if there is one) is still dominant in social psychology.

Allport had complained in the 1968–1969 *Handbook* of the expanding array of topics, each defined more or less by practical or technical research issues, generating concepts, hypotheses, and methods. The "progressive fragmentation" continues (Bronfenbrenner et al., 1986; Cartwright, 1979). Topics arise, attain great popularity, then lose their constituency (Zander, 1979). Some recapture attention with new theoretical developments or methods (Cialdini, Petty, & Cacioppo, 1981; Cooper & Croyle, 1984; Lindzey & Aronson, 1985; McGrath & Kravitz, 1982). Areas also persist and impose a possibly restrictive standard perception that impedes development of new formulations (Berscheid, 1985). Most social psychologists identify themselves with one or a small number of specializations, sometimes as narrow as a particular problem area or method (Gergen, 1985a). Parochial mini-theories abound, mostly devoted to accounting for relatively narrow domains of phenomena. Even within areas, such as attitudes or attribution, they offer competing explanations (Cialdini et al. 1981; Harvey & Weary, 1984).

The multiplicity and diversity of concepts and theoretical interpretations only rarely are regretted, however. More commonly they are found "refreshing"—a positive contribution to a creative, dynamic intellectual enterprise (Clark, 1986; Eagly & Himmelfarb, 1978; Jones, 1985). Clearly there is little imperative toward unification of the field or general theory, except as something over the horizon, to be aspired to but not realistically expected. The exceptions may be those who anticipate that general psychological theories, such as cognitive or behaviorist, ultimately will suffice to account for social phenomena (Jones, 1985; Lott & Lott, 1985; Markus & Zajonc, 1985).

Throughout its history, social psychology—at least the major segment of it within psychology—has primarily studied *individuals* in a social context. With little exception, their attitudes, perceptions, thoughts, motives, and behavior in response to one or more other persons continue to be the subject matter of the contemporary field. Observers agree that an individualist perspective dominates research; although, as we have seen, there is no consensus as to its desirability (Abelson & Levi, 1985; Bar-Tal, 1984; Brewer & Kramer, 1985; Clark, 1985; Manicas & Secord, 1983; McClintock, Kramer, & Keil, 1984; McGrath & Kravitz, 1982; Pepitone, 1981; Steiner, 1986; Stephan, 1985). Even when this individualist orientation is not made explicit, it is implicit in theory and research: for example, in Krebs and Miller's (1985) scheme for ordering studies of altruism and aggression; and in their theoretical explanation of normative behavior.

Theory in social psychology has derived mostly from general theories of psychology. Psychodynamic, behaviorist, and cognitive orientations have provided competing explanations of social phenomena. During the past decade, however, the overwhelming ascendancy of the cognitive orientation has emerged, with the at least partial eclipse of competitors. The new *Handbook* omits the customary chapter on psychoanalytic theory; and personalistic approaches are in disfavor (Lindzey & Aronson, 1985). Behaviorists acknowledge that interest in their theoretical orientation has waned, except among the true believers (Lott & Lott, 1985). Cognitive thinkers triumphantly proclaim that social psychology and cognitive social psychology are "nearly synonymous" (Markus & Zajonc, 1985). The "cognitive revolution," for better or worse, has arrived in social psychology (Gergen, 1985a).

In almost every area of the contemporary field, problems and methods reflect this emphasis upon "getting inside the head" (Taylor & Fiske, 1981). For example, in research on attitudes and persuasion (Cialdini et al., 1981; Cooper & Croyle, 1984), attribution (Harvey & Weary, 1984; Kelley & Michela, 1980), interpersonal attraction (Huston & Levinger, 1978), small groups (Levine, 1985; Steiner, 1986), and intergroup relations (Stephan, 1985).

Without doubt, social psychology has made considerable progress in dissecting the complex cognitive processes of individuals involved in social relations. As we have seen, many contributors believe that an expanded and developed cognitive psychology will serve social psychology well, as a subdivision of general psychology (Brody, 1980; Jones, 1985; Markus & Zajonc, 1985). But others complain of a regression to Wundt and Titchener's introspectionism, that solipsism is encompassing the discipline to the exclusion of the truly *social* in theories and research (Fiske & Taylor, 1984; Steiner, 1986; Tajfel, 1982). One is reminded of G. H. Mead's (1930) denunciation of Cooley's phenomenological approach, discussed earlier.

A closer examination of contemporary theories and research, however, reveals that the cognitive orientation itself is undergoing extensive modification and expansion in attempts to deal with empirical data and observed social phenomena. It is likely that what is beginning to emerge will only faintly resemble the classical cognitive model. It may lead to a new, more integrative and comprehensive theoretical orientation. In the next section, we review the major trends in contemporary social psychology, as we perceive them, that appear to be moving in that direction.

Current Trends in Social Psychology

As we have seen, a small but relatively influential minority of social psychologists reject the prevailing "paradigm" to some degree. They have begun to sketch out guidelines for a substantially different social psychology, less wedded to, or completely divorced from its traditional positivist heritage. These somewhat inchoate formulations are catholic in their intellectual and empirical antecedents, which range across Kant, Wittgenstein, Marx, Dewey, Mead, Piaget, Vigotsky, linguistics, dialectics, modern philosophy, and empirical developments in neurology, psychology, and social psychology. Most of these antecedents have been alluded to previously, or are discussed briefly in the final chapter. Inevitably, such revolutionary formulations are more philosophical and polemical than constructive, and offer little basis from which to derive new research problems or designs. Yet they have spawned a considerable literature of books, articles, and reviews in major journals. It is too early to evaluate any lasting influence; although the vehemence of denunciations (Jones, 1985) suggests that traditional social psychologists are paying some attention.

Even though this dissident literature ultimately may prove to have been highly influential, it still lies outside the main stream of contemporary social psychology. Perhaps more significant, in spite of the general appearance of little change, are major trends appearing within the established framework of theory, methods, and metatheory. It is not uncommon for reviewers of major areas of the field to report the inadequacies of the existing orientation, as in research on equity and social exchange (McClintock et al., 1984), or on expectancies and interpersonal processes (Miller & Turnbull, 1986). Some also note that a paradigm-like change is occurring, for example, in the study of deviance (Archer, 1985), social cognition (Showers & Cantor, 1985), intergroup relations (Brewer & Kramer, 1985; Tajfel, 1982), and social influence and conformity (Moscovici, 1985).

The main body of social psychology is highly interrelated with and derivative from the assumptions and theories of general psychology and, as mentioned previously, sometimes indistinguishable from that parent discipline. Mounting evidence suggests that shifts in psychology's "paradigm" also may be occurring, and might be viewed as a major source of current trends in social psychology (Bronfenbrenner et al., 1986; de Charms & Muir, 1978; Howard, 1985; Manicas & Secord, 1983; Sullivan, 1984; Tyler, 1981). The direction of influence would not be unilateral, however, but reciprocal, considering the fuzzy boundary between the two fields. Criticisms that first arose during social psychology's crisis period have spread to all of psychology; indeed there are proposals, reminiscent of Dewey, George Mead, Baldwin and Harry Stack Sullivan, that social psychology should be the parent discipline since all human action is social (Gergen, 1984, 1985; Harré, 1984).

In his discussion of scientific revolutions, Kuhn (1962) observed that "normal science" continued its course even after the introduction of a new paradigm. Although pre-paradigmatic, contemporary social psychology may be in a similar transitional stage. The trends that seem evident in many areas, if they continue to win adherents, may have the potential for a major but evolutionary transformation of the discipline.

Trends are constructed by the analyst from a partial and biased view of an indefinitely large domain of phenomena. It may be useful, nevertheless, to describe the tendencies that appear in the eye of this beholder, and that can be documented by selective reference to the literature. Each of the following six trends is rooted in the past: Various forms of their critiques and proposals can be found throughout the history of social psychology. But in the current period they appear to be more robust, directed, and empirically grounded.

1. Expansion of the unit of analysis
2. Change in the model of a person
3. Movement toward self as a reflexive, multiplex process
4. Increased inclusion of complex reference processes
5. Increased inclusion of complex normative processes
6. From a static time frame toward a bounded unitary period

Expansion of the Unit of Analysis. One of the major trends in contemporary social psychology is an expansion of the unit of analysis from *molecular* to *molar*, to extend Tolman's (1932) useage. Widespread dissatifaction with the restricted emphasis on psychological processes of isolated individuals has led to investigations of more inclusive phenomena.

In almost every area, work reflects the desirability of including larger contexts in studies of persons. Personalities must be understood in terms of "social settings" (Snyder & Ickes, 1985). For example, *achievement motivation* is found to be influenced by situational and contextual factors (Brislin, 1983) and by diverse cultural meanings (Segall, 1986). *Machiavellianism* varies by social contexts (Geis, 1979). Attitude change requires a "larger canvas" for interpretation (Cialdini et al., 1981). Attribution theory demands a "broader unit" (Kelley & Michela, 1980) and should be studied in a "social context" (Harvey & Weary, 1984). Supporting evidence is supplied, for example, by reports of intercultural differences in the attribution of causality and achievement (Brislin, 1983; Segall, 1986). In relations between groups, the categorization, stereotyping, and ethnocentrism are seen to originate in a "cultural context" rather than in individual psychological processes (Brewer & Kramer, 1985; Segall, 1986; Tajfel, 1982).

Broader social contexts, whether situational or cultural, typically involve multiperson units: relationships between persons, interaction, and processes of reciprocal influence. Increasingly, social psychology's focus is shifting to interpersonal relations and processes of interaction. Moscovici (1985) proposed that social influence be studied as a reciprocal rather than a unilateral process, in the context of interaction. Support is found in the reciprocal regulation of behavior in interaction between parents and infants (Parke & Asher, 1983). Similarly, McClintock et al. (1984) concluded that progress in the study of exchange and equity requires that research substitute an interest in interdependence for the current disposition to study unilateral effects.

Interactive relationships between and among persons also require a situational and cultural context for proper interpretation, because all human action occurs in a *natural social context* (Berscheid, 1985; Brenner, 1980). Investigators are developing new methods for naturalistic situations. Romantic attraction and relationships, for example, are not very suitable for experimental investigations in the laboratory: They are "real world" events (Huston & Levinger, 1978; McGrath & Kravitz, 1982). Altruism and aggression similarly require naturalistic studies

(Krebs & Miller, 1985). The study of language *use* rather than *structure* requires observation and analysis of social activities, involving the coordination of two or more persons (Clark, 1985).

Investigators are beginning to ask: What are people doing together in this situation? What are they trying to accomplish? What is happening to them? For example, Fitzpatrick (1984) proposed a taxonomy for categorizing the strategies spouses employ to gain compliance in marital interaction. Studies of social development show that quite young children have "goals for interaction" that change their roles in different games; and that even infants modify their interaction patterns in different situations (Parke & Asher, 1983). This relatively new approach involves the exploration of how people select and influence social situations (Snyder & Ickes, 1985) and is sometimes called *modern dynamic interactionism* (Krebs & Miller, 1985).

The trend toward a more comprehensive unit of analysis in American social psychology also has been influenced by increased awareness of movement in a vigorous European social psychology, from an intrapersonal or interpersonal focus toward greater emphasis on cultural contexts (Semin & Manstead, 1983).

New "subdisciplines," *environmental social psychology* (Holahan, 1986) and *cross-cultural psychology* (Brislin, 1983; Segall, 1986), responses to dissent from narrow, artificial, and parochial formulations in experimental social psychology, also have stimulated a large volume of research in natural situations. They have induced attempts to conceptualize and measure more inclusive realms of phenomena. Another thriving specialty, *applied social psychology*, also stimulated by the crisis, has moved from unsuccessful attempts to directly apply findings from laboratory experiments on individuals to formulation of broader concepts and theory, more adequate to investigation of real-world problem situations (Rodin, 1985). Although the increased fragmentation of social psychology is regrettable, as is the inordinate amount of effort expended in these new specialties on problems of boundary-definition and institutional identities, they have stimulated cohorts of researchers who contribute to an expanded vision of social psychology's task.

Change in the Model of a Person. Social psychology has never had a single, agreed-upon model of a person. One can view its history as a quest for such a unified conception of human nature. The traditional theoretical orientations that underly much of its theory and research, *psychodynamic, behaviorist*, and *cognitive*, make divergent assumptions about the nature of a person. Yet, in spite of the theoretical diversity and controversy, social psychology has developed a working model of a person, generated implicitly by the dictates of experimental research. This model's implicit assumptions, that a person is essentially a *passive, unreflexive, autonomous* individual whose behavior is activated by aspects of the external world, has increasingly been challenged (de Charms & Muir, 1978; Gergen, 1984; Howard, 1985; Kanfer, 1979; Koch, 1981). In accord with everyday observations and empirical findings, contemporary theory and research is moving toward contrary assumptions: that a person is *active, reflexive,* and *interdependent* with others.

As discussed in an earlier chapter, many feared that the idea of a person exercising choice and initiating action threatened the status of social psychology as a true positivistic science. Much research still is designed to study unilateral effects, for example, viewing the "targets of influence as passive" (Miller & Turnbull, 1986, p. 241). Yet moving from a mechanistic model to one of "agency" does not necessarily negate a scientific approach to social phenomena. What Gergen (1984) called "agency smuggling," the introduction of implicit assumptions about human initiative and choice, is occurring in many areas: for example, in Bandura's (1982) *reciprocal interactionism,* and in research on *self-schemas* and *causal attribution.* There is increased awareness among investigators that a person is an active, intentional agent engaged in making choices (Krebs & Miller, 1985; Tyler, 1981).

Toward Self as a Reflexive, Multiplex Process. With the exception of the long taboo imposed by Watson's radical behaviorism, the problem of the "self" always has been important for social psychology (Gordon & Gergen, 1968). From a psychodynamic perspective, it has been represented as a central part of the personality: *self, ego,* or related conceptions that generated processes of *self-defense* and *self-esteem.* In the cognitive theoretical orientation it has been reified as a *self-concept,* a part, or even the core, of a relatively stable cognitive structure. In contemporary social psychology, the self is assuming even greater centrality; but unitary, fixed, structural conceptions are being replaced by multiple, dynamic, reflexive processes (Berkowitz, 1984; Gergen, 1984, 1985a; Loevinger & Knoll, 1983; Tyler, 1981).

Social influences upon the self and its formation were recognized, of course, by James, Dewey, Baldwin, Mead, Cooley, and many others. An extensive body of differentiated research has provided support for that classical postulate (Rosenberg & Gara, 1985; Stryker & Statham, 1985). The question of *reflexivity,* a, persons' ability to focus their attention on themselves, their own behavior, thoughts, and feelings, also has been a traditional problem. With the changing model of a person, however, both interpersonal and intrapersonal reflexivity have assumed increasing significance in research on self-processes. Goffman's (1959, 1961a, 1961b, 1963) insightful analyses of the presentation of self in social encounters led social psychologists to contemporary theories and research on self-presentation and impression management (Cialdini et al.,1981; Dion, 1985; Eagly & Himmelfarb, 1978; Markus & Zajonc, 1985; Schlenker, 1980; Tedeschi, 1981).

The recognition of a person's strategic activity in shaping, presenting, and adapting an impression of self to others has made salient the possibilities of multiple selves or identities, another classical conception (Brislin, 1983; Markus & Nurius, 1986; Rosenberg & Gara, 1985). *Social identity* and *situated identity* theories have specified conditions and processes involved in the assumption of identities for different purposes and situations (Brewer & Kramer, 1985; Cialdini et al., 1981; Schlenker, 1982; Stryker & Statham, 1985; Tajfel, 1982). The conception of a unitary, persistent, "real" self has not been abandoned, however, even in the newer formulations. It persists, for example, in the question of consistency between self and image or identity; and in the problem of organization and priority of multiple identities.

Increased Inclusion of Complex Reference Processes. The concept *reference group* was introduced in the early days of modern social psychology, but was relegated to a narrow segment of social activity, called *reference group behavior*. The main body of social psychological theorizing and research thus could proceed untroubled by this segregated idea. Another classical concept, *significant other(s)*, also has been available for sporadic use when convenient. Popular theories in social psychology, such as *social comparison theory*, have involved reference processes without using these older concepts. Only recently, however, has there been an increasing acknowledgment that reference processes are an intrinsic part of all social behavior.

Many areas of contemporary research and theory assume that a person's perceptions, thoughts, and feelings about one or more others whom the person selects as significant in a situation are essential to understanding the persons's resultant behavior. From an early age, for example, persons seek out emotional information from significant others, called *social referencing* (Klinnert, Campos, Sorce, Emde, & Svejda, 1982; Parke & Asher, 1983). Clearly, reference processes are central in theories of *impression management* and *self-presentation*, previously discussed. Interest in *social networks*, the cohort of others with whom a person has actual contact, has increased as investigators recognize the constraints they impose on attraction between persons (Berscheid, 1985). Stephan (1985) reviewed many studies on interracial behavior that explore the influence of reference processes. In the area of application, investigators have conducted field experiments on tobacco smoking, weight reduction, and other personal and social problems, and emphasize concepts such as *peer pressure, referent power*, and *social support* in accounting for changes in behavior (Rodin, 1985).

We see a development and broadening, concomitant with the changing unit of analysis in social psychology, from an individual reference process, perceptual or judgmental, to an interactive, reciprocal one. Reference processes are sometimes being conceived as *reflexive-interactive*, in which each of the interactants refer their evaluations and actions both to internal and external significant others, much as Mead (1934) proposed. An even more comprehensive *situated-reflexive-interactive* reference process recognizes its situational specificity.

Increased Inclusion of Complex Normative Processes. Sherif's classical experiments won an honorable place for norm in social psychology's conceptual panoply. Yet, the concept has remained peripheral to the main body of theory and research. It often has been included in the expositions of a problem area, or in the post hoc explanations of data that did not fit the initial hypotheses or theory.

But definitions and measurement models, with some exceptions (Jackson, 1960, 1975), have not been sufficiently comprehensive nor clear to generate much agreement. Most investigators have spoken about norms rather than investigated them in rigorous research.

The trend in contemporary social psychology, however, involves increased recognition of the influence of norms, more extensive inclusion of them in formulation of studies, and analysis of the relationship between complex normative processes and social behavior. A shift is under way from the traditional conception of *internalized norms* inculcated by socialization, to an appreciation of external, objective normative processes of influence—a change in emphasis from "self-control" to "social control" (Krebs & Miller, 1985; Spence, Deaux, & Helmreich, 1985). Accompanying this eviction of norms from the personality is an awareness that norms do not invariably imply conformity: The relation with behavior is contingent and complex, requiring understanding of the conditions that affect their selection, activation, and change (Campbell, 1978; Krebs & Miller, 1985; Stryker & Statham, 1985).

Empirical findings distinguish among various bases of norms— situational, group, or cultural—with implications for the generality of their influence upon behavior (Huston & Levinger, 1978; Krebs & Miller, 1985; Parke & Asher, 1983; Segall, 1986; Spence et al., 1985; Turner, 1975). A number of generic norms have been identified that appear to be widespread in our society: norms of *reciprocity, social responsibility*, and *equity* (Berkowitz, 1984; Berkowitz & Daniels, 1963; Gouldner, 1960; Walster, Walster & Berscheid, 1978). Investigators are exploring their diverse forms, distribution, and effects in this and other cultural areas.

The reification of *norm* increasingly is being replaced by a conception of a normative process of influence that pervades social activity. Normative explanations are being considered in most topical areas of social psychological theory and research: for example, in the study of attitudes (Cialdini et al., 1981; Eagly & Himmelfarb, 1978; Fishbein, 1980; Fishbein & Ajzen, 1975; Triandis, 1977), altruism and aggression (Krebs & Miller, 1985; Schwartz & Howard, 1981), equity and social exchange (McClintock et al., 1984), and in various applied studies (Rodin, 1985). Role theory, of course, must be added to any list, because its assumptions are inherently normative (Biddle, 1979; Jackson, 1966; Stryker & Statham, 1985).

In spite of psychologists' tendency to reinvent the wheel in their exploration of the intricacies of normative process—they could benefit from reading the extensive work of their colleagues in sociology and anthropology—clearly this current trend in social psychology is a positive move toward a more comprehensive, realistic, and integrated theory. Its intrinsic relatedness to the other trends discussed also must be evident.

From a Static Time Frame Toward a Bounded Unitary Period. Nothing is more apparent to observers of naturally occurring social life than the flux in persons and their relationships over time. Yet most research in social psychology has studied social behavior within an essentially static time frame: snapshots of attribution, attitude, judgment, or response. Or investigators have frozen data collection at two periods, before and after an experimental change. This discrepancy between the domain of natural social events and their representation in research certainly is not attributable to investigators' lack of sophistication. For example, recent reviewers of decision theory had to "treat decisions as though they were one-shot responses," at the same time acknowledging the ecological invalidity of most of the research (Abelson & Levi, 1985). The malady undoubtedly can be traced to the difficulty, complexity, expense, and lack of experimental rigor of research involving extended periods of time.

During the past decade, however, social psychologists have been recognizing that the temporal dimension must be taken into consideration in their theories and research. In her APA presidential address, Tyler (1981) pointed out that "time is an essential component" of all process models. Investigators have been constructing such models of interpersonal interaction, the development of a relationship over its *life course* (Altman, Vinsel, & Brown, 1981; Huston & Levinger, 1978), and are studying participation patterns over time (McGrath & Kravitz, 1982). The growing interest in close affective relationships has stimulated research on temporal stages and patterns of interpersonal attraction (Berscheid, 1985). Investigators of personality and social development also are conducting more longitudinal studies (Parke & Asher, 1983). McGrath (1984; McGrath & Kelly, 1986) has drawn attention to this changing focus of research, from a static time frame to a bounded, extended period; which is consistent and interrelated with the move toward more naturalistic studies of encounters, events, episodes, and social acts.

In a number of places previously we have referred to the traditional *theoretical orientations* that have been so influential in shaping social psychology. The term is a more general, inclusive one than *theory*: essentially a device for classifying theories, theorizing, hypotheses, concepts—even research techniques—which implicitly assume a particular model of human nature. Each of the traditional theoretical orientations assumes a different model of a person that is, to a considerable degree, shared by the theories, fragmentary theorizing, and methods in its category.

A general trend in contemporary social psychology that cuts across all of the six trends just discussed is a tendency toward the mixing and merging of the traditional orientations, with the possibility that an integrated theoretical orientation might eventually emerge. Although this eclecticism is resisted strenuously by theoretical purists in the behaviorist and psychodynamic orientations, it is especially evident in the dominant cognitive orientation, which is undergoing extensive modification reflecting all of the current trends.

In the next section, we sketch out possible stages in this transformation of the cognitive orientation into a more integrative one. In the final chapter we describe one formulation of an integrative theoretical orientation that reflects these trends in theory and research.

FROM A COGNITIVE TO AN INTEGRATIVE THEORETICAL ORIENTATION

The Cognitive Theoretical Orientation

The traditional cognitive model in social psychology assumes that a person is like a computer or information-processing system. The person is programmed to perform logical (rational) operations upon data selected in an immediate situation. From this perspective, social behavior is like that of a robot activated by computer output, the product of particular programs and accumulated stored information acting upon available informational inputs and translated into motoric activity.

Because the cognitive theoretical orientation is almost synonymous with contemporary work in social psychology, the trends reviewed in the preceding section primarily reflect extensive modifications and development of this traditional cognitive model (Fiske & Taylor, 1984; Forgas, 1983; Gergen, 1984, 1985a; Markus & Zajonc, 1985). Examples of these changes in the unit of analysis, model of a person, representations of self, reference, and normative processes, and in the time frame, can be found in cognitively oriented theory and research.

Toward an Integrative Theoretical Orientation

In addition to these trends, there appears to be a movement—not uncontested—toward increased theoretical integration in social psychology. The boundaries between the traditional orientations are becoming fuzzy. The behaviorist orientation always has included cognitive conceptions (Tolman, 1948), except for the radical behaviorists Watson and Skinner. In modern times, behaviorist social learning theories have incorporated cognitive terms and processes (Bandura, 1977, 1982; Rotter, 1966). Cognitive social psychology is replacing a single-process "cold" cognition with a "hot" version that includes affective and motivational processes (Markus & Zajonc, 1985), thus partially incorporating the psychodynamic orientation's motivational-emotional emphasis. Within sociological social psychology a similar integrative trend seems evident with the attempted theoretical synthesis of role and symbolic interaction perspectives (Stryker & Statham, 1985).

Psychological and sociological social psychologists still maintain their separate identities and show little tolerance for ecumenical movement. But their knowledge of each others' contributions and problems is becoming less superficial. Stryker and Statham's (1985) analysis makes availabe to psychologists a sophisticated treatment of the strengths and weaknesses of two important areas of sociological theorizing. A comparison of attribution and symbolic interaction theories provides a sociological perspective to this major area of psychologists' research activity (Stryker & Gottlieb, 1981). Many of the trends just discussed, for example, toward increased consideration of the context of social action, or greater emphasis on field studies and longitudinal research, have implications for disciplinary integration.

Many new metatheoretical proposals for psychology and social psychology appear to contain assumptions similar to those advanced recently in other social sciences. Gergen (1985b) envisioned the possibility of a "unified reconstruction in social psychology . . . within the broader intellectual milieu" (p. 551). Rather than a paradigmatic revolution, however, with its implications of sudden and cataclysmic change, with a razing of the edifice so painstakingly constructed and a new beginning, it is more probable that social psychology is in the midst of a prolonged period of evolutionary reformation. A more integrative theoretical orientation may emerge eventually to reinterpret and make more meaningful social psychology's accumulated empirical achievements.

Model of the Change Process in Social Psychology

Assuming the trends in contemporary social psychology persist, one can construct a model of the change process and can envision the outlines of a developing integrative theoretical orientation. Each of the trends identified refers to one *component* of such an orientation, and each component is moving through a number of *stages*, from the traditional formulation to an integrative one. For example, the traditional unit of analysis in social psychology has been the psychological processes or behavior of an *individual*. As the trend toward an expanded unit of analysis proceeds, its integrative culmination could be a *social act*, a multi-person bounded social event. Summarized on the next page are the components and stages of a model of social psychology's change process.

It must be apparent that the "stages" in this model are quite arbitrary, certainly not exhaustive, and do not necessarily represent a linear progression. The polar extremes may be more reliable, although even there objections can be raised. The "traditional" pole is almost a caricature of an individualistic, nonsocial social psychology: Except that examples of this category are common in the literature. Questions also can be asked regarding the *integrative* pole, because the term has been used in a number of different ways. In addition to theoretical, disciplinary, and metatheoretical integration, briefly discussed previously, an additional as-

Components	Stages
Unit of analysis	Individual . . . Interaction . . . Event-Episode . . . Social Act.
Model of a Person	Passive Reactive . . . Active-Initiating. . . Active-Choice. . . Active-Reflexive-Choice . . . Active-Initiating-Reflexive-Choice . . . Active-Reflexive-Social.
Psychological Modality	Cognitive . . . Cognitive-Behavioral . . . Cognitive-Motivational-Emotional . . . Cognitive-Motivational-Emotional-Behavioral.
Self	None . . . Self-Concept . . . Self-Esteem . . . Self-Process . . . Self-Reflexive-Process . . . Identity . . . Situated Identity.
Reference Process	None . . . Individual-Comparative . . . Interactive . . . Reflexive-Interactive . . . Situated-Reflexive-Interactive.
Normative Process	None . . . Individual Morality . . . Internalized Norms . . . Group/Cultural Norms . . . Situated Norms . . . Roles . . . Situated Role Behavior.
Time frame	Static . . . Brief Period . . . Longitudinal . . . Unitary Bounded Period.

sumption is involved in this category: That the separate topical areas, and the "specialities" of social psychology—such as *cross-cultural, environmental,* and *applied*—will become integrated with the main discipline to the degree that its theoretical orientation represents as completely as possible the characteristics of naturalistic social action.

Although social psychology is evolving, the rate of change is uneven and varies with different components of the model. Any particular theoretical or research contribution will encompass many if not all of the components, yet little consistency will be found among them. Traditional and integrative formulations coexist. One can find almost every mix of component stages. Students are challenged, as they read social psychology, to attempt to code specific contributions in terms of their component stages, and to identify alternative formulations of problems. In spite of its manifest inadequacies, we hope this crude model of social psychology's change process may help to foster a more analytical view of the contemporary literature.

In the final chapter we describe in greater detail the theoretical and empirical grounds, the assumptions, and the component processes of a possible integrative theoretical orientation for social psychology.

Chapter 7
An Integrative Theoretical Orientation

Contemporary social psychology is the product of all the beliefs, observation, imagination, and discoveries of its past. Perhaps our best estimate of its future state can be obtained from projecting current trends and developments. In this chapter, an *integrative* theoretical orientation is proposed for social psychology, an attempted synthesis of the culmination of movements discussed in the previous chapter and related intellectual and empirical contributions. It is apparent that none of this model of a social psychology is totally new: Every aspect of it can be found in the theoretical and research literature. Yet, it may prove useful to view it whole in some explicit brevity, as one possible construction of the future derived from contemporary developments and their implications.

PREREQUISITES FOR AN INTEGRATIVE ORIENTATION

Some Theoretical and Empirical Antecedents

The trends in contemporary social psychology that we have identified are the product of many significant influences from outside the field, in addition to the social psychological contributions just reviewed. Some of these influences are relatively recent developments, such as major changes in thinking about traditional areas of psychology, and new understandings of human brain processes. Others are classical contributions whose significance and relevance are being appreciated more fully, such as the theorizing of Dewey and Mead. The implications of these achievements in other fields for a changing social psychology have yet to be fully realized.

Advances in Psychological Theory. For decades, psychology's core areas of perception, learning, and motivation have rested on certain bedrock assumptions. This "metaphysics of psychological thinking" no longer is capable of organizing the new knowledge (Tyler, 1981). A movement began with Hebb's (1949) revolutionary neuropsychological theory and his associates' dramatic demonstrations of *sensory deprivation*, supportive evidence for an active person in continuous informational interchange with its environment. A new model of a person, active and reflexive, also emerged from White's (1959) questioning of traditional motivation theory, Hunt's (1965) research and attacks on "deficit theories" of motivation, and Mischel's (1968, 1973) proposal of an interactionist theory of personality. In perception, although not everyone accepted Gibson's (1950) substitution of an active, holistic person orienting itself to an environment, for the passive, camera-like individual of traditional theory, his influence has been immense. Another basic area also has been reformulated, with implications for a different model of human nature. Jenkins' (1974) contextualist theory of memory, stemming from Peirce, James, and Dewey, and reminiscent of Bartlett's classical work, analyzed memory processes in the context of a person's important, purposeful, and interesting events.

Advances in Related Sciences. Dramatic expansion of knowledge about human brain processes has resulted from revolutionary research techniques, including the implantation of electrodes directly into animals' brains, and scalp-recording of "event-related potential" in humans. Important for social psychology is how well the emerging picture supports Dewey's *functional psychology*, the basis for Mead's social psychology. In his classical attack on the *reflex arc*, Dewey (1896) criticized psychology's artificial separation of sensory and motor processes. Researchers now conclude that memory, sensation, and perception are not separable but interrelated functions, involving interactions among many regions of the brain, and related to a person's ongoing activity. The function of the brain is to perform, not "to contemplate serenely" (von Bonin, 1965, p. 151). The most parsimonious interpretation of scalp-recording research is that a person evaluates incoming information "in the context of expectations derived from previous experience" (John & Schwartz, 1978, p. 25), a conclusion which surely would have delighted but not surprised G.H. Mead, and which is consistent with the reflexive person of contemporary neo-cognitive and identity theories.

Tyler (1981) has drawn psychologists' attention to recent research rooted in evolutionary biology that concludes that human beings have almost unlimited possibilities of human choice, behavior, and creativity (Mayr, 1976; Young, 1978). The emerging picture supports a model of an active, reflexive, selective person.

The Heritage of Dewey and Mead. Although John Dewey had been a president of the APA and both he and George Mead were among the small group of early members, their position in psychology has been peripheral. Their formal identification as philosophers militated against complete acceptance by an experimentally oriented discipline. In recent years, however, psychologists increasingly are recognizing their contributions.

In his 1899 presidential address, Dewey criticized psychology's molecular emphasis. He insisted that behavior could not be understood in isolation from its encompassing social order (Sarason, 1981). He recognized that the Kantian dilemma between subjective and objective perspectives—what we have called in social psychology the *problem of combining subjectivities*— could be resolved only by adopting a more holistic unit of analysis. Dewey (1922) proposed the *trans-action* between an individual and its environment; which maintains the "integrity of the act" consistent with an ecological orientation in contemporary psychology (Gibbs, 1979).

In chapter 2 we described Mead as a social behaviorist who contributed, with Dewey and Angell, to the new *functional psychology* at the University of Chicago. Although he has been adopted by sociologists as one of their own and relatively ignored by psychologists, his recognition as a pioneering psychologist is increasing. Unfortunately, his theoretical position frequently has been distorted, especially in symbolic interactionist writings. He is portrayed, with Cooley, as a cognitive–phenomenologist. His thinking has been used by some as justification for an anti-quantitative or even an anti-scientific approach to social behavior. Familiarity with Mead's published articles and reviews of scientific works and his papers at APA meetings dispels that image. Clearly he was contributing to the central issues of psychology of his era, which included psychological measurement, deriving from psychophysics and the mind-body problem (Mead 1893, 1894a, 1894b, 1895).

The influence of his ideas is increasing among contemporary social psychologists: for example, his social behaviorist, anti-solipsist position (Pepitone, 1981; Sampson, 1981; Woodward, 1982), and the central role of activity in his model of a person. His theory is recognized as "strikingly similar" to that of the currently influential Vygotsky, seen as a Russian version of Mead (Kozulin, 1986). It also is indirectly supported, as in Gergen's (1984) argument, from Ryle (1949), that it is unnecessary to posit internal processes behind action; and the anticognitive quote from Thomas Huxley, whose evolutionary theory influenced Mead, that "the great end of life is not knowledge but action" (Spence, Deaux, & Helmreich, 1985, p. 171).

Empirical evidence also is mounting in support of Mead, for example, his theory of the social origin of mind in the role-taking process. Hoffman (1977) reviewed research that "indicates that very young children (even 2-year-olds) may demonstrate awareness of other perspectives" (p. 298). Zajonc's (1980) speculation, based on empirical data, that cognitive processes do not have to precede affective states, also is well in accord with Mead's model of the behavioral process.

Integrative Stages of Trends in Social Psychology

The trends in contemporary social psychology influenced by these developments from within and outside the discipline supply the prerequisites for an *integrative theoretical orientation*. In the preceding chapter we outlined the possible stages through which these trends appear to be moving, each culminating in an "integrative stage." These stages can be taken together as the components of an interrelated system. We summarize them here and in the following sections describe them more fully, with their assumptions and implications for a new orientation to social psychology.

1. *Unit of analysis*: The Social Act
2. *Model of a person*: Active-Reflexive-Social
3. *Psychological modality*: Cognitive–Motivational–Emotional–Behavioral
4. *Self process*: Situated Identity
5. *Reference process*: Situated-Reflexive-Interactive
6. *Normative process*: Situated Role Behavior
7. *Time frame*: Unitary Bounded Period

THE SOCIAL ACT AS A UNIT OF ANALYSIS

The Integrative Orientation conceives of human social conduct as occurring within meaningful, bounded social contexts, or social acts. This section provides the background, meaning, and assumptions of this central concept. Social acts do not exist as part of objective nature: They must be achieved. We discuss the initiation, course, and conclusion of a social act, and some of the problems of constructing a pattern of participation from diverse meanings and purposes.

Background, Meaning, and Assumptions

Mead defined the *social act* as a cooperative process that involved two or more persons who have, for the purpose of the action, a common end. "Cooperation" here does not have the usual meaning of helping one another or furthering each other's progress toward a goal (Deutsch, 1949). Two fighters in a boxing match, for example, each striving to demolish the other, are engaged in a cooperative activity in this sense, along with the referee, judges, trainers, audience, and others. What these participants in the social act share are common definitions of the situation, common symbolic objects, such as the *ring, rounds, bell*, and *gloves*, and a common objective, *having a boxing match*. A social act is an organization of multi-individual overt and covert meanings and bounded, directed activity.

Certain conditions are necessary for such cooperative action. Participants must share common meanings of the situation, the social objects, and their own and others' behavior. They also must be able to coordinate their activity according to shared norms. For example, the audience at a prizefight cheers and jeers. It is vociferous and raucous. A completely silent audience would indicate that the social act is not proceeding satisfactorily. Compare this with an audience at a Wimbledon tennis match, or a championship chess match, where silence and decorum is required conduct.

A social act has been called a *constructed social reality*, made up of shared definitions of the situation and symbolic meanings. Our language is the major source of such frameworks of meaning, for example, *wedding, funeral, opera*. Each word provides a definition of the situation and many social objects, with sufficiently common meanings. Erving Goffman (1961b) analyzed social process in terms of *encounters*, episodes involving interaction between persons who have engaged each others' attention and have to deal with one another. People who have been socialized within the same cultural system enter these encounters with *frames*, or *scripts* (Abelson, 1981; Goffman, 1974), systems of meaning that provide guidelines for the particular social act. But even standardized cultural meanings vary among individuals depending on their past experience. A social act, to be viable, involves continuous adaptation and coordination of participants' meanings and activity.

Initiation, Course, and Conclusion

A social act is bounded by space and time. It has a beginning, runs its course, and concludes. In using this idea, we sometimes find it difficult to determine the precise beginning of a social act. The observed social process appears to be continuous. Some events occur within larger events that are part of even larger events, like the nested boxes found in novelty shops. The analyst must decide arbitrarily how to delimit the social act, depending on the questions being asked. Sometimes, however, there is apparent discontinuity, a clear break in the social process: for example, when people enter an elevator, or the check-out line in a supermarket. Some social acts are brief encounters, unanticipated and novel. Others are part of larger "social agendas." In the integrative orientation, a social act begins when persons begin taking specific others into account in shaping their adaptations to their immediate evironment. This involves beginning to construct a situated identity for others' acceptance and confirmation.

Blueprints for many social acts are part of a culture, but they are drawn in blurred lines. Details are missing. People know the difference between an employment interview and an office party, but they do not know, and cannot know in advance, precisely how to present themselves. In all societies, however, some social acts are highly formalized. The culture has developed precise and detailed blueprints for them. Acceptable identities in these rituals appear to be completely standardized, as in religious ceremonies, inaugurations, ordinations—or university lectures. A closer examination reveals, however, that each occurrence of even formalized social acts has its own emergent characteristics. Participants find ways of constructing and confirming unique identities.

Most social acts in everyday situations proceed smoothly. Persons are unaware of the fragility of social acts, of the cooperation involved in maintaining them. Even routine social acts are problematic. In the next section, we discuss the confusion and emotion generated when persons do not share meanings nor confirm one anothers' situated identities. Implied in this interdependence of both meanings and conduct is a *concern* by participants that others behave appropriately. This implication becomes significant in our discussion of norms and normative behavior, in a following section. Thus, social acts are maintained, to run their course to a satisfactory conclusion, by a process of reciprocal adaptation of identities and action.

The conclusion of some social acts, like their beginning, is easy to identify. There is a discontinuity in the social process. The person leaves the elevator or the supermarket for a different location and enters into interaction with a new set of others defining a new shared purpose. A change in spatial location often indicates such a discontinuity, as Barker (1968, 1978) has observed in his studies of behavior settings, permitting us to carve up the social process into different social acts. A social act can terminate and a new one can begin without a setting change, however, as when business or political negotiations conclude and informal friendly relations are resumed; or frequently in domestic settings in which affective, economic, and other interests and purposes are intertwined.

Construction and Maintenance of a Social Act

People assume that if their behavior can be observed that it will be interpreted and evaluated. They attempt to avoid negative evaluation in the process of constructing their conduct, before it "emerges" for public inspection. In a social situation, participants monitor others' reactions to their own conduct. Their behavior acquires a situated meaning, specific to the social act. If one's conduct means something different to others than what one had intended or assumed, one makes verbal and behavioral adjustments until one obtains the desired reactions.

The problem for each person is to construct a pattern of activity—to "present a self"—that is acceptable to the other participants who will confirm it by their own patterned activity. But there are limits to the adjustments a person can or will make in the course of interaction. One's activity must have some coherence. One cannot behave in a random, incoherent manner, shifting one's implied definition of the situation, meanings, and purpose, without turning off the others, confusing and inhibiting them. Others are interacting with a *person*, not a disconnected series of responses for interpretation. Thus, each participant is constructing, by the way they play their role, a certain kind of person, a situated identity for the others' acceptance and confirmation.

A person cannot decide unilaterally how to play a role, and still participate successfully in a social act. An instructor at the beginning of a course may present a self to the students that implies "I am a respected scholar, to be taken seriously and treated with respect." This has implications for the ways students must play their roles. The instructor's situated identity cannot be maintained if students do not play their roles in confirming ways. If, for example, they ask facetious questions or interrupt solemn disquisitions with irrelevant observations, they disrupt the social act. Yet, one will not validate another's identity if it implies a drastic revision of one's own, except when coerced by superior power.

Each person in a social act is affected by reference processes that go beyond the immediate encounter. Persons respond to absent others—teachers, parents, friends, colleagues, heroes, gods—who have taught them ideal ways of playing a role and ideal outcomes of the social act in that type of social situation. Adapting one's situated identity to immediate participants may involve violating the demands of these reference processes.

One also has oneself to deal with. A person cannot be a chameleon without imposing insufferable stress on oneself. Although individuals differ in their tolerance, there are limits to the malleability of identity construction. Some consistency of roles in one's life, from one social act to another, seems to be required to remain a viable person. From an individual participant's viewpoint, the problem of interaction is: How do I participate in this social act in order to achieve my purpose while maintaining a viable identity? Each participant must find some patterned way of participation that is acceptable both to self and others. In any social act, therefore, the construction and confirmation of identities is problematic. Yet solutions must emerge from the interaction for the social act to proceed.

Even when individual backgrounds are similar, people often fail to understand each others' purposes in a situation. Verbally expressed purposes seem to imply certain actions, but the consequent behavior frequently appears inconsistent. People experience confusion or anxiety. They say things like: "I don't know what's happening," or We're not communicating," or "I don't know where you're coming from." When a person attempts to construct a pattern of activity for the occasion only to find other participants not responding appropriately, and feeling that their own pattern construction is impeded, the social act is disrupted and sometimes terminated. More frequently, a process of apparently aimless interaction occurs during which negotiations and reciprocal adjustments of purposes, meanings, and activities occur. The ultimate characteristics and direction of the social act emerges from this process.

NORMATIVE PROCESSES IN THE SOCIAL ACT

Introduction and Background

The Integrative Orientation is a normative conception of social psychology. That statement may be taken in stride by the reader or may cause some perplexity. What does it really say? The terms *norm* and *normative* are favorites in all of social science. They appear as explanatory concepts in discussions of almost every topic. For social psychologists they have many of the properties of Garfinkel's (1967) taken-for-granted everyday knowledge. They conceal hidden, shared assumptions that permit social psychologists to communicate with a presumption that they understand one another. We explore briefly the background, phenomena, meanings, and use in the integrative orientation of these ubiquitous concepts.

We observe around us a vast amount of uniformity and regularity of human activity. People in various categories or situations dress, speak, and act similarly. The exceptions attract attention, are considered humorous, tasteless, uninformed, or "sick." In earlier chapters we reviewed investigations of these social phenomena: Sumner's *folkways* and *mores*, Sherif's pioneering experiments on *norms*, and the transformation of this work by Asch, Milgram, and many others into social psychological problems of conformity, deviation, and social influence processes.

The term *norm* became accepted in social psychology to refer to accepted standards for social conduct, definitions of correct judgment and appropriate activity or attitude. The distinction between the everyday term *normal*, in the sense of typical or average, and the terms *norm* or *normative*, to imply propriety or impropriety, is recognized by most social psychologists. They generally agree that persons expect others to conduct themselves appropriately, within limits, in particular situations; and are affected by others' expectations. Normative regulation of social behavior is a process of influence that occurs either because of, or in the formation of a structure of norms.

Norms and Roles: Structure and Process

For analytical purposes we can think of individual norms, but the organized activity of social life requires a more holistic concept, *roles*, or normative systems. A *female role*, for example, can be defined in terms of a system of interrelated norms, each specifying for a a category of actors, a set of referent others, and a particular situation, certain appropriate or inappropriate conduct (Jackson, 1960, 1966). Role theory in social psychology takes two forms that derive from different intellectual antecedents and make divergent assumptions about human nature and society. *Structural role theory* has developed from "sociological" sociology and cultural anthropology. *Process role theory* derives from American pragmatism and "psychological" sociology. These early influences upon social psychology were discussed in chapter 2.

Some of the best examples of structural role theory were contributed by anthropological studies of small, isolated, preliterate societies that had experienced little cultural change prior to World War II. A blueprint of the role structure could be drawn, showing the roles members of each sex would be called on to play at each stage of life. The members of these societies agreed on sharply defined expectations for appropriate behavior and imposed severe sanctions if the limits of permissible conduct were violated. Traditional American sociology adopted this model—although in recent years quesions have been raised about the validity of some early studies. Implicit in structural role theory is a consensual model of society, organized and stable; and a passive-receptive model of a person, socialized by and conforming to the prevalent cultural system, what Wrong (1961) called the "oversocialized conception of man."

Process role theory makes different assumptions about the nature of persons and society. Persons are active and reflexive, capable of selecting, adopting or rejecting, and constructing roles in particular situations. Role relationships are not entirely predetermined but are negotiated and emerge from the interaction process. Society is less organized, coherent, and stable: It is constantly in a state of tension and flux, in the process of attempting to construct solutions for divergent meanings and interests.

Examples of this perspective typically are found in studies of interaction among people under naturally occurring conditions. For example, Davis (1961) observed how a physiotherapist tried to convert a person with a temporary physical handicap into a *patient*. The therapist emphasized the disability's seriousness, to persuade the person to relinquish "normal" roles usually played in favor of total patienthood. The person responded by emphasizing the handicap's temporary character and the imminent prospect of recovery. The person attempted to establish friendly relations by providing personal details about self, asking the therapist personal questions, extending social invitations and in other ways attempting to avoid becoming "only" a patient. The therapist could not play a completely professional role unless the person became a complete patient, however, so that offers of friendship and intimacy were rejected. But the therapist still could not afford to be viewed as cold and distant by either patient or colleagues. A "distant cordiality" was maintained as a role relationship emerged from the negotiation.

Normative Processes in the Integrative Orientation

Persons come to a situation and begin interaction with some cultural preparation. They may be unaware of their normative expectations, which derive from implicit answers to questions such as: What's happening? Who are you? Who am I? What are we doing here together? The social process is normative to the degree that participants in a social act attempt to coordinate action by taking each others' meanings into account in constructing their behavior. Participants react and respond to others' role taking with their own, a normative process of identity construction and negotiation.

Normative in the integrative orientation encompasses both structural and process perspectives. Situations vary, from those that fully constrain and regulate human activity to those where interaction processes are in a relatively free state of flux, with few shared meanings or directives for conduct. When normative processes are stable and regular, we can analyze them as normative structure. When persons' evaluative reactions and responses to specific conduct are shared and stabilized, we speak of a norm. When the normative process regulating an area of a person's conduct is patterned and stabilized, we can treat this as a structure of related and compatible norms, or a *role*. Normative structure is an analytical device, a way of "freezing" normative process in order to examine its regularities and relationships. Normative process is intrinsic to a social act, but the degree of normative regulation and stability is an empirical question.

If another person says a word to you and you laugh, you define it as funny. If you become angry, it is an insult. The meaning of another's behavior emerges in your reaction to it. The meaning of your own behavior becomes apparent in others' reactions. How often do we recognize a different, perhaps embarrassing, interpretation of what we said, only when others react to it in an unexpected way? The ongoing process of interaction involves continuous anticipation of others' reactions, observation of responses to our constructed conduct, recognition of others' and our own meanings, and adaptation of meanings and behavior. When coordination of activity occurs, it rests upon common evaluations of own and others' conduct. Negotiating those shared meanings in the social act is a normative process.

IDENTITY PROCESSES IN THE SOCIAL ACT

When our close acquaintances are inconsistent in their conduct, expressions, or appearance, we tell them: "You're not yourself today." We try to push them back into playing their role in the customary way, so that we can continue to play ours without alteration. A student who worked as a part-time cashier in a supermarket was shocked to find one of her professors standing before her with his purchases. "Wh—what—are you doing here?" she stammered. Typically we interact with others in only one or a few related social acts and assume we are dealing with the whole person. Yet we ourselves play different roles, or play our roles differently—what we call here assuming *identities*—in different situations, or as the social act changes.

It is imperative in a particular situation that we construct for others a coherent, believable identity that permits the other participants to do the same. We need to believe that we are dealing with a *person*, not a mere verbal expression or performance. We can trust others' conduct only if it conveys some substance, stability, and integrity. Otherwise we are hesitant to commit ourselves to an identity. For interaction to occur smoothly and a social act to proceeed, persons must be able to accept and confirm each others' constructed identities.

When Goffman, in his *dramaturgical* approach, described the process of self-presentation and construction of an unflawed performance for others' consumption, he was accused of cynically proposing a negative model of human nature: the person as a confidence man (woman?). The criticism derived from the traditional assumption of a true self: "To thine own self be true and thou canst not then be false to any man." With a different view of human nature and social process, however, the assumption of multiple identities does not imply hypocrisy nor moral blemish. As we have seen, theory and research on self-presentation and impression management has become a significant area of contemporary social psychology, complementary to the work on attribution processes.

In the integrative orientation, processes of identity construction and validation are intrinsic to a social act. There is no moral connotation, since all communication and interaction is inherently manipulative. It involves reciprocal processes of exerting and adapting to social influence.

Situated Identity in the Social Act

In the theater, an actor cannot play a role if other members of the cast do not play their roles in a coherent manner. For any social act to be maintained and proceed toward a satisfactory conclusion, coordination of behavior must occur. When one boxer dances in the middle of the ring and the other lolls against the ropes, the audience boos and the referee has to threaten disqualification. The social act is endangered. Activity cannot be coordinated, however, unless each participant in a social act constructs a coherent pattern of conduct. One cannot carry on a conversation with someone who is incoherent. Random activity by one participant does not permit the others to construct identities. A successful social act requires that participants together construct meaningful situated identities, so that coordination of action can occur.

A social act is an abstraction from the continuous flow of experienced social process. It is a unit of analysis with arbitrary boundaries, created by the analyst for the purpose of studying and understanding social life. Situated identities, the roles persons jointly construct to participate in a social act, persist as long as the social act. The duration of a social act and a situated identity can vary in any way an analyst finds useful. This may be for only a fleeting period, or for an actor's lifetime. The question for a social psychologist is: If I use this framework, does it help me impose order upon the phenomena? If I conceive of a particular segment carved out of social process as a bounded social act, with actors, shared definitions and purposes, roles played and identities validated, does it make the phenomena more meaningful?

A person's *career* can be conceived as a social act, with the constructed identities of the person and relevant others. Phases of the career, too: A student's academic or athletic career might be analyzed usefully in terms of a sequence of social acts and identities. People play different games, live in different social worlds: family, business, work, sports, adventure, friendship, love. Each has its cast of characters, its domain of language and symbols, its objectives, processes of normative evaluation, and constructed identities. A social world may persist for a long time, but the person may enter it only intermittently. Yet, the symbolic meanings and constructed identities may be reassumed and the social act proceed with little interruption.

Identity Validation

Previous direct experience may supply little guidance for playing a role in a new social act. An applicant in a job interview confronted by a youngish personnel executive, for example, may have acquired information, expectations, and exhortations from many sources. All of this assorted material must be organized into some initial pattern for presenting a self, for being a coherent, meaningful person in the social act. The applicant must avoid an image of an inconsistent or insincere person. The advice to "be yourself" or to "act natural" is not particularly helpful, because the person has a wide repertoire of behavior patterns and has to determine "who to be" in the immediate situation.

Regardless of initial intentions, interaction inevitably produces changes in the role played. As the social act proceeds, the meaning of the situation and the applicant's behavior are redefined: It may be a preliminary, information-gathering interview to screen out applicants; the position may become more or less attractive than initially; the applicant's previous experience and credentials may be more or less relevant than assumed at first; the interviewer may be seen as possessing relatively low or high decision-making power. The reactions and responses of one or more relevant other persons may be critical. The applicant's situated identity is validated when they respond in a pattern that confirms it as appropriate for the social act. When an identity is validated by referent others, persons feel no pressure to alter the way they are playing their roles.

Even in situations of unequal power, identity validation is a reciprocal process. To continue the example, the junior personnel executive may come on strong in the interview, playing an authoritative role. The applicant may validate this identity by being appropriately deferential, at the cost of being forced into assuming an unwanted identity. Another alternative might be to provide minimal deference but to ask questions to elicit the actual power position of the other. Efforts also might be made to structure a more equal relationship by making reference to common backgounds, persons known, and experiences shared.

The identities that emerge in a social act are those that each participant is willing to assume and to validate. They negotiate and strike an identity bargain. The more participants in a social act, the more protracted this process of negotiation will be. Unlike a formal, overt agreement, identity bargains are covert and temporary, always open to renegotiation as soon as validation is withdrawn.

Even though it was initially possible for persons to coordinate their action, new developments may make it increasingly difficult and lead to disruption of interaction. Identities are not validated as completely, their legitimacy has slipped. Mistakes occur when people are not skillful in playing their roles. Vestiges of roles played in other social acts may intrude into present role-playing. Sometimes persons may not recognize the internal logic or pattern of others' identities and may view their conduct as inappropriate or inconsistent. Even when participants appear to be communicating well, an unexpected and startling response may be received. If it is tolerably appropriate, it may be defined and accepted as humorous. But inappropriate conduct sometimes creates shock, confusion, embarrassment, or anger. Participants become aware that an actor's identity is flawed, and they begin to question their common purpose and definition of the situation. Either the social act is terminated—sometimes called a *temporary adjournment*—or renegotiation and validation of identities must occur.

Stability and Change of Identity

Biological endowments or cultural imperatives do not enslave persons, but they do affect their freedom to construct particular identities. Biology imposes limits on the behavior of members of all species. Stages of a person's life cycle, although culturally defined, do have a physiological basis. A person's size, shape, gender, race, ethnic origin, temperament, physical perfection or deformity, and other physical and intellectual capacities directly affect a person's choice of identities. An obese person is unlikely to choose to be a sprinter; although stammerers, like Demosthenes, become orators. The paramount effect of biological properties is introduced by their cultural meanings. Although these vary tremendously across and within societies and undergo continuous change, they impose restraints upon identity choice and construction.

Social structure is no myth. As discussed previously, it is a useful invention to describe the stable regularities and continuities of social process in every aspect of social life. Distinctive social acts in many institutional settings are culturally defined: the classroom with its single teacher and many students; the university lecture or seminar; the examination in a doctor's office or dentist's chair; the factory assembly line; the singles' bar. Although, as mentioned, cultural role expectations provide only crude blueprints for playing roles, they foster and perpetuate particular identities and restrict freedom to construct deviant ones. Although social structure restricts the choice of identities, it does not foreclose innovation and change, because the processes of negotiation and adaptation in social acts is continuous and endless.

The most effective method of changing persons' conduct is to change the social act in which they are engaged. Sometimes it is difficult to recognize the same person in a different milieu. Not only does appearance change, but also posture, movements, expression, and speech. People also make different evaluations when they play different roles: Social objects acquire new negotiated meanings. When the social act changes, it is not possible to maintain the same conduct and meanings, because these emerge from interaction with a new set of participants in a redefined situation with different shared purposes. A change of social act leads to a transformation of a person's identity.

REFERENCE PROCESSES IN THE SOCIAL ACT

The idea of *reference*, the consideration of other persons' thoughts, feelings, attitudes, or behavior in the process of forming our own, has been central in social psychology. It has appeared throughout its history under a variety of rubrics, such as *reference group, social influence, social comparison, social reality, significant others, referent others*, and *looking- glass self*. It has been embedded in different theoretical orientations with different assumptions about the nature of a person. Reference concepts have reflected the universal observation that a person's activity is not the product of an autonomous, isolated individual organism, but partakes of aspects of other persons' activities. In that sense, *reference processes* are inherent in a truly *social social psychology*.

Examples of the use of the reference idea within different theoretical orientations are numerous. In psychodynamic theories, reference others always have been considered central, from Freud's *superego* to Sullivan's *significant others*. Behaviorist approaches have considered the *social stimulus value* of other persons and the *reinforcements* they provide in shaping an individual's behavior. The cognitive orientation's information-processing person is assumed in *comparative reference groups* and the various forms of *social comparison* theory, not greatly different from Hyman's initial *frame of reference* conception.

Because reference processes are an integral aspect of the integrative orientation, they have been discussed previously together with the social act, normative, and identity processes. Clearly, the different components of the theoretical orientation are only analytically separable: They are interrelated in our conception of the process involved in any social event.

Cognitive and Integrative Theoretical Orientations

Although there is a superficial resemblance between the traditional cognitive orientation and the integrative orientation proposed here, the two approaches make different assumptions about the nature of persons and social process. The distinction is manifest in the treatment of meaning, either *cognitive* or *symbolic*. In the integrative orientation, construction of conduct is a reciprocal process: In contrast to the cognitive orientation, it involves more than perceiving others' evaluations and being influenced by them, but an exchange and adaptation of meanings. Another difference is in the treatment of self. Identity processes are also reference processes in the integrative orientation. They require that persons reciprocally construct acceptable ways of playing their roles. From the integrative perspective, reference processes are inherent in a person being social, in seeking and having validated a situated identity.

Reference Processes and Meaning

When we sit on a wooden box, it becomes a "seat." By using it differently, as a platform to stand on or as a table to work on, we change its meaning. The pragmatic theory of meaning says that meaning develops out of use and activity. From an integrative perspective, the meaning of our own and others' conduct emerges from interaction between us. When meanings have been adapted and modified until they are shared, conduct acquires symbolic significance and persons can anticipate each other's reactions. In the cognitive orientation, information may have its source in reference groups or individuals, but its meaning derives from its relationships with other information in a person's cognitive structure. Meaning thus exists within a single person rather than between persons.

The cognitive orientation considers reality to exist as an external state, to be perceived more or less accurately by a person; or to be a mental state encapsulated within an individual's private *phenomenal world*. People use reference others to influence their inner reality or their perception of the objective external world. In the integrative orientation, reality is social, constructed by interaction among persons. An external objective world exists, but its meanings are the creations of social activities. As an example, consider the social act of "taking a college course." The meaning of the social objects, *examinations* and *grades*, are not fixed nor universal. They emerge from the interaction among instructor, students, and administrative oficials, and the way they play their roles. The social act creates a distinctive social reality by the reciprocal adaptive conduct of its participants. Meanings in the social act emerge from its reference processes.

Reference Processes and Self Processes

Cooley's concept, the *looking-glass self*, has become a model in social psychology for a social conception of self. Cooley (1922) said that "A self-idea of this sort seems to have three principal elements: the imagination of our appearance to the other person; the imagination of his judgment of that appearance, and some sort of self-feeling, such as pride or mortification" (p. 184). This conception of self clearly embodies a cognitive theoretical orientation towards reference processes, one that Mead (1930) criticized as too subjective. He pointed out that in Cooley's doctrine of mind "the action of the others upon the self and of the self upon the others becomes simply the interaction of ideas upon each other within mind...in the same consciousness" (p. 700). Mead insisted that selves belong to an objective realm "which we distinguish from our imagination and our ideas." He said that "a society of selves in advance of inner experiences opens the door to an analysis which is behavioristic" (Mead 1930, pp. 704-705). The distinction between Mead and Cooley epitomizes the difference between the integrative and cognitive approaches to self and reference processes.

IMPLICATIONS OF THE INTEGRATIVE THEORETICAL ORIENTATION

The concepts and definitions adopted in a science are not just matters of clarity or convenience. They embody commitments to a particular view of the world, assumptions that have implications for theory construction and the conduct of research. The choice of the *social act* as the unit of analysis in the integrative orientation, with its normative, identity, and reference processes, has implications for a different social psychology that we review here briefly.

Metatheoretical Implications

Distinction Between Individual and Social Psychology. All psychology is in some sense social. Human behavior from birth invariably is affected by social and cultural influences. But most of social psychology has been developed essentially as an extrapolation from principles of the psychology of the individual. These principles have been derived from studies of isolated organisms—human and nonhuman. The consequence is a social psychology that is difficult to distinguish from individual psychology. The integrative orientation recognizes that there are inherently social processes not reducible to the principles of individual psychology. It does not deny a biological organism making inputs into behavior, but assumes that in social situations, conduct is constructed and emerges from interaction. Social psychology from this perspective is clearly distinguishable from individual or general psychology.

Emphasis on Process Rather than Structure. When the continuous movement and change that constitutes *process* exhibits recognizable regularities, we abstract these patterns from the ongoing activity and describe them as *structure*. Much of social psychology freezes social process, often in the interests of statistical method, by describing it in terms of interdependent "factors": for example, factors relating to individuals and their relationships, to characteristics of the task or problem, and to characteristics of the location and facilities (Sherif & Sherif, 1969). These abstracted, structural factors interact only in a statistical sense, as an operation on the data. In contrast, the integrative orientation assumes that social interaction processes and their emergents are central to all social phenomena.

The Person as an Identity Constructing Social Being. Social psychology as the study of social acts views a person as inherently social, adapting to other persons as a requirement for essential participation in social life. A person's identity, or way of playing a role in a social situation, is negotiated with others who are significant. It is a mutually acceptable product of interaction, and is subject to renegotiation as a social act changes. A person has an indefinitely large potential of identities, depending on the extent and variety of social experience. Yet, to varying degrees, persons maintain coherence among their identities by internal negotiations, reference processes that impose limits on identity change.

Meanings are Socially Constructed. We have referred several times previously to Moscovici's important distinction between *cognitive* and *symbolic* meaning. The integrative orientation views meaning as symbolic, a joint construction emergent from social interaction. When one person's activity implies a particular reaction and response from others, and the various participants in the social act share that implication, then the meaning of the activity is symbolic: not within one person's mind, but supra-individual, "combining subjectivities." In practice, is it possible to make this distinction between individual, cognitive meaning and shared, symbolic meaning? The test is the coordination of action in a social act.

Bounded Unitary Time Period. The negotiation of meanings, purposes, and identities in a social act require some duration of time. Social acts have a beginning, run their course, and come to an end. The integrative orientation implies that social psychologists must study interaction processes within bounded periods of time rather than static states and their relationships.

Implications for Conducting Research

Conducting research in social psychology has been treated traditionally as the application of a technology with an internal logic. In developing the logical structure of research procedures, social psychological theory has been deemed irrelevant. From this perspective, the particular theory or hypothesis under investigation should in principle not affect the choice of correct technology. Yet in practice, it seems clear that different theoretical orientations with their diverse assumptions about human nature imply different methods of research. Behaviorists do not interview subjects to explore their ideas and beliefs. A projective test makes sense only with the model of a person assumed in psychodynamic theories. Theory and methods are not really separable. In evaluating and understanding research, therefore, we must ask: What theoretical assumptions were made in using these particular methods? The assumptions made in the integrative theoretical orientation about persons and social processes imply a different approach and a new evaluation of many traditional problems of conducting research.

The integrative orientation assumes that all research involves the construction of a social act, whose participants include the subjects, investigators, their collaborators or assistants, and perhaps others absent from the immediate situation. The interaction among participants necessarily will generate normative, reference, and identity processes. People will be concerned that they are conducting themselves appropriately in terms of others' expectations and will reciprocally construct patterns of participation that are mutually acceptable.

A number of traditional "problems" in conducting research disappear with this conception of the research process. For example, investigators typically guard against subjects' psychological states or behavior being affected by anything except the intended inputs, such as the experimental situation, task, independent variables, interview questions, or questionnaire items. For example, *experimenter effects, observer effects, interviewer effects, demand characteristics*, and *social desirability*, introduce "error" and contaminate the data. The integrative orientation recognizes that these are aspects of the normal process of interaction in the social act. Rather than being weeded out or neutralized, they afford opportunities for experimental variation, and must be studied and understood.

In a talk at the University of Michigan in the late 1950s, Herbert Simon criticized laboratory experiments in social psychology for preventing or restricting interaction among subjects. He said that there were no emergents, nothing new was being discovered. The outputs were just recombinations of the inputs, and the research might just as well be performed by computers. The integrative orientation does not assume that persons, social behavior, or social situations have stable, invariant properties but that they constantly change during the course of a social act and new emergents appear. This has implications for problems of observation of social behavior, such as *sampling* and *categorizing*. Samples are not representative of the total social process and lose their contextual meaning. Categories change depending on the course of the action. Investigators must focus on more holistic processes, such as identity construction and validation, the emergence and sequential patterning of meanings, symbols, and relationships.

Measurement theory has great scientific prestige among most social psychologists. Its aura of implacable rigor attracts the hard-headed disciples of science but repels or intimidates soft-headed humanists. From an integrative perspective, measurement is an unavoidable human activity that needs to be understood and utilized properly. It begins with the recognition of variability in phenomena: one person is more friendly than another, a situation is highly threatening, a relationship between persons is only slightly competitive. Measurement occurs when a property is located on a scale of possible values. As Coombs (1950, 1964) has demonstrated, the scale may be crude and nonquantitative, such as *high–low* or *more–less*. Advanced measurement techniques provide mathematical precision and logical rigor, but the level of measurement should correspond to the complexity of the questions asked. Precise quantification must justify itself by contributing more to the ordering of experience than less precise measurement.

Two of the pillars of scientific respectability in social psychological research are the concepts *reliability* and *validity*. In brief, reliability concerns the accuracy of measurement and validity refers to the accuracy of naming what is measured. Without reliability, one is not measuring anything. Therefore, whatever you think you are measuring, you are wrong. Without reliability there can be no validity. Reliability assumes static properties and relationships that yield the same values under repeated measurement. The integrative orientation assumes reciprocal changing and emergent processes, which militates against achieving an acceptable level of reliability and implies that validity of measurement also will be low. This will be so only if we assume that the properties we attempt to measure are stable and invariant in nature, for example, *authoritarianism*. But if we recognize that this is an idea created to impose order upon our experience, a different kind of validity is more appropriate, *construct validity* (Landy, 1986; Whitely, 1983). It refers to the degree that our measure succeeds in imposing the particular order upon observations that we anticipate. The emphasis in the integrative orientation is on a pragmatic use of measurement to help impose meaningful order on social phenomena rather than arbitrarily defined acceptable levels of reliability and validity.

Statistics is a tool to prevent self-deception. We ask: How representative is an event we observe of all such events? What risk are we incurring if we believe that a result in our research is more than just chance? Social psychologists abide by the verdicts yielded by statistical analysis of their data; although in practice all of the mathematical assumptions that justify use of rigorous techniques are rarely met. Clyde Coombs once said that investigators can choose between being purists—and becoming methodologists—or doing research. As Donald Hebb once pointed out, and demonstrated by his own innovative studies, the most creative research is imprecise, imperfect, and fails to meet methodological criteria. It is based upon imagination and skeptical curiosity. A good part of scientific research consists of "i-dotting and t-crossing." From the integrative perspective, statistical techniques can be useful tools in attempts to impose order and meaning on experience. It is just important to cultivate the proper attitude of irreverence, to ensure that statistics remains the slave rather than becoming the master.

Reinterpretation of Accumulated Research Findings

Some recent proposals for a new paradigm in social psychology have asserted that a fresh start must be made with a clean slate, discarding as illusory and valueless all the achievements of the past. The integrative theoretical orientation does not have that implication. Even if a shift to this orientation were seen as one of Kuhn's paradigmatic revolutions—which is questionable—we know that in the physical sciences, at least, a new paradigm does not negate previous accomplishments but only reinterprets them. Einstein's relativity theory included Newton's laws as a special case, true under specified conditions.

Research is always being reinterpreted, of course, when its methods are reexamined or its results placed within a different theoretical framework, as in continued attempts to understand cognitive dissonance research, or Zajonc's reformulation of classical social facilitation research. But a reinterpretation of social psychology's accumulated findings demands more than a new look at methods and theory. It requires an inclusion of the context of research, the roles played by subjects and researchers, the implicit definitions of the research situation, and the normative and reference processes that were activated or emerge, as in Alexander's and others' reinterpretations of Sherif's and Asch's classical studies.

Not all of social psychology's vast inventory of empirical findings will survive such a reexamination. With a different definition of social psychology, the contributions of much of its accumulated research will belong to individual, general psychology. Only where the conditions, instructions, and total context of a study permit its reinterpretation can it be understood within the proposed framework. It is likely, however, that from such an intensive analysis and revised understandings, a comprehensive and more significant body of empirical knowledge will emerge, like old masters' paintings rescued from the accumulated obscuring grime.

From the integrative perspective, every research study in social psychology has constructed a social act, and all research is cultural in that it studies social conduct in the context of symbolic meanings and normative processes. The particular cultural context of a study can be identified by delineation of the social act and its processes. The "same" problem studied within diverse social acts—for example the relations between leaders and followers in trade unions or in congressional committees—will lead to different results. Understanding the differences in normative, reference, and identity processes attributable to different social acts is a central focus of the integrative orientation. It is not necessary to travel to foreign lands, however, to discover cultural diversity. Like charity, cross-cultural research can begin at home. The significant emphasis, from the integrative perspective, is not where or when research is done, but that it provides increased knowlege of active, reflexive, social persons participating in social acts as they pursue their interests and purposes in life.

References

Abelson, R. P. (1981). Psychological status of the script concept. *American Psychologist, 36,* 715–729.
Abelson, R. P. (1982). Three modes of attitude-behavior consistency. In M. P. Zanna, E. T. Higgins, & C. P. Herman (Eds.), *Consistancy in social behavior: The Ontario symposium* (Vol. 2, pp. 131–146). Hillsdale, NJ: Lawrence Erlbaum Associates.
Abelson, R. P., & Levi, A. (1985). Decision making and decision theory. In G. Lindzey & E. Aronson (Eds.), *The handbook of social psychology* (3rd ed., Vol. 1, pp. 231–309). New York: Random House.
Adler, A. (1924). *The practice and theory of individual psychology.* New York: Harcourt Brace.
Adorno, T. W., Frenkel-Brunswik, E., Levinson, D. J., & Sanford, R. N. (1950). *The authoritarian personality.* New York: Harper.
Allport, F. H. (1924). *Social psychology.* Boston: Houghton Mifflin.
Allport, F. H. (1933). *Institutional behavior.* Chapel Hill: University of North Carolina Press.
Allport, F. H. (1962). A structuronomic conception of behavior: Individual and collective: I. Structural theory and the master problem of social psychology. *Journal of Abnormal and Social Psychology, 64,* 3–30.
Allport, G. W. (1943). The ego in contemporary psychology. *Psychological Review, 50,* 451–478.
Allport, G. W. (1954). The historical background of social psychology. In G. Lindzey (Ed.), *Handbook of social psychology* (Vol. 1, pp. 3–56). Cambridge, MA: Addison-Wesley.
Allport, G. W. (1968). The historical background of modern social psychology. In G. Lindzey & E. Aronson (Eds.), *The handbook of social psychology* (2nd ed., Vol. 1, pp. 1–80). Reading, MA: Addison-Wesley.
Altman, I. (1976). A response to Epstein, Proshansky and Stokols. *Personality and Social Psychology Bulletin, 2,* 364–370.
Altman, I., Vinsel, A., & Brown, B. B. (1981). Dialectic conceptions in social psychology: An application to social penetration and privacy regulation. In L. Berkowitz (Ed.), *Advances in experimental social psychology* (Vol. 14, pp. 107–160). New York: Academic Press.

REFERENCES

American Sociological Society, Committee on the Implications of Certification Legislation. (1958). Legal certification of psychology as viewed by sociologists. *American Sociological Review, 23,* 301.

Amrine, M., & Sanford, F. H. (1956). In the matter of juries, democracy, science, truth, senators, and bugs. *American Psychologist, 11,* 54-60.

Ancona, L. (1954). *Social psychology in U. S. A.* (Italian) *Milan: Publications of the Catholic University of the Sacred Heart, Contributions of the Psychology Laboratory, 45* (Serial No. 17).

Angell, J. R. (1907). The province of functional psychology. *Psychological Review, 14,* 61-91.

APA Committee on Ethical Standards in Psychological Research. (1973). *Ethical principles in the conduct of research with human participants.* Washington DC: American Psychological Association.

Archer, D. (1985). Social deviance. In G. Lindzey & E. Aronson (Eds.), *The handbook of social psychology* (3rd ed., Vol. 2, pp. 743-804). New York: Random House.

Archibald, W. P. (1976). Psychology, sociology, and social psychology: Bad fences make bad neighbours. *British Journal of Sociology, 27,* 115-129.

Argyris, C. (1969). The incompleteness of social-psychological theory: Examples from small group, cognitive consistency, and attribution research. *American Psychologist, 24,* 893-908.

Argyris, C. (1975). Dangers in applying results from experimental social psychology. *American Psychologist, 30,* 469-485.

Aronson, E., & Carlsmith, J. M. (1968). Experimentation in social psychology. In G. Lindzey & E. Aronson (Eds.), *The handbook of social psychology* (2nd ed., Vol. 2, pp. 1-79). Reading, MA: Addison-Wesley.

Asch, S. E. (1946). Forming impressions of personality. *Journal of Abnormal and Social Psychology, 41,* 258-290.

Asch, S. E. (1948). The doctrine of suggestion, prestige and imitation in social psychology. *Psychological Review, 55,* 250-277.

Asch, S. E. (1952). *Social psychology.* Englewood Cliffs, NJ: Prentice-Hall.

Asch, S. E. (1956). Studies of independence and conformity. *Psychological Monographs, 70,* 1-70.

Asch, S. E., Block, H., & Hertzman, M. (1938). Studies in the principles of judgments and attitudes: I. Two basic principles of judgment. *Journal of Psychology, 5,* 219-251.

Back, K. (1963). The proper scope of social psychology. *Social Forces, 41,* 368-376.

Back, K. W., Hood, T. C., & Brehm, M. L. (1964). The subject role in small group experiments. *Social Forces,* 43, 181-187.

Bagehot, W. (1875). *Physics and politics.* New York: D. Appleton.

Baldwin, J. M. (1895). *Mental development in the child and in the race.* New York: Macmillan (1962).

Bandura, A. (1962). Social learning through imitation. In M. R. Jones (Ed.), *Nebraska symposium on motivation* (Vol. 10, pp. 211-269). Lincoln, NE: University of Nebraska Press.

Bandura, A. (1977). Self-efficacy: Toward a unifying theory of behavior change. *Psychological Review, 84,* 191-215.

Bandura, A. (1982). The self and mechanisms of agency. In J. Suls (Ed.), *Psychological perspectives on the self* (Vol. 1, pp. 3-39). Hillsdale, NJ: Lawrence Erlbaum Associates.

Bandura, A., & Walters, R. H. (1963). *Social learning and personality development.* New York: Holt, Rinehart & Winston.

Barker, R. G. (1968). *Ecological psychology: Concepts and methods for studying the environment of human behavior.* Stanford, CA: Stanford University Press.

Barker, R. G. (1978). *Habitats, environments, and human behavior.* San Francisco: Jossey-Bass.

REFERENCES

Barker, R. G., Dembo, T., & Lewin, K. (1941). Frustration and regression: An experiment with young children. *University of Iowa Studies in Child Welfare, 18* (1).
Barker, R. G., & Wright, H. F. (1955). *Midwest and its children.* New York: Harper & Row.
Bar-Tal, D. (1984). American study of helping behavior—what? why? and where? In E. Staub, D. Bar-Tal, J. Karylowski, & J. Reykowski (Eds.), *Development and maintenance of pro-social behavior: International perspectives* (pp. 5–27). New York: Plenum Press.
Bartlett, F. C. (1932). *Remembering: A study in experimental and social psychology.* Cambridge England: Cambridge University Press.
Baumgardner, S. R. (1976). Critical history and social psychology's "crisis." *Personality and Social Psychology Bulletin, 2,* 460–465.
Baumgardner, S. R. (1977). Critical studies in the history of social psychology. *Personality and Social Psychology Bulletin, 3,* 681–687.
Bem, D. (1967). Self-perception: An alternative interpretation of cognitive dissonance phenomena. *Psychological Review, 74,* 183–200.
Benedict, R. (1934). *Patterns of culture.* Boston: Houghton Mifflin.
Benedict, R. (1938). Continuities and discontinuities in cultural conditioning. *Psychiatry, 1,* 161–167.
Benne, K., Bradford, L., Gibb, J., & Lippitt, R. (Eds.). (1975). *The laboratory method of changing and learning: Theory and application.* Palo Alto, CA: Science and Behavior Books.
Berelson, B. (1954). Content analysis. In G. Lindzey (Ed.), *Handbook of social psychology* (Vol. 1, pp. 488–522). Cambridge, MA: Addison-Wesley.
Berger, S., & Lambert, W. W. (1968). Stimulus-response theory in contemporary social psychology. In G. Lindzey & E. Aronson (Eds.), *The handbook of social psychology* (2nd ed., Vol. 1, pp. 81–178). Reading, MA: Addison-Wesley.
Berkowitz, L. (1962). *Aggression: A social psychological analysis.* New York: McGraw-Hill.
Berkowitz, L. (1964). *The development of motives and values in the child.* New York: Basic Books.
Berkowitz, L. (1969). Social motivation. In G. Lindzey & E. Aronson (Eds.), *The handbook of social psychology* (2nd ed., Vol. 3, pp. 50–135). Reading, MA: Addison-Wesley.
Berkowitz, L. (Ed.). (1984). *Advances in experimental social psychology* (Vol. 18). New York: Academic Press.
Berkowitz, L., & Daniels, L. R. (1963). Responsibility and dependency. *Journal of Abnormal and Social Psychology, 66,* 429–437.
Berkowitz, L., & Daniels, L. R. (1964). Affecting the salience of the social responsibility norm: Effects of past help on the response to dependency relationships. *Journal of Abnormal and Social Psychology, 68,* 275–281.
Berkowitz, L., & Donnerstein, E. (1982). External validity is more than skin deep: Some answers to criticisms of laboratory experiments. *American Psychologist, 37,* 245–257.
Berkowitz, L., & Walster, E. (1976). Equity theory: Toward a general theory of social interaction. In L. Berkowitz (Ed.), *Advances in experimental social psychology* (Vol. 9). New York: Academic Press.
Bernard, L. L. (1921). The misuse of instinct in the social sciences. *Psychological Review, 28,* 96–119.
Bernard, L. L. (1924). *Instinct: A study in social psychology.* New York: Holt.
Berscheid, E. (1985). Interpersonal attraction. In G. Lindzey & E. Aronson (Eds.), *The handbook of social psychology* (3rd ed., Vol. 2, pp. 413–484). New York: Random House.
Bickman, L. (1976). Fulfilling the promise: A response to Helmreich. *Personality and Social Psychology Bulletin, 2,* 131–133.
Biddle, B. J. (1979). *Role theory: Expectations, identities, and behaviors.* New York: Academic Press.
Bion, W. R. (1948–1951). Experiences in groups I–VII. *Human Relations, 1–4.*

REFERENCES

Blank, T. O. (1978). Two social psychologies: Is segregation inevitable? *Personality and Social Psychology Bulletin, 4,* 553-556.
Boas, F. (Ed.). (1911). *Handbook of American Indian languages.* Bureau of American Ethnology, Bulletin No. 40.
Bogardus, E. S. (1928). *Immigration and race attitudes.* Boston: Heath.
Bogardus, E. S. (1933). A social distance scale. *Sociology and Social Research, 17,* 265-271.
Bonner, H. (1953). *Social psychology: An interdisciplinary approach.* New York: American Book.
Boring, E. G. (1929). *A history of experimental psychology.* New York: Appleton-Century.
Boulding, K. E. (1962). *Conflict and defense: A general theory.* New York: Harper.
Boulding, K. E. (1967). Dare we take the social sciences seriously? *American Behavioral Scientist, 10,* 12-16.
Bradford, L., Gibb, J. R., & Benne, K. D. (1964). *T-group theory and laboratory method.* New York: Wiley.
Braid, J. (1889). *Neurypnology.* London: G. Redway. (Originally published 1843)
Brenner, M. (1980). Introduction. In M. Brenner (Ed.), *The structure of action* (pp. 1-27). New York: St. Martin's Press.
Brewer, M. B., & Kramer, R. M. (1985). The psychology of intergroup attitudes and behavior. In M. R. Rozenzweig & L. W. Porter (Eds.), *Annual review of psychology* (Vol. 36, pp. 219-243). Palo Alto, CA: Annual Reviews.
Brislin, R. W. (1983). Cross-cultural research in psychology. In M. R. Rozenzweig & L. W. Porter (Eds.), *annual review of psychology* (Vol. 34, pp. 363-400). Palo Alto, CA: Annual Reviews.
Britt, S. H. (1941). *Social psychology of modern life.* New York: Rinehart.
Brody, N. (1980). Social motivation. In M. R. Rozenzweig & L. W. Porter (Eds.), *Annual review of psychology* (Vol. 31, pp. 143-168). Palo Alto, CA: Annual Reviews.
Bronfenbrenner, U. (1963). Developmental theory in transition. In H. W. Stevenson (Ed.), *Child psychology* (NSSE Yearbook, Part I, pp. 517-542). Chicago: University of Chicago Press.
Bronfenbrenner, U., Kessel, F., Kessen, W., & White, S. (1986). Toward a critical social history of developmental psychology: A propaedeutic discussion. *American Psychologist, 41,* 1218-1230.
Brown, T. (1820). *Lectures on the philosophy of the human mind.* Edinburgh: J. Ballantyne for W. Tait & C. Tait.
Bruner, J. S. (1941). The dimensions of propaganda: German shortwave broadcasts to America. *Journal of Abnormal and Social Psychology, 36,* 311-337.
Bruner, J. S. (1950). Social psychology and group processes. *Annual review of psychology* (Vol. 1, pp. 119-150). Palo Alto, CA: Annual Reviews.
Bruner, J. S. (1951). Personality dynamics and the process of perceiving. In R. G. Blake & G. V. Ramsey (Eds.), *Perception: An approach to personality* (pp. 121-147). New York: Ronald Press.
Bruner, J. S., & Tagiuri, R. (1954). The perception of people. In G. Lindzey (Ed.), *Handbook of social psychology* (Vol. 2, pp. 634-654). Cambridge, MA: Addison-Wesley.
Burgess, R. (1977). The withering away of social psychology. *American Sociologist, 12,* 12-13.
Buss, D. M. (1986). Review of L. Berkowitz (Ed.), *Advances in experimental social psychology* (Vol. 18, 1984). *Contemporary Psychology, 31,* 190.
Campbell, A. A. (1946). Measuring public attitudes. *Journal of Social Issues 2,* 1-69.
Campbell, D. T. (1978). On the genetics of altruism and the counterhedonic component in human culture. In L. Wispé (Ed.), *Altruism, sympathy, and helping* (pp. 39-57). New York: Academic Press.
Cantil, H. (1940). Experiments in the wording of questions. *Public Opinion Quarterly, 4,* 330-332.

REFERENCES

Cartwright, D. (1945). American social psychology and the war. *Journal of Consulting Psychology, 9,* 67-72.
Cartwright, D. (1948). Social psychology in the United States during the Second World War. *Human Relations, 1,* 333-352.
Cartwright, D. (1949a). Basic and applied social psychology. *Philosophy of Science, 16,* 198-208.
Cartwright, D. (1949b). Some principles of mass persuasion: Selected findings of research on the sale of United States war bonds. *Human Relations, 2,* 253-267.
Cartwright, D. (1959). Power: A neglected variable in social psychology. In D. Cartwright (Ed.), *Studies in social power* (pp. 1-14). Ann Arbor: University of Michigan Press.
Cartwright, D. (1961). A decade of social psychology. In R. Patton (Ed.), *Current trends in psychological theory* (pp. 9-30). Pittsburgh, PA: University of Pittsburgh Press.
Cartwright, D. (1979). Contemporary social psychology in historical perspective. *Social Psychology Quarterly, 42,* 82-93.
Cartwright, D., & Zander, A. (1960). *Group dynamics: Research and theory.* Evanston, IL: Row, Peterson.
Cattell, R. B. (1951). New concepts for measuring leadership in terms of group syntality. *Human Relations, 4,* 161-184.
Chapanis, N. P., & Chapanis, A. (1964). Cognitive dissonance. *Psychological Bulletin, 61,* 1-22.
Chapman, D. W., & Volkmann, J. A. (1939). A social determinant of the level of aspiration. *Journal of Abnormal and Social Psychology, 34,* 225-238.
Chapple, E. D., & Arensberg, C. M. (1940). Measuring human relations: An introduction to the study of the interaction of individuals. *Genetic Psychology Monographs, 22,* 3-147.
Christie, R., & Geis, F. L. (Eds.). (1970). *Studies in Machiavellianism.* New York: Academic Press.
Christie, R., & Jahoda, M. (Eds.). (1954). *Studies in the scope and method of "The Authoritarian Personality."* New York: The Free Press.
Cialdini, R. B., Petty, R. E., & Cacioppo, J. T. (1981). Attitudes and attitude change. In M. R. Rozenzweig & L. W. Porter (Eds.), *Annual review of psychology* (Vol. 32, pp. 357-404). Palo Alto, CA: Annual Reviews.
Clark, H. H. (1985). Language use and language users. In G. Lindzey & E. Aronson (Eds.), *The handbook of social psychology* (3rd ed., Vol. 2, pp. 179-231). New York: Random House.
Clark, K. B. (1965). Problems of power and social change: Toward a relevant social psychology. *Journal of Social Issues, 21,* 4-20.
Clark, M. S. (1986). Review of Volume 17, *Advances in experimental social psychology,* 1984. *Contemporary Psychology, 31,* 412-413.
Clark, R. D., III. (1986). Review of Staub, Bar-Tal, Karylowski, & Reykowski (Eds.), *Development and maintenance of pro-social behavior: International perspectives. Contemporary Psychology, 31,* 60-61.
Clore, G. L., Bnay, R. M., Itkin, S. M., & Murphy, P. (1978). Interracial attitudes and behavior at a summer camp. *Journal of Personality and Social Psychology, 36,* 107-116.
Cloward, R. A., & Ohlin, L. E. (1960). *Delinquency and opportunity.* New York: The Free Press.
Cohen, A. K. (1955). *Delinquent boys: The culture of the gang.* New York: The Free Press.
Cohen, A. K. (1966). *Deviance and control.* Englewood Cliffs, NJ: Prentice-Hall.
Collins, B. E., & Raven, B. H. (1969). Group structure: Attraction, coalitions, communication, and power. In G. Lindzey & E. Aronson (Eds.), *The handbook of social psychology* (2nd ed., Vol. 4, pp. 102-204). Reading, MA: Addison-Wesley.
Comte, A. (1853). *The positive philosophy* (Vol. 1). London: Trubner. (Originally published in French in 1830)

REFERENCES

Cooley, C. H. (1902). *Human nature and the social order.* New York: Charles Scribner's Sons.
Cooley, C. H. (1909). *Social organization.* New York: Charles Scribner's Sons.
Cooley, C. H. (1918). The social process. New York: Charles Scribner's Sons.
Coombs, C. H. (1950). Psychological scaling without a unit of measurement. *Psychological Review, 57,* 145-158.
Coombs, C. H. (1964). *A theory of data.* New York: Wiley.
Cooper, J., & Croyle, R. T. (1984). Attitudes and attitude change. In M. R. Rozenzweig & L. W. Porter (Eds.), *Annual review of psychology* (Vol. 35, pp. 395-426). Palo Alto, CA: Annual Reviews.
Coopersmith, S. (1967). *The antecedents of self-esteem.* San Francisco: W. H. Freeman.
Cronbach, L. J. (1955). Processes affecting scores on 'understanding of others' and 'assumed similarity.' *Psychological Bulletin, 52,* 177-193.
Cronbach, L. J. (1975). Beyond the two disciplines of scientific psychology. *American Psychologist, 30,* 116-127.
Crow, W. J., & Hammond, K. R. (1957). The generality of accuracy and response sets in interpersonal perception. *Journal of Abnormal and Social Psychology, 54,* 384-390.
Cumberland, R. (1672). *A philosophical examination of natural law.* Cambridge: Cambridge University.
Darley, J. G. (1951). Five years of social science research: Retrospect and prospect. In H. Guetzkow (Ed.), *Groups, leadership and men: Research in human relations* (pp. 3-15). Pittsburgh, PA: Carnegie Press.
Darwin, C. (1859). *On the origin of species.* London: J. Murray.
Darwin, C. (1872). *The expression of the emotions in man and animals.* London: J. Murray.
Davis, A., Gardner, B. B., & Gardner, M. R. (1941). *Deep south: A social anthropological study of caste and class.* Chicago: University of Chicago Press.
Davis, F. (1961). Deviance disavowal: The management of strained interaction by the visibly handicapped. *Social Problems, 9,* 120-132.
Dawson, C. A., & Gettys, W. E. (1948). The ecological approach to the study of man and his institutions. *An introduction to sociology* (3rd ed., Part II). New York: Ronald Press.
Deaux, K., & Wrightsman, L. S. (1984). *Social psychology in the 80s* (4th ed.). Monterey, CA: Brooks/Cole.
de Charms, R., & Muir, M. S. (1978). Motivation: Social approaches. In M. R. Rozenzweig & L. W. Porter (Eds.), *Annual review of psychology* (Vol. 29, pp. 91-114). Palo Alto, CA: Annual Reviews.
de Charms, R., & Shea, D. J. (1976). Beyond attribution theory: The human conception of motivation and causality. In L. H. Strickland, F. E. Aboud, & K. J. Gergen (Eds.), *Social psychology in transition* (pp. 253-267). New York: Plenum Press.
Dennis, W. (Ed.). (1948). *Current trends in social psychology.* Pittsburgh, PA: University of Pittsburgh Press.
Deutch, M. (1949). An experimental study of the effects of cooperation and competition upon group processes. *Human Relations, 2,* 199-232.
Deutsch, M. (1962). Cooperation and trust: Some theoretical notes. In M. Jones (Ed.), *Nebraska symposium on motivation* (Vol. 10, pp. 275-320). Lincoln, NE: University of Nebraska Press.
Deutsch, M. (1968-1969). Field theory in social psychology. In G. Lindzey & E. Aronson (Eds.), *The handbook of social psychology* (2nd ed., Vol. 1, pp. 412-487). Reading, MA: Addison-Wesley.
Deutsch, M. (1976). Theorizing in social psychology. *Personality and Social Psychology Bulletin, 2,* 134-141.
Deutsch, M., & Krauss, R. M. (1965). *Theories in social psychology.* New York: Basic Books.
Dewey, J. (1896). The reflex arc concept in psychology. *Psychological Review, 3,* 357-370.
Dewey, J. (1899). *Psychology as philosophic method.* Berkeley, CA: University Chronicle.

REFERENCES

Dewey, J. (1910). *How we think.* Boston: Heath.
Dewey, J. (1917). The need for social psychology. *Psychological Review, 24,* 266-276.
Dewey, J. (1922). *Human nature and conduct: An introduction to social psychology.* New York: Carlton House.
Dion, K. K. (1985). Socialization in adulthood. In G. Lindzey & E. Aronson (Eds.), *The handbook of social psychology* (3rd ed., Vol. 2, pp. 123-147). New York: Random House.
Diggory, J. C. (1966). *Self-evaluation: Concepts and studies.* New York: Wiley.
Dollard, J., Doob, L. W., Miller, N. E., Mower, O. H., & Sears, R. R. (1939). *Frustration and aggression.* New Haven, CT: Yale University Press.
Dollard, J., & Miller, N. E. (1950). *Personality and psychotherapy.* New York: McGraw-Hill.
Dunham, H. W., & Weinberg, S. K. (1960). *The culture of the state mental hospital.* Detroit, MI: Wayne State University Press.
Dunlap, K. (1919). Are there any instincts? *Journal of Abnormal Psychology, 14,* 307-311.
Durkheim, E. (1897). *Suicide.* Paris: F. Alcan.
Durkheim, E. (1912). *The elementary forms of religious life.* Paris: F. Alcan.
Duval, S., & Wicklund, R. A. (1972). *A theory of objective self-awareness.* New York: Academic Press.
Eagly, A. H., & Himmelfarb, S. (1978). Attitudes and opinions. In M. R. Rozenzweig & L. W. Porter (Eds.), *Annual review of psychology* (Vol. 29, pp. 517-554). Palo Alto, CA: Annual Reviews.
Elms, A. C. (1975). The crisis of confidence in social psychology. *American Psychologist, 30,* 967-976.
Epstein, Y. M. (1976). Comments on "environmental psychology and social psychology." *Personality and Social Psychology Bulletin, 2,* 346-349.
Ex, J. (1960). Analysis of the experimental situation and the experiment in social psychology. (Dutch) *Z. exp. angew andt. Pschol., 7,* 100-125.
Feather, N. T. (1964). A structural balance model of communication effects. *Psychological Review, 71,* 291-313.
Feather, N. T. (1965). A structural balance model of evaluative behavior. *Human Relations, 18,* 171-185.
Fechner, G. T. (1860). *Elements of psychophysics* (German). Leipzig, Germany: Brettkopf & Hantel.
Ferguson, G. A. (1966). *Statistical analysis in psychology and education.* New York: McGraw-Hill.
Festinger, L. (1942).Wish, expectation, and group performance as factors influencing level of aspiration. *Journal of Abnormal and Social Psychology, 37,* 184-200.
Festinger, L. (1950a). Experiments in group belongingness. In J. Miller (Ed.), *Experiments in social process* (pp. 31-46). New York: McGraw-Hill.
Festinger, L. (1950b). Informal social communication. *Psychological Review, 57,* 271-282.
Festinger, L. (1957). *A theory of cognitive dissonance.* Stanford, CA: Stanford University Press.
Festinger, L., Schachter, S., & Back, K. (1950). *Social pressures in informal groups: A study of human factors in housing.* Stanford, CA: Stanford University Press.
Fishbein, M. (1980). A theory of reasoned action: Some applications and implications. In M. Page (Ed.), *Nebraska symposium on motivation* (Vol. 27, pp. 65-116). Lincoln, NE: University of Nebraska Press.
Fishbein, M., & Ajzen, I. (1975). *Belief, attitude, intention and behavior: An introduction to theory and research.* Reading, MA: Addison-Wesley.
Fiske, S. T., & Taylor, S. E. (1984). *Social cognition.* Reading, MA: Addison-Wesley.
Fitzpatrick, M. A. (1984). A typological approach to marital interaction. In L. Berkowitz (Ed.), *Advances in experimental social psychology* (Vol. 18, pp. 1-47). New York: Academic Press.

Forgas, J. P. (1983). What is social about social cognition? *British Journal of Social Psychology, 22,* 129-144.
Fouillée, A. (1908). *Morale des idées-forces* (2nd ed.). Paris: F. Alcan.
Fouraker, L. E., & Siegel, S. (1963). *Bargaining behavior.* New York: McGraw-Hill.
Franke, R. H. (1979). Comment. *American Sociological Review, 44,* 861-867.
Franke, R. H., & Kaul, J. D. (1978). The Hawthorne experiments: First statistical interpretation. *American Sociological Review, 43,* 623-643.
French, J. R. P., Jr. (1941). The disruption and cohesion of groups. *Journal of Abnormal and Social Psychology, 36,* 361-377.
French, J. R. P., Jr., & Raven, B. H. (1959). The bases of social power. In D. Cartwright (Ed.), *Studies in social power* (pp. 150-167). Ann Arbor: University of Michigan Press.
Frenkel-Brunswik, E. (1952). Social psychology. In D. Brower & L. E. Abt (Eds.), *Progress in clinical psychology* (Vol. 1, pp. 508-518). New York: Grune & Stratton.
Freud, S. (1913). *Totem and taboo.* New York: W. W. Norton.
Freud, S. (1922). *Group psychology and the analysis of the ego.* London: Hogarth.
Freud, S. (1930). *Civilization and its discontents.* Garden City, NY: Doubleday.
Fromm, E. (1941). *Escape from freedom.* New York: Farrar & Rinehart.
Fromm, E. (1947). *Man for himself.* Boston: Houghton Mifflin.
Gamson, W. A. (1964). Experimental studies of coalition formation. In L. Berkowitz (Ed.), *Advances in experimental social psychology* (Vol. 1, pp.81-110). New York: Academic Press.
Garfinkel, H. (1967). *Studies in ethnomethodology.* Englewood Cliffs, NJ: Prentice-Hall.
Geis, F. (1979). Machiavellianism: A cross-cultural perspective of manipulative social behavior. In L. Eckensberger, W. Lonner, & Y. Poortinga (Eds.), *Cross-cultural contributions to psychology* (pp. 151-162). Amsterdam: Swets & Zeitlinger.
Gergen, K. J. (1973). Social psychology and history. *Journal of Personality and Social Psychology, 26,* 309-320.
Gergen, K. J. (1976). Social psychology, science and history. *Personality and Social Psychology Bulletin, 2,* 373-383.
Gergen, K. J. (1984). Theory of the self: Impasse and evolution. In L. Berkowitz (Ed.), *Advances in experimental social psychology,* Vol. 17. *Theorizing in social psychology: Special topics* (pp. 49-115). New York: Academic Press.
Gergen, K. J. (1985a). The social constructionist movement in modern psychology. *American Psychologist, 40,* 266-275.
Gergen, K. J. (1985b). Social psychology and the phoenix of realism. In S. Koch & D. E. Leary (Eds.), *A century of psychology as a science* (pp. 528-557). New York: McGraw Hill.
Gibbs, J. C. (1979). The meaning of ecologically oriented inquiry in contemporary psychology. *American Psychologist, 34,* 127-140.
Gibson, J. J. (1950). *The perception of the visual world.* Boston: Houghton Mifflin.
Giddings, F. H. (1896). *The principles of sociology.* New York: Macmillan.
Goffman, E. (1959). *The presentation of self in everyday life.* Garden City, NY: Doubleday Anchor Books.
Goffman, E. (1961a). *Asylums.* Garden City, NY: Anchor Books.
Goffman, E. (1961b). *Encounters.* Indianapolis, IN: Bobbs-Merrill.
Goffman, E. (1963). *Stigma.* Englewood Cliffs, NJ: Prentice-Hall.
Goffman, E. (1974). *Frame analysis.* New York: Colophon Books.
Goldstein, J. W. (1963). *Level of aspiration, social comparison, and wish: A reexamination of Festinger.* Unpublished master's thesis, University of Kansas, Lawrence, KS.
Gordon, C., & Gergen, K. J. (Eds.). (1968). *The self in social interaction: Classic and contemporary perspectives.* New York: Wiley.
Gottlieb, A. (1977). Social psychology as history or science: An addendum. *Personality and Social Psychology Bulletin, 3,* 207-210.

Gouldner, A. W. (1960). The norm of reciprocity: A preliminary statement. *American Sociological Review, 25,* 161-179.

Gouldner A. W. (1970). *The coming crisis in Western sociology.* New York: Basic Boors.

Greenblatt, M. D., Levinson, D. J., & Williams, R. H. (Eds.). (1957). *The patient and the mental hospital.* Glencoe, IL: The Free Press.

Greenwald, A. G. (1976). Transhistorical lawfulness of behavior: A comment on two papers. *Personality and Social Psychology Bulletin, 2,* 391.

Gross, E. (1956). Social science techniques: A problem of power and responsibility. *Scientific Monthly, 83,* 242-247.

Gross, G. (1974). Unnatural selection. In N. Armistead (Ed.), *Reconstructing social psychology* (pp. 42-51). Harmondsworth, England: Penguin Education.

Guetzkow, H. (Ed.). (1951). *Groups, leadership and men: Research in human relations.* Pittsburgh, PA: Carnegie Press.

Gurmund, L. (1955). *The problem of correct symbolism as related to some problems of social psychology.* Goteborg, Sweden: Elandere Boktryckeri Aktiebolag.

Guttentag, M. (1976). Presidential Message - Division 8, A.P.A. *Personality and Social Psychology Bulletin, 2,* 1-2.

Guttman, L. (1941). The quantification of a class of attributes: A theory and method of scale construction. In P. Horst (Ed.), *The prediction of personal adjustment* (pp. 319-348). New York: Social Science Research Council, Bulletin No. 48.

Haan, N. (1982). Can research on morality be "scientific?" *American Psychologist, 37,* 1096-1104.

Hall, C. S., & Lindzey, G. (1954). Psychoanalytic theory and its applications in the social sciences. In G. Lindzey (Ed.), *Handbook of social psychology* (Vol. 1, pp. 143-180). Cambridge, MA: Addison-Wesley.

Hall, C. S., & Lindzey, G. (1968-1969). The relevance of Freudian psychology and related viewpoints for the social sciences. In G. Lindzey & E. Aronson (Eds.), *The handbook of social psychology* (2nd ed., Vol. 1, pp. 245-319). Reading, MA: Addision-Wesley.

Hamilton, W. (1861). *Lectures on metaphysics.* Boston: Gould & Lincoln.

Harary, F., & Norman, R. Z. (1953). *Graph theory as a mathematical model in social science.* Ann Arbor, MI: Institute for Social Research.

Harary, F., Norman, R., & Cartwright, D. (1965). *Structural models.* New York: Wiley.

Harré, R. (1972). The analysis of episodes. In J. Israel & H. Tajfel (Eds.), *The context of social psychology: A critical assessment.* London: Academic Press.

Harré, R. (1984). *Personal being: A theory for individual psychology.* Cambridge, MA: Harvard University Press.

Harré, R., & Secord, P. (1972). *The explanation of social behavior.* Totowa, NJ: Rowman & Littlefield.

Harvey, J. H., & Weary, G. (1984). Current issues in attribution theory and research. In M. R. Rosenzweig & L. W. Porter (Eds.), *Annual review of psychology* (Vol. 35, pp. 427-460). Palo Alto, CA: Annual Reviews.

Hebb, D. O. (1949). *The organization of behavior.* New York: Wiley.

Heider, F. (1944). Social perception and phenomenal causality. *Psychological Review, 51,* 358-374.

Heider, F. (1946). Attitudes and cognitive organization. *Journal of Psychology, 21,* 107-112.

Heider, F. (1958). *The psychology of interpersonal relations.* New York: Wiley.

Helmreich, R. (1975). Applied social psychology: The unfulfilled promise. *Personality and Social Psychology Bulletin, 1,* 548-560.

Hendrick, C. (1974). Social psychology as history: A bibliography. *Catalog of Selected Documents in Psychology, 4,* 125-126.

Herskovits, M. J. (1953). *Franz Boas: The science of man in the making.* New York: Scribners.

REFERENCES

Hewitt, J. P. (1976). *Self and society: A symbolic interactionist social psychology.* Boston, MA: Allyn & Bacon.
Höffding, H. (1955). A history of modern philosophy (Vol. 2). New York: Dover Publications.
Hoffman, M. L. (1977). Personality and social development. In M. R. Rosenzweig & L. W. Porter (Eds.), *Annual review of psychology* (Vol. 28, pp. 295-322). Palo Alto, CA: Annual Reviews.
Holahan, C. J. (1986). Environmental psychology. In M. R. Rosenzweig & L. W. Porter (Eds.), *Annual review of psychology* (Vol. 37, pp. 381-408). Palo Alto, CA: Annual Reviews.
Hollander, E. P. (1975). Independence, conformity, and civil liberties: Some implications from social psychological research. *Journal of Social Issues, 31,* 55-67.
Homans, G. C. (1961). *Social behavior: Its elementary forms.* New York: Harcourt.
Homans, G. C. (1964). Bringing men back in. *American Sociological Review, 29,* 809-818.
Horney, K. (1937). *The neurotic personality of our time.* New York: W. W. Norton.
Horney, K. (1945). *Our inner conflicts.* New York: W. W. Norton.
House, J. S. (1977). The three faces of social psychology. *Sociometry, 40,* 161-177.
Hovland, C. I. (Ed.). (1957). *The order of presentation in persuasion.* New Haven, CT: Yale University Press.
Hovland, C. I., Janis, I. L., & Kelley, H. H. (1953). *Communication and persuasion.* New Haven, CT: Yale University Press.
Howard, G. S. (1985). The role of values in the science of psychology. *American Psychologist, 40,* 255-265.
Hulett, J. E., Jr., & Stagner, R. (Eds.). (1952). *Problems in social psychology: An interdisciplinary inquiry.* Urbana, IL: University of Illinois.
Hull, C. L. (1943). *Principles of behavior.* New York: Appleton.
Hunt, J. (1965). Traditional personality theory in the light of recent evidence. *American Scientist, 53,* 60-96.
Hunt, K. (1975). Do we really need more replications? *Psychological Reports, 36,* 587-593.
Hunyady, G. (1966). Psychology and the social sciences. (Hungarian) *Magyar Pszichologiai Szemle, 23,* 97-107.
Huston, T. L., & Levinger, G. (1978). Interpersonal attraction and relationships. In M. R. Rosenzweig & L. W. Porter (Eds.), *Annual review of psychology* (Vol. 29, pp. 115-156). Palo Alto, CA: Annual Reviews.
Huxley, A. (1932). *Brave new world.* New York: Harper.
Inkeles, A., & Levinson, D. J. (1968-1969). National character: The study of modal personality and sociocultural systems. In G. Lindzey & E. Aronson (Eds.), *The handbook of social psychology* (2nd ed., Vol. 4, pp. 418-506). Reading, MA: Addison-Wesley.
Israel, J. (1972). Stipulations and construction in the social sciences. In J. Israel & H. Tajfel (Eds.), *The context of social psychology: A critical assessment* (pp. 123-211). London: Academic Press.
Israel, J., & Tajfel, H. (Eds.). (1972). *The context of social psychology: A critical assessment.* London: Academic Press.
Jackson, J. M. (1960). Structural characteristics of norms. In N. B. Henry (Ed.), *Dynamics of instructional groups* (pp. 136-163). Chicago, IL: University of Chicago Press.
Jackson, J. M. (1964). The normative regulation of authoritative behavior. In W. J. Gore & J. W. Dyson (Eds.), *The making of decisions: A reader in administrative behavior* (pp. 213-241). New York: The Free Press.
Jackson, J. M. (1966). A conceptual and measurement model for norms and roles. *The Pacific Sociological Review, 9,* 35-47.
Jackson, J. M. (1975). Normative power and conflict potential. *Sociological Methods and Research, 4,* 237-263.

REFERENCES

Jackson, J. M., & McGehee, C. (1965). Group structure and role behavior. *The Annals of the American Academy of Political and Social Science.* (Vol. 361, pp. 130-140.) Philadelphia, PA.
Jahoda, G. (1976). Critique: On Triandis's "social psychology and cultural analysis." In L. H. Strickland, F. E. Aboud, & K. J. Gergen (Eds.), *Social psychology in transition* (pp. 247-251). New York: Plenum Press.
James, W. (1890). *Principles of psychology* (2 vols.). New York: Holt.
James, W. (1892). *Psychology: Briefer course.* New York: Holt.
Janowitz, M. (1954). Some observations on the ideology of professional psychologists. *American Psychologist, 9,* 528-532.
Jaques, E. (1951). *The changing culture of a factory.* London: Tavistock.
Jenkins, J. (1974). Remember that old theory of memory? Well, forget it! *American Psychologist, 29,* 785-795.
Jennings, H. H. (1937). Structure of leadership. *Sociometry, 1,* 99-143.
Jennings, H. H. (1943). *Leadership and isolation.* New York: Longmans, Green.
Jennings, H. S. (1904). *Contributions to the study of the behavior of lower organisms.* Washington: Carnegie Institution of Washington.
Jennings, H. S. (1906). *Behavior of the lower organisms.* New York: The Columbia University Press.
John, E. R., & Schwartz, E. L. (1978). The neurophysiology of information processing and cognition. In M. R. Rosenzweig & L. W. Porter (Eds.), *Annual review of psychology* (Vol. 29, pp. 1-29). Palo Alto, CA: Annual Reviews.
Jones, E. E. (1985). Major developments in social psychology during the past five decades. In G. Lindzey & E. Aronson (Eds.), *The handbook of social psychology* (3rd ed., Vol. 1, pp. 47-107). New York: Random House.
Jones, E. E., Kanouse, D. E., Kelley, H. H., Nisbett, R. E., Valins, S., & Weiner, B. (1971). *Attribution: Perceiving the causes of behavior.* Morristown, NJ: General Learning Press.
Jones, M. (1953). *The therapeutic community.* New York: Basic Books.
Jung, C. G. (1953). *The collected works of C. G. Jung.* New York: Bollingen Foundation.
Kahn, R. L., Wolfe, D. M., Quinn, R. P., Snoek, J. D., & Rosenthal, R. A. (1964). *Organizational stress: Studies in conflict and ambiguity.* New York: Wiley.
Kanfer, F. H. (1979). Personal control, social control, and altruism. *American Psychologist, 34,* 231-239.
Kaplan, A. (1964). *The conduct of inquiry.* San Francisco, CA: Chandler.
Kardiner, A. (1939). *The individual and his society: The psychodynamics of primitive social organization.* New York: Columbia University Press.
Kardiner, A. (1945). *The psychological frontiers of society.* New York: Columbia University Press.
Karpf, F. B. (1952). American social psychology—1951. *American Journal of Sociology, a58,* 187-193.
Katz, D. (1935). *The world of colour.* London: K. Paul, Trench, Trubner.
Katz, D. (1942). Do interviewers bias poll results? *Public Opinion Quarterly, 6,* 248-268.
Katz, D. (1960). The functional approach to the study of attitudes. *Public Opinion Quarterly, 24,* 163-204.
Katz, D. (1967). Editorial. *Journal of Personality and Social Psychology, 7,* 341-344.
Kelley, H. H., & Michela, J. L. (1980). Attribution theory and research. In M. R. Rosenzweig & L. W. Porter (Eds.), *Annual review of psychology* (Vol. 31, pp. 457-502). Palo Alto, CA: Annual Reviews.
Kelley, H. H., & Thibaut, J. W. (1968-1969). Group problem solving. In G. Lindzey & E. Aronson (Eds.), *The handbook of social psychology* (2nd ed., Vol. 4. pp. 1-101). Reading, MA: Addison-Wesley.
Kelman, H. C. (1967). Human use of human subjects: The problem of deception in social

psychological experiments. *Psychological Bulletin, 67,* 1-11.

Kiesler, C. A., & Lucke, J. (1976). Some metatheoretical issues in social psychology. In L. H. Strickland, F. E. Aboud, & K. J. Gergen (Eds.), *Social psychology in transition* (pp. 141-151). New York: Plenum Press.

Klineberg, O. (1956). The place of psychology in UNESCO's social science program. *Transactions of the New York Academy of Science, 18,* 456-461.

Klinnert, M. D., Campos, J. J., Sorce, J. F., Emde, R., & Svejda, M. (1982). Emotions as behavior regulators: Social referencing in infancy. In R. Plutchik & H. Kellerman (Eds.), *Emotion: Theory, research, and experience* (Vol. 2). *Emotions in early development* (pp. 57-86). New York: Academic Press.

Kluckhohn, C. (1954). Culture and behavior. In G. Lindzey (Ed.), *Handbook of social psychology* (Vol. 2, pp. 921-976). Cambridge, MA: Addison-Wesley.

Koch, S. (1981). The nature and limits of psychological knowledge: Lessons of a century qua "science." *American Psychologist, 36,* 257-269.

Koffka, K. (1924). *The growth of the mind: An introduction to child psychology.* New York: Harcourt, Brace. (Originally published in German in 1921)

Köhler, W. (1925). *The mentality of apes.* New York: Harcourt, Brace. (Originally published in German in 1917)

Kozulin, A. (1986). The concept of activity in Soviet psychology: Vygotsky, his disciples and critics. *American Psychologist, 41,* 264-274.

Krebs, D. L., & Miller, D. T. (1985). Altruism and aggression. In G. Lindzey & E. Aronson (Eds.), *The handbook of social psychology* (3rd ed., Vol. 2, pp. 1-71). New York: Random House.

Krech, D. (1951). A reformulation of a basic orientation for social psychological theory. *Transactions of the New York Academy of Science, 13,* 333-337.

Krech, D., & Crutchfield, R. S. (1948). *Theory and problems of social psychology.* New York: McGraw-Hill.

Kroeber, A. L. (1939). Totem and taboo in retrospect. *American Journal of Sociology, 45,* 446-451.

Kroger, R. O. (1982). Explorations in ethology: With special reference to the rules of address. *American Psychologist, 37,* 810-820.

Kropotkin, P. A. (1902). *Mutual aid, a factor of evolution.* New York: McClure, Phillips.

Kruglanski, A. W. (1975). Theory, experiment and the shifting publication scene in personality and social psychology. *Personality and Social Psychology Bulletin, 1,* 489-492.

Krupat, E. (1977). Environmental and social psychology—how different *must* they be? *Personality and Social Psychology Bulletin, 3,* 51-53.

Kuethe, J. L. (1962). Social schema. *Journal of Abnormal and Social Psychology, 64,* 31-38.

Kuhn, M. H. (1964). Major trends in Symbolic Interaction theory in the past twenty-five years. *The Sociological Quarterly, 5,* 61-84.

Kuhn, T. S. (1962). *The structure of scientific revolutions.* Chicago: University of Chicago Press.

Kuhn, T. S. (1970). *The structure of scientific revolutions* (2nd ed.). Chicago: University of Chicago Press.

Lachman, R., & Lachman, J. L. (1979). Review of Kuhn, T. S., *The essential tension: Selected studies in scientific tradition and change,* 1977. *Contemporary Psychology, 24,* 4-5.

Landy, F. J. (1986). Stamp collecting versus science: Validation as hypothesis testing. *American Psychologist, 41,* 1183-1192.

La Sorte, M. A. (1972). Replication as a verification technique in survey research: A paradigm. *Sociological Quarterly, 13,* 218-227.

Lasswell, H. D. (1938). A provisional classification of symbol data. *Psychiatry, 1,* 197-204.

Latané, B., & Darley, J. (1968). Group inhibition of bystander intervention in emergencies. *Journal of Personality and Social Psychology, 10,* 215-221.

Lauer, R. H., & Handel, W. H. (1977). *Social psychology: The theory and application of*

symbolic interactionism. Boston: Houghton Mifflin.
Lazarsfeld, P. F. (1935). The art of asking why. *National Marketing Review, 1,* 26-38.
Lazarsfeld, P. F., Berelson, B., & Gaudet, H. (1944). *The people's choice*. New York: Duell, Sloan & Pearce.
Lazarsfeld, P. F., & Fiske, M. (1938). The panel as a new tool for measuring opinion. *Public Opinion Quarterly, 2,* 596-613.
Lazarus, M., & Steinthal, H. (1860-1890). *Journal of Folk Psychology and Philology* (German, 20 vol.). Berlin: F. Dummler.
Le Bon, G. (1896). *The crowd*. London: T. Fisher Unwin. (Originally published in French, Paris 1895)
Lecky, P. (1945). *Self-consistency: A theory of personality*. New York: Island Press.
Leighton, A. H. (1945). *The governing of men*. Princeton, NJ: Princeton University Press.
Lentz, T. F. (1950). The attitudes of world citizenship. *Journal of Social Psychology, 32,* 207-214.
Levine, J. M. (1985). Review of J. E. McGrath, *Groups: Interaction and performance. Contemporary Psychology, 30,* 102-103.
Levinson, D. J. (1964). Toward a new social psychology: The convergence of sociology and psychology. *Merrill-Palmer Quarterly, 10,* 77-88.
Lewin, K. (1935). *A dynamic theory of personality*. New York: McGraw-Hill.
Lewin, K. (1936). *Principles of topological psychology*. New York: McGraw-Hill.
Lewin, K. (1943). Forces behind food habits and methods of change. *Bulletin of the National Research Council, 108,* 35-65. (Reprinted in Lewin, 1951).
Lewin, K. (1944). Constructs in psychology and psychological ecology. *University of Iowa Studies in Child Welfare, 20,* 1-29.
Lewin, K. (1947). Group decision and social change. In T. M. Newcomb & E. L. Hartley (Eds.), *Readings in social psychology* (pp. 330-344). New York: Holt.
Lewin, K. (1948). *Resolving social conflicts*. New York: Harper.
Lewin, K. (1951). *Field theory in social science*. New York: Harper.
Lewin, K., Dembo, T., Festinger, L., & Sears, P. (1944). Level of aspiration. In J. M. Hunt (Ed.), *Personality and the behavior disorders* (pp. 333-378). New York: Ronald Press.
Lewin, K., Lippitt, R., & Escalona, S., (Eds.). (1940). Studies in topological and vector psychology I . *University of Iowa Studies in Child Welfare, 16* (Whole No. 3).
Lewin, K., Lippitt, R., & White, R. K. (1939). Patterns of aggressive behavior in experimentally created "social climates." *Journal of Social Psychology, 10,* 271-299.
Likert, R. (1932). A technique for the measurement of attitudes. *Archives of Psychology,* 140.
Lindzey, G. (Ed.). (1954). *Handbook of social psychology* (Vol. 1-2). Cambridge, MA: Addison-Wesley.
Lindzey, G., & Aronson, E. (Eds.). (1968-1969). *The handbook of social psychology* (2nd ed., Vol. 1-5). Reading, MA: Addison-Wesley.
Lindzey, G., & Aronson, E. (Eds.). (1985). *The handbook of social psychology* (3rd ed., Vol. 1-2). New York: Random House.
Linton, R. (1936). *The study of man*. New York: Appleton.
Linton, R. (1945). *The cultural background of personality*. New York: Appleton.
Lippitt, R. (1940). An experimental study of the effect of democratic and authoritarian group atmospheres. In K. Lewin, R. Lippitt, & S. K. Escalona (Eds.), *Studies in topological and vector psychology. University of Iowa Studies in Child Welfare, 16,* (Whole No. 3).
Lippitt, R. (1948). A program of experimentation on group functioning and group productivity. In W. Dennis (Ed.), *Current trends in social psychology* (pp. 14-49). Pittsburgh, PA: University of Pittsburgh Press.
Liska, A. E. (1977). The dissipation of sociological social psychology. *American Sociologist, 12,* 2-8.
Loevinger, J., & Knoll, E. (1983). Personality: Stages, traits, and the self. In M. R. Rosenzweig & L. W. Porter (Eds.), *Annual review of psychology* (Vol. 34, pp. 195-222).

Palo Alto, CA: Annual Reviews.

Loomis, C. P., & Davidson, D. M., Jr. (1939). Measurement of the dissolution of ingroups in the integration of a rural resettlement project. *Sociometry, 2,* 84-94.

Lorge, I. (1936). Prestige, suggestion, and attitudes. *Journal of Social Psychology, 7,* 386-402.

Lott, B., & Lott, A. J. (1985). Learning theory in contemporary social psychology. In G. Lindzey & E. Aronson (Eds.), *The handbook of social psychology* (3rd ed., Vol. 1, pp. 109-135). New York: Random House.

Lundberg, G. A., & Steele, M. (1938). Social attraction patterns in a village. *Sociometry, 1,* 375-419.

Lynd, R. S., & Lynd, H. M. (1929). *Middletown.* New York: Harcourt Brace.

Lynd, R. S., & Lynd, H. M. (1937). *Middletown in transition.* New York: Harcourt Brace.

Mach, E. (1897). *Contributions to the analysis of sensations.* Chicago: The Open Court. (Originally published in German in 1886)

Malinowski, B. (1927). *Sex and repression in savage society.* New York: Harcourt Brace.

Manicas, P. T., & Secord, P. F. (1983). Implications for psychology of the new philosophy of science. *American Psychologist, 38,* 399-413.

Manis, J. G., & Meltzer, B. N. (Eds.). (1978). *Symbolic interaction: A reader in social psychology* (3rd ed.). Boston: Allyn & Bacon.

Manis, M. (1975). Comments on Gergen's "social psychology as history." *Personality and Social Psychology Bulletin, 1,* 450-455.

Manis, M. (1976). Is social psychology really different? *Personality and Social Psychology Bulletin, 2,* 428-437.

Mannheim, K. (1936). *Ideology and utopia.* New York: Harcourt Brace.

Markus, H. (1977). Self-schemata and processing information about the self. *Journal of Personality and Social Psychology, 35,* 63-78.

Markus, H., & Nurius, P. (1986). Possible selves. *American Psychologist, 41,* 954-969.

Markus, H., & Zajonc, R. B. (1985). Cognitive perspectives in social psychology. In G. Lindzey & E. Aronson (Eds.), *The handbook of social psychology* (3rd ed., Vol. 1. pp. 137-230). New York: Random House.

Marx, K., & Engels, F. (1937). *The German ideology.* New York: International Publishers. (Originally published in German in 1846)

Maslow, A. H. (1954). *Motivation and personality.* New York: Harper.

May, M. A., & Doob, L. W. (1937). *Competition and cooperation.* New York: Social Science Research Council, Bulletin No. 25.

Mayo, E. (1933). *The human problems of an industrial civilization.* New York: Macmillan.

Mayr, E. (1976). *Evolution and the diversity of life.* Cambridge: Harvard University Press.

McClelland, D. C. (1961). *The achieving society.* Princeton, NJ: Van Nostrand.

McClintock, C. G., Kramer, R. M., & Keil, L. J. (1984). Equity and social exchange in human relationships. In L. Berkowitz (Ed.), *Advances in experimental social psychology* (Vol. 17, pp. 183-228). New York: Academic Press.

McDougall, W. (1908). *Introduction to social psychology.* London: Methuen.

McDougall, W. (1926). *Introduction to social psychology* (Rev. ed.). Boston: Luce. (Originally published in 1908)

McDougall, W. (1920).*The group mind.* New York: Putnam.

McGrath, J. E. (Ed.). (1970). *Social and psychological factors in stress.* New York: Holt, Rinehart & Winston.

McGrath, J. E. (1984). *Groups: Interaction and performance.* Englewood Cliffs, NJ: Prentice-Hall.

McGrath, J. E., & Kelly, J. R. (1986). *Time and human interaction: Toward a social psychology of time.* New York: Guilford.

McGrath, J. E., & Kravitz, D. A. (1982). Group research. In M. R. Rosenzweig & L. W. Porter (Eds.), *Annual review of psychology* (Vol. 33, pp. 195-230). Palo Alto, CA: Annual Reviews.

McGuire, W. J. (1966a). Attitudes and opinions. In P. R. Farnsworth (Ed.), *Annual review of psychology* (Vol. 17, pp. 475-514). Palo Alto, CA: Annual Reviews.

McGuire, W. J. (1966b). The current status of cognitive consistency theories. In S. Feldman (Ed.), *Cognitive consistency: Motivational antecedents and behavioral consequences* (pp. 1-46). New York: Academic Press.

McGuire, W. J. (1967). Some impending reorientations in social psychology: Some thoughts provoked by Kenneth Ring. *Journal of Experimental Social Psychology, 3,* 124-139.

McGuire, W. J. (1968-1969). The nature of attitudes and attitude change. In G. Lindzey & E. Aronson (Eds.), *The handbook of social psychology* (2nd ed., Vol. 3, pp. 136-314). Reading, MA: Addison-Wesley.

McGuire, W. J. (1973). The yin and yang of progress in social psychology: Seven Koan. *Journal of Personality and Social Psychology, 26,* 446-456.

McGuire, W. J. (1985). Toward social psychology's second century. In S. Koch & D. E. Leary (Eds.), *A century of psychology as science* (pp. 558-590). New York: McGraw-Hill.

Mead, G. H. (1893, December). *The problem of psychological measurement.* Paper presented at the second annual meeting of the American Psychological Association, Columbia College, New York.

Mead, G. H. (1894a). Review of K. Lasswitz: *Energy and epistemology. The Psychological Review, 1,* 172-175; 210-213.

Mead, G. H. (1894b, December). *A theory of emotion from the physiological standpoint.* Paper presented at the third annual meeting of the American Psychological Association, Princeton University, Princeton NJ.

Mead, G. H. (1895). Review of C. L. Morgan, *An introduction to comparative psychology. The Psychological Review, 3,* 399-402.

Mead, G. H. (1903). The definition of the psychical. *The Decennial Publications.* University of Chicago, *3,* 77-112.

Mead, G. H. (1924-1925). The genesis of the self and social control. *International Journal of Ethicsa, 35,* 251-277.

Mead, G. H. (1930). Cooley's contribution to American social thought. *The American Journal of Sociology, 35,* 693-706.

Mead, G. H. (1934). *Mind, self, and society.* Chicago: University of Chicago Press.

Mead, M. (1928). *Coming of age in Samoa.* New York: Morrow.

Mead, M. (1930). *Growing up in New Guinea.* New York: Morrow.

Mead, M. (1935). *Sex and temperament in three primitive societies.* New York: Morrow.

Mead, M. (1937). *Cooperation and competition among primitive peoples.* New York: McGraw-Hill.

Meltzer, L. (1961). The need for a dual orientation in social psychology. *Journal of Social Psychology, 55,* 43-48.

Merton, R. K. (1949). The role of applied social science in the formation of policy: A research memorandum. *Philosophy of Science, 16,* 161-181.

Merton, R. K., & Lazarsfeld, P. F. (Eds.). (1950). *Studies in the scope and method of "the American soldier."* Glencoe, IL: The Free Press.

Mesmer, F. A. (1948). *Mesmerism.* London: MacDonald. (Originally published in French in 1779)

Milgram S. (1963). Behavioral study of obedience. *Journal of Abnormal and Social Psychology, 67,* 371-378.

Milgram, S. (1964). Issues in the study of obedience: A reply to Baumrind. *American Psychologist, 19,* 848-852.

Milgram, S. (1974). *Obedience to authority.* New York: Harper & Row.

Miller, A. G. (Ed.). (1972). *The social psychology of psychological research.* New York: The Free Press.

Miller, D. T., & Turnbull, W. (1986) Expectancies and interpersonal processes. In M. R.

Rosenzweig & L. W. Porter (Eds.), *Annual review of psychology* (Vol. 37, pp. 233-256). Palo Alto, CA: Annual Reviews.

Miller, N. E., & Dollard, J. (1941). *Social learning and imitation.* New Haven: Yale University Press.

Mischel, W. (1968). *Personality and assessment.* New York: Wiley.

Mischel, W. (1973). Toward a cognitive social learning reconceptualization of personality. *Psychological Review, 80,* 252-283.

Moede, W. (1920). *Experimental social psychology* (German). Leipzig: S. Herzel.

Moore, H. T. (1921). The comparative influence of majority and expert opinion. *American Journal of Psychology, 32,* 16-20.

Moreno, J. L. (1934). *Who shall survive?* Beacon, NY: Beacon House.

Moreno, J. L. (1948). Experimental sociometry and the experimental method in science. In W. Dennis (Ed.), *Current trends in social psychology* (pp. 119-162). Pittsburgh, PA: University of Pittsburgh Press.

Morgan, C. L. (1891). *Animal life and intelligence.* Boston: Ginn.

Moscovici, S. (1963). Attitudes and opinions. In P. R. Farnsworth (Ed.), *Annual review of psychology* (Vol. 14, pp. 231-260). Palo Alto, CA: Annual Reviews.

Moscovici, S. (1972). Society and theory in social psychology. In J. Israel & H. Tajfel (Eds.), *The context of social psychology: A critical assessment* (pp. 17-68). London: Academic Press.

Moscovici, S. (1985). Social influence and conformity. In G. Lindzey & E. Aronson (Eds.), *The handbook of social psychology* (3rd ed., Vol. 2, pp. 347-412). New York: Random House.

Mukerjee, R. (1932). The concepts of distribution and succession in social ecology. *Social Forces, 11,* 1-7.

Murdock, G. P. (1949). *Social structure.* New York: Macmillan.

Murphy, G. (1954). Social motivation. In G. Lindzey (Ed.), *Handbook of social psychology* (Vol. 2, pp. 601-633). Cambridge, MA: Addison-Wesley.

Murphy, G. (1956). The current impact of Freud upon psychology. *American Psychologist, 11,* 663-672.

Murphy, G., & Likert, R. (1938). *Public opinion and the individual: A psychological study of student attitudes on public questions, with a retest five years later.* New York: Harper.

Murphy, G., & Murphy, L. B. (1931). *Experimental social psychology.* New York: Harper.

Murphy, G., Murphy, L. B., & Newcomb, T. M. (1937). *Experimental social psychology* (rev. ed.). New York: Harper.

Murphy, L. B. (1937). *Social behavior and child personality: An exploratory study of some roots of sympathy.* New York: Columbia University Press.

Murray, H. A. (1938). *Explorations in personality.* New York: Oxford University Press.

Murray, H. A. (1949). Research planning: A few propositions. In S. S. Sargent & M. W. Smith (Eds.), *Culture and personality* (pp. 195-212). New York: Viking Fund.

Myrdal, G. (1944). *An American dilemma.* New York: Harper.

Newcomb, T. M. (1943). *Personality and social change.* New York: Dryden.

Newcomb, T. M. (1950). *Social psychology.* New York: Dryden.

Newcomb, T. M. (1951). Social psychological theory: Integrating individual and social approaches. In J. H. Rohrer & M. Sherif (Eds.), *Social psychology at the crossroads: The University of Oklahoma lectures in social psychology* (pp. 31-49). New York: Harper.

Newcomb, T. M., & Hartley, E. L. (Eds.). (1947). *Readings in social psychology.* New York: Holt.

Newcomb, T. M., Koenig, K. E., Flacks, R., & Warwick, D. P. (1967). *Persistence and change: Bennington College and its students after twenty-five years.* New York: Wiley.

Newcomb, T. M., Turner, R. H., & Converse, P. E. (1965). *Social psychology: The study of human interaction.* New York: Holt, Rinehart & Winston.

Northrop, F. S. C. (1949). *The logic of the sciences and the humanities.* New York: Macmillan.
Olmsted, D. W. (1969). Some problems in studying social groups. In E. F. Borgatta (Ed.), *Social psychology: Readings and perspective* (pp. 613–624). Chicago: Rand McNally.
Orne, M. T. (1959). The nature of hypothesis: Artiface and essence. *Journal of Abnormal and Social Psychology, 58,* 277–299.
Orne, M. T. (1962). On the social psychology of the psychological experiment: With particular reference to demand characteristics and their implications. *American Psychologist, 17,* 776–783.
Orwell, G. (1949). *Nineteen eighty-four. New York:* Harcourt.
Osgood, C. E., Suci, G. J., & Tannenbaum, P. H. (1957). *The measurement of meaning.* Urbana, IL: University of Illinois Press.
O.S.S. Assessment Staff. (1948). *The assessment of men.* New York: Rinehart.
Park, R. E. (1924). Experience and race relations. *Journal of Applied Sociology, 9,* 18–24.
Park, R. E. (1936). Succession: An ecological concept. *American Sociological Review, 1,* 171–179.
Park, R. E., & Burgess, E. W. (Eds.). (1925). *The city.* Chicago: University of Chicago Press.
Parke, R. D., & Asher, S. R. (1983). Social and personality development. In M. R. Rosenzweig & L. W. Porter (Eds.), *Annual review of psychology* (Vol. 34, pp. 465–510). Palo Alto, CA: Annual Reviews.
Parrington, V. L. (1927). *Main currents in American thought.* Harcourt Brace.
Parsons, T., & Shils, E. A. (Eds.). (1951). *Toward a general theory of action.* Cambridge: Harvard University Press.
Partington, J. T. (1976). Critique: The interdependent mode of personal causality. In L. H. Strickland, F. E. Aboud, & K. J. Gergen (Eds.), *Social psychology in transition* (pp. 269–274). New York: Plenum Press.
Patton, R. A. (Ed.). (1954). *Current trends in psychology and the behavioral sciences.* Pittsburgh, PA: University of Pittsburgh Press.
Pepitone, A. (1976). Toward a normative and comparative social psychology. *Journal of Personality and Social Psychology, 34,* 641–653.
Pepitone, A. (1981). Lessons from the history of social psychology. *American Psychologist, 36,* 972–985.
Perlmutter, H. V., & de Montmollin, G. (1952). Group learning of nonsense syllables. *Journal of Abnormal and Social Psychology, 47,* 762–769.
Petrinovich, L. (1979). Probabilistic functionalism: A conception of research method. *American Psychologist, 34,* 373–390.
Piaget, J. (1932). *The moral judgment of the child.* London: Kegan Paul.
Proshansky, H. M. (1976). Comment on "environment and social psychology." *Personality and Social Psychology Bulletin, 2,* 359–363.
Proshansky, H., Ittelson, W., & Rivlin, L. (Eds.). (1970). *Environmental psychology: Man and his physical setting.* New York: Holt, Rinehart & Winston.
Quinn, J. A. (1934). Ecological and social interaction. *Sociology and Social Research, 18,* 565–570.
Raven, B. H. (1965). Social influence and power. In I. D. Steiner & M. Fishbein (Eds.), *Current studies in social psychology* (pp. 371–382). New York: Holt, Rinehart & Winston.
Ribot, T. (1897). *The psychology of the emotions.* London: W. Scott Ltd.
Riecken, H. W. (1965). Research developments in the social sciences. In O. Klineberg & R. Christie (Eds.), *Perspectives in social psychology* (pp. 12–20). New York: Holt, Rinehart & Winston.
Riesman, D. (1950). *The lonely crowd.* New Haven, CT: Yale University Press.
Riley, J. W., Jr. (1947). Opinion research in liberated Normandy. *American Sociological Review, 12,* 698–703.
Ring, K. (1967). Experimental social psychology: Some sober questions about some frivolous

values. *Journal of Experimental Social Psychology, 3,* 113-123.
Rodin, J. (1985). The application of social psychology. In G. Lindzey & E. Aronson (Eds.), *The handbook of social psychology* (3rd ed., Vol. 2, pp. 805-881). New York: Random House.
Roethlisberger, F. J. (1941). *Management and morale.* Cambridge, MA: Harvard University Press.
Roethlisberger, F. J., & Dickson, W. J. (1939). *Management and the worker: An account of a research program conducted by the Western Electric Company, Hawthorne Works, Chicago.* Cambridge, MA: Harvard University Press.
Rohrer, J. H., & Sherif, M. (1951). *Social psychology at the crossroads: The University of Oklahoma lectures in social psychology.* New York: Harper.
Rokeach, M. (1960). *The open and closed mind.* New York: Basic Books.
Rommetveit, R. (1976). On "emancipatory" social psychology. In L. H. Strickland, F. E. Aboud, & K. J. Gergen (Eds.), *Social psychology in transition* (pp. 107-120). New York: Plenum Press.
Rorer, L. G., & Widiger, T. A. (1983). Personality structure and assessment. In M. R. Rosenzweig & L. W. Porter (Eds.), *Annual review of psychology* (Vol. 34, pp. 431-464). Palo Alto, CA: Annual Reviews.
Rosenberg, S., & Gara, M. A. (1985). The multiplicity of personal identity. In P. Shaver (Ed.), *Review of personality and social psychology* (Vol. 6, pp. 87-113). Beverly Hills, CA: Sage.
Rosenthal, R. (1963). On the social psychology of the psychological experiment: The experimenter's hypothesis as unintended determinant of the experimental results. *American Scientist, 51,* 268-283.
Rosenthal, R. (1966). *Experimenter effects in behavioral science.* New York: Appleton-Century-Crofts.
Rosenthal, R. (1978). Combining results of independent studies. *Psychological Bulletin, 85,* 185-193.
Rosenthal, R., & Rosnow, R. L. (Eds.). (1969). *Artifact in behavioral research.* New York: Academic Press.
Ross, E. A. (1908). *Social psychology: An outline and source book.* New York: Macmillan.
Rotter, J. B. (1954). *Social learning and clinical psychology.* Englewood Cliffs, NJ: Prentice-Hall.
Rotter, J. B. (1966). Generalized expectancies for internal versus external control of reinforcement. *Psychological Monographs, 80,* 1-28.
Ruitenbeek, H. M. (1970). *The new group therapies.* New York: Avon.
Ryckman, R. M. (1976). Applied social psychology--a haven for the comfortable radical pussycat: A response to Helmreich. *Personality and Social Psychology Bulletin, 2,* 127-130.
Ryle, G. (1949). *The concept of mind.* New York: Barnes & Noble.
Sahakian, W. S. (1974). *Systematic social psychology.* New York: Chandler.
Samelson, F. (1974). History, origin, myth, and ideology: Comte's "discovery" of social psychology. *Journal for the Theory of Social Behavior, 4,* 217-231.
Sampson, E. E. (1975). On justice as equality. *Journal of Social Issues, 31,* 45-64.
Sampson, E. E. (1977). Psychology and the American Ideal. *Journal of Personality and Social Psychology, 35,* 767-782.
Sampson, E. E. (1981). Cognitive psychology as ideology. *American Psychologist, 36,* 730-743.
Sapir, E. (1929). The status of linguistics as a science. *Language, 5,* 207-214.
Sarason, S. B. (1981). An asocial psychology and misdirected clinical psychology. *American Psychologist, 36,* 827-836.
Sarbin, T. R. (1954). Role theory. In G. Lindzey (Ed.), *Handbook of social psychology* (Vol. 1, pp. 223-258). Cambridge, MA: Addison-Wesley.
Sarbin, T. R., & Allen, V. L. (1968-1969). Role theory. In G. Lindzey & E. Aronson (Eds.),

The handbook of social psychology (2nd ed., Vol. 1, pp. 488–567). Reading, MA: Addison-Wesley.

Sargent, S. S. (1951). Conceptions of roles and ego in contemporary psychology. In J. H. Rohrer & M. Sherif (Eds.), *Social psychology at the crossroads: The University of Oklahoma lectures in social psychology* (pp. 355–370). New York: Harper.

Sargent, S. S. (1952). The problem posed: Interdisciplinary contributions and cooperation in the developmment of social psychology. In J. E. Hulett, Jr. & R. Stagner (Eds.), *Problems in social psychology: An interdisciplinary inquiry* (pp. 7–15). Urbana, IL: University of Illinois.

Schachter, S. (1959). *The psychology of affiliation: Experimental studies of the sources of gregariousness.* Stanford, CA: Stanford University Press.

Schachter, S. (1964). The interaction of cognitive and physiological determinants of emotional state. In L. Berkowitz (Ed.), *Advances in experimental social psychology* (Vol. 1, pp. 49–80). New York: Academic Press.

Scheerer, M. (1954). Cognitive theory. In G. Lindzey (Ed.), *Handbook of social psychology* (Vol. 1, pp. 91–142). Cambridge, MA: Addison-Wesley.

Scheler, M. (1923). *The nature and forms of sympathy.* Bonn: Friedrich Cohen.

Schlenker, B. R. (1974). Social psychology and science. *Journal of Personality and Social Psychology, 29,* 1–15.

Schlenker, B. R. (1980). *Impression management: The self-concept, social identity, and interpersonal relations.* Monterey, CA: Brooks/Cole.

Schlenker, B. R. (1982). Translating actions into attitudes: An identity-analytic approach to the explanation of social conduct. In L. Berkowitz (Ed.), *Advances in experimental social psychology* (Vol. 15, pp. 194–247). New York: Academic Press.

Schneirla, T. C. (1951). The "levels" concept in the study of social organization in animals. In J. H. Rohrer & M. Sherif (Eds.), *Social psychology at the crossroads: The University of Oklahoma lectures in social psychology* (pp. 83–120). New York: Harper.

Schwartz, S. H., & Howard, J. A. (1981). A normative decision-making model of altruism. In J. P. Rushton & R. M. Sorrentino (Eds.), *Altruism and helping behavior* (pp. 189–211). Hillsdale, NJ: Lawrence Erlbaum Associates.

Scott, W. A. (1968–1969). Attitude measurement. In G. Lindzey & E. Aronson (Eds.), *The handbook of social psychology* (2nd ed., Vol. 2, pp. 204–273). Reading, MA: Addison-Wesley.

Secord, P. F. (1976). Transhistorical and transcultural theory. *Personality and Social Psychology Bulletin, 2,* 418–420.

Secord, P. F. (1977). Social psychology in search of a paradigm. *Personality and Social Psychology Bulletin, 3,* 41–50.

Secord, P. F., & Backman, C. W. (1964). *Social psychology.* New York: McGraw-Hill.

Segal, D. R., & Segal, M. W. (1972). How sociological is social psychology? *American Sociologist, 7,* 15.

Segall, M. H. (1986). Culture and behavior: Psychology in global perspective. In M. R. Rosenzweig & L. W. Porter (Eds.), *Annual review of psychology* (Vol. 37, pp. 523–564). Palo Alto, CA: Annual Reviews.

Semin, G. R., & Manstead, A. S. K. (1983). *The accountability of conduct: A social psychological analysis.* London: Academic Press.

Shaw, C. R. (1930). *The jack roller.* Chicago: University of Chicago Press.

Shaw, M. E. (1974). New science or non-science? *Contemporary Psychology, 19,* 96–97.

Sherif, M. (1935). A study of some social factors in perception. *Archives of Psychology, 187,* 5–60.

Sherif, M. (1936). *The psychology of social norms.* New York: Harper.

Sherif, M. (1948). *An outline of social psychology.* New York: Harper.

Sherif, M. (1951). Introduction. In J. H. Rohrer & M. Sherif (Eds.), *Social psychology at the*

crossroads: The University of Oklahoma lectures in social psychology (pp. 1-28). New York: Harper.
Sherif, M. (1970). On the relevance of social psychology. *American Psychologist, 25,* 144-156.
Sherif, M. (1977). Crisis in social psychology: Some remarks towards breaking through the crisis. *Personality and Social Psychology Bulletin, 3,* 368-382.
Sherif, M., & Cantril, H. (1947). *The psychology of ego-involvements.* New York: Wiley.
Sherif, M., Harvey, O. J., White, B. J., Hood, W. R., & Sherif, C. W. (1961). *Intergroup conflict and cooperation: The Robbers Cave experiment.* Norman, OK: University of Oklahoma.
Sherif, M., & Hovland, C. I. (1953). Judgmental phenomena and scales of attitude measurement: Placement of items with individual choice of number categories. *Journal of Abnormal and Social Psychology, 48,* 135-141.
Sherif, M., & Hovland, C. I. (1961). *Social judgment: Assimilation and contrast effects in communication and attitude change.* New Haven, CT: Yale University Press.
Sherif, M., & Sherif, C.W. (1969). *Social psychology.* New York: Harper & Row.
Sherif, M., & Wilson, M. O. (1957). *Emerging problems in social psychology.* Norman, OK: University of Oklahoma Book Exchange.
Shils, E. A. (1948). *The present situation in American sociology.* Glencoe, IL: The Free Press.
Showers, C., & Cantor, N. (1985). Social cognition: A look at motivated strategies. In *Annual review of psychology* (Vol. 36, pp. 275-305). Palo Alto, CA: Annual Reviews.
Silverman, I. (1977). Why social psychology fails. *Canadian Psychological Review, 18,* 353-358.
Skinner, B. F. (1948). *Walden two.* New York: Macmillan.
Skinner, B. F. (1953). *Science and human behavior.* New York: Macmillan.
Smith, A. (1759). *The theory of moral sentiments.* London: A. Miller.
Smith, A. (1776). *An inquiry into the nature and causes of the wealth of nations.* London: W. Strahan & T. Cadell.
Smith, M. B. (1966). Three textbooks: A special review. *Journal of Experimental Social Psychology, 2,* 109-118.
Smith, M. B. (1973). Is psychology relevant to new priorities? *American Psychologist, 28,* 463-471.
Smith, M. B. (1976). Some perspectives on ethical/political issues in social science research. *Personality and Social Psychology Bulletin, 2,* 445-453.
Smith, M. B. (1977). A dialectical social psychology? Comments on a symposium. *Personality and Social Psychology Bulletin, 3,* 719-724.
Smith, M. B. (1983). The shaping of American social psychology: A personal perspective from the periphery. *Personality and Social Psychology Bulletin, 9,* 165-180.
Smith, N. C. (1970). Replication studies: A neglected aspect of psychological research. *American Psychologist, 25,* 970-975.
Smith, R. J. (1978). The future of an illusion: American social psychology. *Personality and Social Psychology Bulletin, 4,* 172-176.
Snyder, M. (1979). Self-monitoring processes. In L. Berkowitz (Ed.), *Advances in experimental social psychology* (Vol. 12, pp. 85-128). New York: Academic Press.
Snyder, M., & Ickes, W. (1985). Personality and social behavior. In G. Lindzey & E. Aronson (Eds.), *The handbook of social psychology* (3rd ed., Vol. 2, pp. 883-947). New York: Random House.
Sofer, C. (1961). *The organization from within.* London: Tavistock.
Souief, M. (1954). The problem of concepts in social psychology. (Arabic) *Egyptian Yearbook of Psychology, 1,* 223-232.
Spence, J. T., Deaux, K., & Helmreich, R. L. (1985). Sex roles in contemporary American society. In G. Lindzey & E. Aronson (Eds.), *The handbook of social psychology* (3rd ed., Vol. 2, pp. 149-178). New York: Random House.

Stagner, R. E. (1952). Should social psychology be interdisciplinary? In J. E. Hulett, Jr. & R. Stagner (Eds.), *Problems in social psychology: An interdisciplinary inquiry* (pp. 261-271). Urbana, IL: University of Illinois.

Stanton, A. H., & Schwartz, M. S. (1954). *The mental hospital: A study of institutional participation in psychiatric illness and treatment.* New York: Basic Books.

Staub, E., Bar-Tal, D., Karylowski, J., & Reykowski, J. (Eds.). (1984). *Development and maintenance of pro-social behavior: International perspectives.* New York: Plenum Press.

Steiner, I. D. (1964). Group dynamics. In P. R. Farnsworth (Ed.), *Annual review of psychology* (Vol. 15, pp. 421-446). Palo Alto, CA: Annual Reviews.

Steiner, I. D. (1974). Whatever happened to the group in social psychology? *Journal of Experimental and Social Psychology, 10,* 93-108.

Steiner, I. D. (1986). Paradigms and groups. In L. Berkowitz (Ed.), *Advances in experimental social psychology* (Vol. 19, pp. 251-289). New York: Academic Press.

Stephan, W. G. (1985). Intergroup relations. In G. Lindzey & E. Aronson (Eds.), *The handbook of social psychology* (3rd ed., Vol. 2, pp. 599-658). New York: Random House.

Stock, D., & Thelen, H. A. (1958). *Emotional dynamics and group culture.* New York: New York University Press.

Stokols, D. (1976). Social-unit analysis as a framework for research in environmental and social psychology. *Personality and Social Psychology Bulletin, 2,* 350-358.

Stone, G. P., & Farberman, H. A. (Eds.). (1970). *Social psychology through symbolic interaction.* Waltham, MA: Ginn-Blaisdell.

Stoodley, B. H. (Ed.). (1962). *Society and self: A reader in social psychology.* Glencoe, IL: The Free Press.

Stouffer, S. A., Suchman, E. A., Devinney, L. C., Star, S. A., & Williams, R. M., Jr. (1949). *Studies in social psychology in World War II* (Vol. 1): *The American soldier, adjustment during army life.* Princeton, NJ: Princeton University Press.

Stouffer, S. A., Lumsdaine, A. A., Lumsdaine, M. H., Williams, R. M., Jr., Smith, M. B., Janis, I. L., Star, S. A., & Cottrell, L. S., Jr. (1950). *Studies in social psychology in World War II* (Vol. 2): *The American soldier, combat and its aftermath.* Princeton, NJ: Princeton University Press.

Strickland, L. H., Aboud, F. E., & Gergen, K. J. (Eds.). (1976). *Social psychology in transition.* New York and London: Plenum.

Strickland, L. H., Aboud, F. E., Gergen, K. J., Jahoda, G., & Tajfel, H. (1976). General theory in social psychology. *Personality and Social Psychology Bulletin, 2,* 148-153.

Stryker, S. (1971). Review symposium: The handbook of social psychology. *American Sociological Review, 36,* 894-898.

Stryker, S. (1977). Developments in "Two Social Psychologies": Toward an appreciation of mutual relevance. *Sociometry, 40,* 145-160.

Stryker, S., & Gottlieb, A. (1981). Attribution theory and symbolic interactionism: A comparison. In J. H. Harvey, W. Ickes, & R. F. Kidd (Eds.), *New directions in attribution research* (Vol. 3, pp. 425-458). Hillsdale, NJ: Lawrence Erlbaum Associates.

Stryker, S., & Statham, A. (1985). Symbolic interaction and role theory. In G. Lindzey & E. Aronson (Eds.), *The handbook of social psychology* (3rd ed., Vol. 1, pp. 311-378). New York: Random House.

Sullivan, E. V. (1984). *A critical psychology: Interpretation of the personal world.* New York: Plenum Press.

Sullivan, H. S. (1947). *Conceptions of modern psychiatry.* New York: Norton.

Sullivan, H. S. (1950). The illusion of individuality. *Psychiatry, 13,* 317-332.

Sullivan, H. S. (1953). *The interpersonal theory of psychiatry.* New York: Norton.

Sumner, W. G. (1906). *Folkways.* Boston, MA: Ginn.

Sutherland, E. H., & Cressey, D. (1966). *Principles of criminology* (7th ed.). Philadelphia, PA: J. B. Lippincott.

Tagiuri, R. (1968-1969). Person perception. In G. Lindzey & E. Aronson (Eds.), *The handbook of social psychology* (2nd ed., Vol. 3, pp. 395-449). Reading, MA: Addison-Wesley.
Tajfel, H. (1972). Experiments in a vacuum. In J. Israel & H. Tajfel (Eds.), *The context of social psychology* (pp. 69-119). London: Academic Press.
Tajfel, H. (1982). Social psycholoty of intergroup relations. In M. R. Rosenzweiz, & L. W. Porter (Eds.), *Annual review of psychology* (Vol. 33, pp. 1-40). Palo Alto, CA: Annual Reviews.
Tarde, G. (1903). *The laws of imitation.* New York: Henry Holt. (Originally published in French in 1901)
Taylor, S. E., & Fiske, S. T. (1981). Getting inside the head: Methodologies for process analysis in attribution and social cognition. In J. H. Harvey, W. Ickes, & R. F. Kidd (Eds.), *New directions in attribution research* (pp. 459-524). Hillsdale, NJ: Lawrence Erlbaum Associates.
Tedeschi, J. T. (Ed.). (1981). *Impression management theory and social psychological research.* New York: Academic Press.
Tesch, F. E. (1977). Debriefing research participants: Though this be method there is madness to it. *Journal of Personality and Social Psychology, 35,* 217-224.
Thibaut, J. W., & Kelley, H. H. (1959). *The social psychology of groups.* New York: Wiley.
Thomas, W. I. (1904). The province of social psychology. *Psychological Bulletin, 1,* 392-393.
Thomas, W. I. (1905). The province of social psychology. *American Journal of Sociology, 11,* 445-455.
Thomas, W. I. (1928). *The unadjusted girl.* Boston, MA: Little, Brown.
Thomas, W. I., & Znaniecki, F. (1918-1920). *The Polish peasant in Europe and America* (5 vols). Boston, MA: Richard G. Badger.
Thorndike, E. L. (1898). Animal intelligence: An experimental study of the associative processes in animals. *Psychological Review* (Monograph Supplement).
Thorngate, W. (1975). Process invariance: Another red herring. *Personality and Social Psychology Bulletin, 1,* 485-488.
Thorngate, W. (1976a). "In general" vs. "it depends": Some comments on the Gergen-Schlenker debate. *Personality and Social Psychology Bulletin 2,* 404-410.
Thorngate, W. (1976b). Ignorance, arrogance, and social psychology: A response to Helmreich. *Personality and Social Psychology Bulletin, 2,* 122-126.
Thrasher, F. M. (1927). *The gang.* Chicago: University of Chicago Press.
Thurstone, L. L. (1927). Attitudes can be measured. *American Journal of Sociology, 33,* 529-554.
Thurstone, L. L., & Chave, E. J. (1929). *The measurement of attitude.* Chicago: University of Chicago Press.
Tolman, E. C. (1932). *Purposive behavior in animals and men.* New York: Century.
Tolman, E. C. (1948). Cognitive maps in rats and men. *Psychological Review, 55,* 189-208.
Tolman, E. C. (1952). A theoretical analysis of the relations between sociology and psychology. *Journal of Abnormal and Social Psychology, 47,* 291-298.
Triandis, H. C. (1976). Social psychology and cultural analysis. In L. H. Strickland, F. E. Aboud, & K. J. Gergen (Eds.), *Social psychology in transition* (pp. 223-241). New York and London: Plenum.
Triandis, H. C. (1977). *Interpersonal behavior.* Monterey, CA: Brooks/Cole.
Triandis, H. C. (1978). Some universals of social behavior. *Psychological Bulletin, 4,* 1-16.
Triplett, N. (1897). The dynamogenic factors in pacemaking and competition. *American Journal of Psychology, 9,* 507-533.
Trotter, W. (1916). *Instincts of the herd in peace and* war. New York: Macmillan.
Tufts, J. H. (1895). Book reviews. *The Psychological Review, 2,* 305-309.
Turner, J. C. (1975). Social comparison and social identity: Some prospects for intergroup

behavior. *European Journal of Social Psychology, 5,* 5-34.
Turner, R. H., & Killian, L. M. (1972). *Collective behavior* (2nd ed.). Englewood Cliffs, NJ: Prentice-Hall.
Tyler, L. E. (1981). More stately mansions—psychology extends its boundaries. In M. R. Rosenzweig & L. W. Porter (Eds.), *Annual review of psychology* (Vol. 32, pp. 1-20). Palo Alto, CA: Annual Reviews.
United States Strategic Bombing Survey. (1946). *The effects of bombing on German morale.* Washington, DC: Government Printing Office.
Vinacke, W. E. (1954). *The miniature social situation.* Honolulu: University of Hawaii.
Volkart, E. H. (1971). Comments in "Review symposium on the Handbook of Social Psychology." *American Sociological Review, 36,* 898-902.
Volkmann, J. (1936). The anchoring of absolute scales. *Psychological Bulletin, 33,* 742-743.
von Bonin, G. (1965). Brain and mind. In F. T. Severin (Ed.), *Humanistic viewpoints in psychology* (pp. 145-158). New York: McGraw-Hill.
Walster, E., Walster, G. W., & Berscheid, E., (1978). *Equity theory and research.* Boston: Allyn & Bacon.
Wardwell, W. I. (1979). Comment. *American Sociological Review, 44,* 858-861.
Warner, W. L., & Low, J. O. (1947). *The social system of the modern factory.* New Haven: Yale University Press.
Warner, W. L., & Lunt, P. S. (1941). *The social life of a modern community.* New Haven: Yale University Press.
Watson, G. (Ed.). (1942). *Civilian morale.* Boston: Houghton Mifflin.
Watson, J. B. (1913). Psychology as the behaviorist views it. *Psychological Review, 20,* 158-177.
Watson, J. B. (1919). *Psychology from the standpoint of a behaviorist.* Philadelphia, PA: J. B. Lippincott.
Watson, J. B. (1936). Autobiography. In C. Murchison (Ed.), *A history of psychology in autobiography* (Vol. 3, pp. 271-281). Worcester, MA: Clark University Press.
Webb, E. J., Campbell, D. T., Schwartz, R. D., & Sechrest, L. (1966). *Unobtrusive measures: Nonreactive research in the social sciences.* Chicago: Rand McNally.
Weissberg, N. C. (1976). Methodology or substance? A response to Helmreich. *Personality and Social Psychology Bulletin, 2,* 119-121.
Wertheimer, M. (1912). Experimental studies of seen movement (German), *Zeitschrift f. Psychologie, 61,* 161-265.
Wertheimer, M. (1945). *Productive thinking.* New York: Harper.
White, R. K. (1938). Democratic and autocratic group atmospheres. *Psychological Bulletin, 35,* 694.
White, R. K., & Lippitt, R. O. (1960). *Autocracy and democracy: An experimental inquiry.* New York: Harper.
White, R. W. (1959). Motivation reconsidered: The concept of competence. *Psychological Review, 66,* 297-334.
Whitely, S. E. (1983). Construct validity: Construct representation versus nomothetic span. *Psychological Bulletin, 93,* 179-197.
Whiting, J. W. M. (1941). *Becoming a Kwoma: Teaching and learning in a New Guinea tribe.* New Haven, CT: Yale University Press.
Whittemore, I. C. (1924). Influence of competition on performance: An experimental study. *Journal of Abnormal and Social Psychology, 19,* 236-253.
Whyte, W. F. (1943). *Street corner society.* Chicago, IL: University of Chicago Press.
Wilson, J. T. (1954). Psychology and the behavioral sciences. In R. A. Patton (Ed.), *Current trends in psychology and the behavioral sciences* (pp. 1-26). Pittsburgh, PA: University of Pittsburgh Press.
Wirth, L. (1928). *The ghetto.* Chicago, IL: University of Chicago Press.

REFERENCES

Wolff, M. (1977). Social psychology as history: Advancing the problem. *Personality and Social Psychology Bulletin, 3,* 211–212.

Woodward, W. (1982). The "discovery" of social behaviorism and social learning theory, 1870–1980. *American Psychologist, 37,* 396–410.

Wright, H. F., & Barker, R. G. (1950). *Methods in psychological ecology.* Lawrence, KS: University of Kansas Press.

Wright, M. E. (1943). The influence of frustration on the social relations of young children. *Character and Personality, 12,* 111–122.

Wrong, D. H. (1961). The oversocialized conception of man in modern sociology. *American Sociological Review, 26,* 183–193.

Wundt, W. (1862). *Contributions to the theory of sense perception.* (German). Leipzig: C. F. Winter.

Wundt, W. (1916). *Folk psychology* (10 vol., 1900–1920). Translated (Vols. 1–3) as *Elements of folk psychology.* New York: Macmillan.

Wylie, R. C. (1961). *The self-concept: A critical survey of pertinent research literature.* Lincoln, NE: University of Nebraska.

Wylie, R. C. (1969). Self theory. In E. Borgatta & W. W. Lambert (Eds.), *Handbook of personality theory and research* (pp. 728–787). Chicago, IL: Rand McNally.

Xydias, N. (1955). Difficulties encountered by the psychologist in the course of psycho-sociological investigations. (French) *Travail Humain, 18,* 57–63.

Young, J. Z. (1978). *Programs of the brain.* New York: Oxford.

Young, K. (1956). *Social psychology* (3rd ed.). New York: Appleton-Century-Crofts.

Zajonc, R. B. (1960). The concepts of balance, congruity, and dissonance. *Public Opinion Quarterly, 24,* 280–296.

Zajonc, R. B. (1965). Social facilitation. *Science, 149,* 269–274.

Zajonc, R. B. (1968–1969). Cognitive theories in social psychology. In G. Lindzey & E. Aronson (Eds.), *The handbook of social psychology* (2nd ed., Vol. 1, pp. 320–411). Reading, MA: Addison-Wesley.

Zajonc, R. B. (1980). Feeling and thinking: Preferences need no inferences. *American Psychologist, 35,* 151–175.

Zander, A. (1979). Psychology of group processes. In M. R. Rosenzweig & L. W. Porter (Eds.), *Annual review of psychology* (Vol. 30, pp. 417–452). Palo Alto, CA: Annual Reviews.

Zorbaugh, H. W. (1929). *The Gold Coast and the slum.* Chicago, IL: University of Chicago Press.

Author Index

A

Abelson R. P., 101, 104, 112, 120
Aboud F. E., 93
Ach N., 28
Adler A., 34
Adorno T. W., 7, 33
Ajzen I., 111
Allen V. L., 39
Allport F. H., 14, 19, 26, 49, 53, 81
Allport G. W., 4, 7, 10, 11, 13, 16, 21, 22, 37, 40, 42, 47, 51, 53, 67, 71, 77, 79, 89, 103
Altman I., 96, 112
American Psychological Association 88
American Sociological Society 70
Amrine M., 84
Ancona L., 67, 83
Angell J. R., 41, 42, 118
Archer D., 106
Archibald W. P., 92
Arensberg C. M., 58
Argyris C., 85, 86
Aronson E., 71, 79, 80, 88, 104
Asch S. E., 19, 30, 31, 73, 75, 84, 123, 135
Asher S. R., 107, 108, 110, 111, 112

B

Back K., 67, 70, 84
Backman C. W., 81
Bagehot W., 16
Baldwin J. M., 41, 42
Bandura A., 74, 109, 113
Bar-Tal D., 100, 101, 104
Barker R. G., 32, 33, 58, 76, 121
Bartlett F. C., 28, 38, 40
Baumgardner S. R., 47, 51
Bem D., 42
Benedict R., 37, 39
Benne K., 42, 72
Bentham J., 12
Berelson B., 63, 64
Berger S., 13, 19, 24, 74
Berkowitz L., 8, 9, 24, 33, 79, 93, 103, 109, 111
Bernard L. L., 47
Berscheid E., 104, 107, 110, 111, 112
Bickman L., 87
Biddle B. J., 111
Bion W. R., 7, 33
Blank T. O., 92
Block H., 19
Blumer H., 80
Boas F., 37, 38
Bogardus E. S., 44, 52
Bonner H., 68
Boring E. G., 15, 23, 25, 28, 29, 79
Boulding K. E., 81, 84
Bradford L., 42, 72
Braid J., 15

161

AUTHOR INDEX

Bray R. M., 101
Brehm M. L., 84
Brenner M., 107
Brentano F., 25, 26, 28, 29
Brewer M. B., 104, 106, 107, 109
Brislin R. W., 101, 107, 108, 109
Britt S. H., 49
Brody N., 100, 105
Bronfenbrenner U., 34, 100, 103, 106
Brown B. B., 112
Brown T., 15
Bruner J. S., 11, 28, 64, 67
Burgess E. W., 76
Burgess, R., 92
Buss D. M., 103

C

Cacioppo J. T., 104
Campbell A. A., 64, 66
Campbell D. T., 86, 111
Campos J. J., 110
Cantor N., 106
Cantril H., 7, 64
Carlsmith J. M., 71, 88
Carlyle T., 16
Cartwright D., 8, 49, 58, 63, 65, 66, 69, 70, 72, 80, 86, 89, 99, 100, 101, 102, 103
Cattell R. B., 67
Chapanis A., 75
Chapanis N. P., 75
Chapman D. W., 59
Chapple E. D., 58
Chave E. J., 27, 52
Christie R., 49, 74
Cialdini R. B., 104, 105, 107, 109, 111
Clark, H. H., 104, 108
Clark K. B., 62, 77
Clark M. S., 100
Clore G. L., 101
Cloward R. A., 76
Cohen A. K., 76
Collins B. E., 78
Comte A., 17, 21
Converse, P. E., 81
Cooley C. H., 36, 42, 43, 50, 80, 105, 118, 131
Coombs C. H., 27, 71, 134, 135
Cooper J., 104, 105
Coopersmith S., 8
Cressey D., 76

Cronbach L. J., 11, 87, 94, 95, 96
Crow W. J., 11
Croyle R. T., 104, 105
Crutchfield R. S., 30, 63, 65, 75
Cumberland R., 10

D

Daniels L. R., 8, 111
Darley J. G., 12, 66
Darwin C., 11, 16, 21, 22, 24, 25, 32, 47
Davidson D. M., Jr., 58
Davis A., 56
Davis F., 124
Dawson C. A., 55, 76
de Charms R., 96, 106, 108
de Montmollin G., 12
Deaux K., 20, 111, 118
Dembo T. 33, 58
Dennis W., 66, 67, 68
Deutsch M., 12, 32, 59, 74, 77, 79, 80, 93, 120
Dewey J., 22, 40, 41, 42, 43, 47, 51, 89, 95, 117, 118
Dickson W. J., 55
Diggory J. C., 76
Dion K. K., 109
Dollard J., 13, 31, 33, 38
Donnerstein E., 103
Doob L. W., 11, 33
Dunham H. W., 76
Dunlap K., 22, 47
Durkheim, E., 40, 41, 48, 58
Duval S., 7

E

Eagly A. H., 100, 104, 109, 111
Elms A. C., 93, 98, 99
Emde R., 110
Engels F., 51
Epstein Y. M., 96
Escalona S., 58
Ex J., 84

F

Farberman H. A., 77
Feather N. T., 75
Fechner G. T., 26, 27
Ferguson G. A., 27

AUTHOR INDEX

Festinger L., 14, 43, 58, 67, 72, 73, 75, 77, 84, 87, 100
Fishbein M., 111
Fiske M., 64
Fiske S. T., 105, 113
Fitzpatrick M. A., 108
Flacks R., 73
Forgas J. P., 113
Fouillé A., 18
Fouraker L. E., 79
Franke R. H., 74
French J. R. P., Jr., 8, 60, 61
Frenkel-Brunswik E., 7, 68
Freud S., 7, 18, 22, 32, 33, 34, 35, 36, 37, 47, 50, 51, 130
Fromm E., 9, 34, 35, 50, 51, 68

G

Gall F. J., 25
Gamson W. A., 79
Gara M. A., 109
Gardner B. B., 56
Gardner, M. R., 56
Garfinkel H., 123
Gaudet H., 64
Geis F., 49, 107
Gergen K. J., 87, 93, 94, 95, 99, 100, 101, 102, 104, 106, 108, 109, 113, 114, 118
Gettys W. E., 76
Gibb J. R., 72, 79
Gibbs J. C., 102, 118
Gibson J. J., 117
Giddings F. H., 10
Goffman E., 8, 36, 76, 78, 109, 120, 126
Goldstein J. W., 87
Gordon C., 76, 109
Gottlieb A., 95, 114
Gouldner A. W., 80, 111
Greenblatt M. D., 76
Greenwald A. G., 94
Gross E., 84
Gross, G., 89
Guetzkow H., 67
Gurmund L., 68, 83
Guttentag M., 93
Guttman L., 27

H

Haan N., 101
Hall C. S., 32, 33, 41

Hamilton W., 15
Hammond K. R., 11
Handel W. H., 42
Harary F., 58
Harr R., 85, 86, 93, 95, 96, 106
Harvey J. H., 100, 104, 105, 107
Harvey O. J., 63
Hebb D. O., 117, 135
Heider F., 14, 25, 28, 30, 32, 73, 75
Helmreich R., 87
Helmreich R. L., 111, 118
Hendrick C., 94
Herskovits M. J., 38
Hertzman M., 19
Hewitt J. P., 96
Himmelfarb S., 100, 104, 109, 111
Höffding H., 13, 17
Hoffman M. L., 118
Holahan C. J., 108
Hollander E. P., 35
Homans G. C., 49, 72, 74, 80
Hood T. C., 84
Hood W. R., 63
Horney K., 34, 35, 50, 51
House J. S., 92
Hovland C. I., 4, 28, 66, 74
Howard G. S., 106, 108
Howard J. A., 111
Hulett J. E., Jr., 68
Hull C. L., 73
Hunt J., 13, 117
Hunt K., 86
Hunyady G., 80
Huston T. L., 105, 107, 111, 112
Huxley A., 17

I

Ickes W., 107, 108
Inkeles A., 35, 37
Israel J., 85, 89
Itkin S. M., 101
Ittelson W., 96

J

Jackson J. M., 39, 75, 81, 111, 124
Jahoda M., 74
Jahoda G., 93, 96
James W., 16, 22, 26, 40, 41, 42, 43, 47, 62

AUTHOR INDEX

Janis I. L., 4, 74
Janowitz M., 70
Jaques E., 72
Jenkins J., 117
Jennings H. H., 58
Jennings H. S., 23
John E. R., 117
Jones, E. E., 74, 98, 99, 104, 105
Jones M., 72
Jung C. G., 34

K

Kahn R. L., 35
Kanfer F. H., 108
Kaplan A., 49
Kardiner A., 35, 39
Karpf F. B., 67
Karylowski J., 101
Katz Daniel, 64, 73, 81
Katz David, 30
Kaul J. D., 74
Keil L. J., 104
Kelley H. H., 4, 8, 72, 74, 105, 107
Kelly J. R., 112
Kelman H. C., 84, 88
Kessel F., 100
Kessen W., 100
Kiesler C. A., 93
Killian L. M., 99
Klineberg O., 67
Klinnert M. D., 110
Kluckhohn C., 38, 47
Knoll E., 109
Koch S., 108
Koenig K. E., 73
Koffka K., 29
Köhler W. 29
Kozulin A., 118
Kramer R. M., 104, 106, 107, 109
Krauss R. M., 74, 77, 78
Kravitz D. A., 100, 101, 103, 104, 107, 112
Krebs D. L., 104, 108, 109, 111
Krech D., 30, 63, 65, 75
Kroeber A. L., 37
Kroger R. O., 101, 102
Kropotkin P. A., 10
Kruglanski A. W., 85
Krupat E., 96
Kuethe J. L., 28

Kuhn M. H., 80
Kuhn T. S., 49, 51, 77, 85, 91, 93, 98, 101, 102, 106, 135

L

La Sorte M. A., 86
Lachman J. L., 99
Lachman, R., 99
Lambert W. W., 13, 19, 24, 74
Landy F. J., 134
Lasswell H. D., 64
Latané B., 12
Lauer R. H., 42
Lazarsfeld P. F., 64, 66, 74
Lazarus M., 24
Le Bon G., 15, 16, 17, 40, 48
Lecky P., 7
Leighton A. H., 63
Lentz T. F., 65
Levi A., 104, 112
Levine J. M., 105
Levinger G., 105, 107, 111, 112
Levinson D. J., 7, 35, 37, 69, 70, 76, 81
Lewin K., 28, 30, 32, 33, 44, 49, 58, 59, 60, 62, 63, 64, 65, 66, 68, 74, 75, 76, 78, 84, 87, 94, 100
Likert R., 27, 52, 64, 66
Lindzey G., 32, 33, 67, 71, 79, 80, 104
Linton R., 39
Lippitt R., 12, 42, 58, 60, 61, 67, 72
Liska A. E., 92
Loevinger J., 109
Loomis C. P., 58
Lorge I., 19
Lott A. J., 104
Lott, B., 104
Low J. O., 56
Lucke J., 93
Lundberg G. A., 58
Lunt P. S., 56
Lynd H. M., 55
Lynd R. S., 55

M

Mach E., 29
MacLeod R. B., 30, 75
Malinowski B., 37
Manicas P. T., 100, 104, 106

AUTHOR INDEX

Manis J. G., 42
Manis, M., 94
Mannheim K., 51
Manstead A. S. K., 108
Markus H., 7, 104, 105, 109, 113
Marx K., 51
Maslow A. H., 9
May M. A., 11
Mayo E., 55
Mayr E., 118
McClelland D. C., 8
McClintock C. G., 104, 106, 107, 111
McDougall W., 11, 18, 21, 22, 26, 47, 48
McGrath J. E., 14, 100, 101, 103, 104, 107, 112
McGuire W. J., 72, 75, 79, 85, 93, 103
Mead G. H., 23, 24, 36, 40, 41, 42, 43, 80, 95, 105, 110, 117, 118, 119, 131
Mead M., 11, 37, 39, 64
Meltzer B. N., 42
Meltzer L., 81
Merton R. K., 66, 67, 74, 77
Mesmer F. A., 15
Michela J. L., 105, 107
Milgram S., 88, 123
Miller A. G., 86
Miller D. T., 104, 106, 108, 109, 111
Miller N. E., 13, 31, 33, 38
Mischel W., 117
Moede W., 53
Moore H. T., 19, 53
Moreno J. L., 57, 58, 83
Morgan C. L., 23
Moscovici S., 73, 85, 87, 89, 90, 95, 106, 107, 132
Mowrer O. H., 33
Muir M. S., 106, 108
Mukerjee R., 76
Murdock G. P., 67
Murphy G., 26, 32, 38, 49, 58, 64, 68
Murphy L. B., 11, 26, 49,
Murphy P., 101
Murray H. A., 8, 65
Myrdal G., 63

N

Newcomb T. M., 26, 49, 51, 54, 57, 58, 60, 65, 66, 68, 73, 81
Norman R. Z., 58

Northrop F. S. C., 6, 68
Nurius P., 109

O

O.S.S. Assessment Staff 63
Ohlin L. E., 76
Olmsted D. W., 72
Orne M. T., 84, 86
Orwell G., 17
Osgood C. E., 73, 75

P

Park R. E., 44, 55, 76
Parke R. D., 107, 108, 110, 111, 112
Parrington V. L., 13
Parsons T., 41, 66, 68, 80
Partington J. T., 95, 96
Patton R. A., 67
Pepitone A., 95, 96, 100, 104, 118
Perlmutter H. V., 12
Petrinovich L., 102
Petty R. E., 104
Piaget J., 40
Proshansky H. M., 96

Q

Quinn, J. A., 76
Quinn R. P., 35

R

Raven B. H., 8, 78
Reykowski J., 101
Ribot T., 10
Riecken H. W., 81
Riesman D., 9
Riley J. W., Jr., 64
Ring K., 84, 85, 87, 88
Rivlin L., 96
Rodin J., 108, 110, 111
Roethlisberger F. J., 55
Rohrer J. H., 67
Rokeach M., 73, 75
Rommetveit R., 86
Rorer L. G., 101
Rosenberg S., 109
Rosenthal R., 76, 84, 86, 103

Rosenthal R. A., 35
Rosnow R. L., 86
Ross E. A., 18, 21
Rotter J. B., 74, 113
Ruitenbeek H. M., 72
Ryckman R. M., 87
Ryle G., 118

S

Sahakian W. S., 21, 24, 39, 58
Samelson F., 51
Sampson E. E., 89, 95, 100, 118
Sanford, F. H., 84
Sanford R. N., 7
Sapir E., 36, 37, 38
Sarason S. B., 118
Sarbin T. R., 39, 41
Sargent S. S., 67, 68
Schachter S., 12, 67, 79
Scheerer M., 27, 28
Scheler M., 10
Schlenker B. R., 94, 109, 110
Schneirla T. C., 68
Schwartz E. L., 117
Schwartz M. S., 36, 76
Schwartz R. D., 86
Schwartz S. H., 111
Scott W. A., 71
Sears P., 58
Sears R. R., 33
Sechrest L., 86
Secord P. F., 81, 85, 86, 93, 95, 96, 100, 104, 106
Segal D. R., 92
Segall M. H., 102, 103, 107, 108, 111
Segal M. W., 92
Semin G. R., 108
Shaw C. R., 54, 55, 58
Shaw M. E., 93, 98
Shea D. J., 96
Sherif C. W., 132
Sherif M., 7, 19, 28, 31, 38, 58, 59, 63, 65, 67, 68, 84, 86, 87, 96, 110, 123, 132, 135
Shils E. A., 41, 56, 68
Showers C., 106
Siegel S., 79
Silverman I., 85
Skinner B. F., 17, 49, 50, 51, 74, 80, 113
Smith A., 10, 12

Smith M. B., 63, 66, 71, 80, 81, 85, 88, 93, 95
Smith, N. C., 86
Smith, R. J., 87, 89
Snoek J. D., 35
Snyder M., 8, 107, 108
Sofer C., 72
Sorce J. F., 110
Souief M., 68, 83
Spence J. T., 111, 118
Stagner R. E., 68
Stanton A. H., 36, 76
Statham A., 42, 109, 110, 111, 113, 114
Staub E., 101
Steele M., 58
Steiner I. D., 72, 96, 99, 100, 104, 105
Steinthal H., 24
Stephan W. G., 101, 103, 104, 105, 110
Stock D., 33
Stokols D., 96
Stone G. P., 77
Stoodley B. H., 76
Stouffer S. A., 64
Strickland L. H., 93, 94
Stryker S., 42, 80, 92, 96, 109, 110, 111, 113, 114
Suci G. J., 73, 75
Sullivan E. V., 106
Sullivan H. S., 34, 35, 36, 130
Sumner W. G., 24, 123
Sutherland E. H., 76
Svejda M., 110

T

Tagiuri R., 11, 25, 73, 78, 79
Tajfel H., 85, 87, 89, 93, 95, 96, 105, 106, 107, 110
Tannenbaum P. H., 73, 75
Tarde G., 14, 16, 18, 48
Taylor S. E., 105, 113
Tedeschi J. T., 109
Tesch F. E., 88
Thelen H. A., 33
Thibaut J. W., 8, 72, 74
Thomas W. I., 43, 44, 52, 54
Thorndike E. L. 23, 47
Thorngate W., 87, 94, 95
Thrasher F. M., 54, 58
Thurstone L. L., 27, 44, 52
Tolman E. C., 68, 107, 113

AUTHOR INDEX

Triandis H. C., 87, 93, 96, 111
Triplett N., 19, 21, 49, 53
Trotter W., 11
Tufts J. H., 48, 49
Turnbull W., 106, 109
Turner J. C., 111
Turner R. H., 81, 99
Tyler L. E., 102, 106, 109, 112, 117

U

U. S. Strategic Bombing Survey 63, 64

V

Vinacke W. E., 88
Vinsel A., 112
Volkart E. H., 79, 80, 83
Volkmann J. A., 59
von Bonin G., 117

W

Walster E., 93, 111
Walster, G. W., 111
Walters R. H., 74
Wardwell W. I., 74
Warner W. L., 56
Warwick D. P., 73
Watson G., 63
Watson J. B., 23, 24
Weary G., 100, 104, 105, 107
Webb E. J., 86
Weinberg S. K., 76
Weissberg N. C., 87
Wertheimer M., 29, 30
Wever E. G., 27
White B. J., 63
White R. K., 60

White R. W., 117
White S., 100
Whitely S. E., 134
Whiting J. W. M., 39
Whittemore I. C., 53
Whyte W. F., 57, 58, 60
Wicklund R. A., 8
Widiger L. G., 101
Williams R. H., 76
Wilson M. O., 67
Wirth L., 54, 55
Wolfe D. M., 35
Wolff M., 95
Woodward W., 118
Wright H. F., 32, 76
Wright M. E., 58
Wrightsman L. S., 20
Wrong D. H., 9, 96, 124
Wundt W., 24, 25, 26, 28, 29, 40, 42
Wylie R. C., 7, 76

X

Xydias N., 68, 83

Y

Young J. Z., 118
Young K., 67

Z

Zajonc R. B., 19, 42, 53, 74, 75, 100, 104, 105, 109, 113, 119, 135
Zander A., 72, 100, 103
Zener K. E., 27
Znaniecki F., 44, 52, 54
Zorbaugh H. W., 54

Subject Index

A

Achievement motivation, 107
Action research, 63-65, 67
Affiliation, 11-12
Aggression, 11, 107, 111
Alone-together, 19, 49, 53
Altruism, 107, 111
American Soldier, 74
Animal magnetism, 14-15
Aristotle, 3, 5
    anticipations of contemporary social psychology, 4
    assumptions and method, 3-4
Association, principles of, 19
Associationists, British, 14-16
Attitude change, 107
Attitude scales, 26
    Bogardus social distance, 44
    Coombs, 27
    Guttman, 27
    Likert, 27
    Thurstone-Chave, 27, 44
Attitudes, 44, 57, 72-73, 111
Attraction, interpersonal, 107, 112
Attribution theory, 25, 74, 107
Authoritarian personality, 7, 33, 73-75
Authority, legitimate, 8

Autokinetic experiment, 58
Autokinetic phenomenon, 31

B

Balance theory, 14, 74
Behavior setting, 121
Behaviorism, 47
    radical, 17, 23
    social, 43
Behaviorist Theory, 14, 16, 19, 74
Bennington Study, 57
Bennington Study, follow-up, 73

C

Causal attribution, 109
Chicago Monographs, 54
Classical contributions, revision, 74
Cognitive dissonance, 14, 73, 75, 100
Cohesiveness, 43
Collective behavior, 18
Communication, 36, 74
Competition, 12
Concepts, sociological 67
Conformity, 2, 16, 31, 111
Consciousness of kind, 10
Consensual validation, 36
Cooperation, 11, 12

SUBJECT INDEX

Crowd behavior, 19, 40, 48
Cultural anthropology
  Freudian influence, 37
  psychologizing of, 37
Cultural relativism, 38
Culture, 39

D

Darwin
  emotions, expression, 25
  emotions, recognition, 25
  theory of evolution, 21
Decision theory, 112
Demand characteristics, 84
Determining tendency, 28
Dissonance reduction, 13
Dogmatism, 73
Dynamogenesis, 16, 19, 53

E

Ecological validity, 112
Ecology
  psychological, 76
  sociological, 76
Economic man, 13
Ego involvement, 7
Egoism, 17
Emotion, James-Lange theory, 42
Empathy, 11
Empiricism, 17, 50, 77
Encounters, 120
Environment
  behaviorist orientation, 76
  cognitive orientation, 75
  psychodynamic orientation, 76
  role theory orientation, 76
  treatment, 76
  urban, 76
Environment and delinquency, 55
Environment, organizational
  mental hospitals, 36
Environment, research, 76
Environmentalism, 47, 77
Equity, 111
Equity theory, 107
European social psychology, 89, 108
Exchange theory, 13, 107
Expectation theory, 28

Experimental research, 19
Experimenter effects, 84

F

Folkways, 24
Four wishes, 44
Frame of reference, 27-28
Frames, 120
Frustration-aggression hypothesis, 33

G

Gestalt principles
  closure, 30
  figure-ground, 30
  prägnanz, 30
Gestalt psychology, 19
  mental development, 29
  productive thinking, 30
Gestaltqualität, 29
Graph theory, 58
Group atmosphere, 43, 49
Group dynamics, 60, 65, 67, 72, 100
  Bion's theory, 33
Group Dynamics, Research Center for, 32, 67
Group learning, 12
Group membership, 55
Group mind, 18, 40, 46, 48-49
Group processes, 42, 67, 72
Group psychology, 18
Group structure, 57
Group vs. individual thinking, 49
Group, primary, 43
Groups
  co-acting, 53
  face-to-face, 53
  informal, 54
  organized vs. unorganized, 49, 60
Groups, small, 72
  field experiments, 55-56

H

Habit, 42
Hawthorne effect, 56
Hawthorne studies, 55, 74
Hedonism, 13-14, 17
  Bentham, 12
  early, 6
  enlightened, 12

Hedonistic calculus, 12
Helping behavior, 12
Heredity-environment, 47
Hobbes, Thomas, 6-9
Human brain processes, 117
Human nature, *see also* Model of a person, 4, 6-7, 10, 17, 19, 46, 50, 85, 96, 101, 108, 112, 126, 130
  benevolence, 9, 11
  desire for self-preservation, 6
  egotistical, 6-7, 9, 12
  gregarious, 12, 17
  hedonistic, 13
  humanistic, 11-12
  power-seeking, 6-7, 9
  selfish, 6, 12, 17
Human subjects, 84, 88
Hypnosis, 14-16, 18
Hypothesis, 28

I

Identities, multiple, 110
Identity, 129
  bargain, 128
  disciplinary, 63, 69, 80
  process, 57, 126
  situated, 36, 44, 109, 115, 119, 122, 126
  validation, 127-128
Ideomotor theory, 16, 53
Ideé-forces, 19
Imageless thought, 28
Imitation, 14, 16-19, 38
  Asch reformulation, 31
  laws of, 18
Impression management, 109-110, 126
Independence, 31
Influence, social, 14
Informed consent, 88
Instinct of human solidarity, 11
Instincts, 16, 22, 47
Instincts, social
  Giddings, 10
  McDougall, 11
  Trotter, 11
Institution
  primary, 39
  secondary, 39
Interdisciplinary relations, 63, 65-70
Interdisciplinary research, 65-66
Interdisciplinary training, 66, 68-69

Intergroup relations, 107
Interracial behavior, 110

J

Journal of Abnormal and Social Psychology, 15
Journal of Personality and Social Psychology, 15, 34

L

Laboratory experiment, 53, 87, 88, 101
  deception, 84
Laissez-faire, 10, 13, 24
Language, 38
Language use, 108
Law of Effect, 23
Leadership, 2, 57
  authoritarian, 12, 60
  democratic, 12, 60
  laissez-faire, 60
  psychoanalytic theory, 7
Learning
  insight, 29
  trial-and-error, 23, 30
Levels of analysis, multiple, *see also* Unit of analysis, 49, 50
Lewin's formula, 44

M

Machiavellianism, 49, 107
Marital interaction, 108
Marxist criticism, 89
Mead
  social behaviorism, 24
Meaning
  cognitive vs. symbolic, 132
  pragmatic theory, 4, 130
Memory
  contextualist theory, 117
  social influences, 28, 40
Mentality
  animal, 22
  human, 23
Mesmerism, 15
Meta-analysis, 103
Middletown studies, 55
Mind-body problem, 23, 27
Modal personality, 35, 39

SUBJECT INDEX

Model of a person, *see also* Human nature, 107-109, 112-114, 117-119, 124, 132
Modern dynamic interactionism, 108
Moral judgment, 40
Mores, 24
Motivation, deficit theories, 13, 117

N

National character, 35
National Training Laboratory for Group Development (NTL), 42, 72
Nativism, 22, 47
Nature-nurture controversy, 46
Normative process, 57, 59, 107, 111, 113, 115, 119, 123, 125
Normative structure, 125
Normative system, 124
Norms, 24, 31, 54, 58-59, 110, 123-124
  equity, 111
  reciprocity, 111
  social responsibility, 8, 111

O

Obedience, 88

P

Paradigm, 77, 85, 91-93, 99-100, 103, 105-106, 135
Perception, 117
  interpersonal, *see also* Social perception, 32, 73-74
  of movement, 29
Person perception, 11, 25, 73
  first impressions, 30
Person-society relationship, 46, 50-52
Personality, 44, 107, 112
  interactionist theory, 117
Personality and attitude change, 57
Phenomenology, 29
Phi phenomenon, 29
Philosophers, classical, 6
Philosophy
  pragmatic, 41
Philosophy of science, 101
Phrenology, 25
Plato, 3, 5, 9, 16
  anticipations of contemporary social psychology, 4
  assumptions and method, 3-4

Polish peasant study, 44
Positivism 17, 101, 103
Power, 49
  coercive, 8
  need for, 8
  theories, 8
Prestige-suggestion, 19
  Asch reformulation, 31
Pro-social behavior, 12
Problem of combining subjectivities, 75, 118, 132
Problem-solving processes, 42
Psychiatry
  interpersonal theory, 35
Psychoanalytic theory, 7
Psychological modality, 119
Psychology
  act, 29
  ecological, 32
  empirical, 25
  experimental, 25-26, 28
  folk, 24, 26, 36
  functional, 42, 43
  physiological, 23, 25
Psychophysics
  measurement and scaling theory, 26

R

Racial prejudice, 33
"Rational-irrational" dichotomy, 31
Reciprocal interactionism, 109
Reductionism, 19, 40, 49-50
Reference group, 110
Reference process, 57, 80, 107, 110, 113, 115, 119, 122, 129-130
Reflected appraisals, 36
Reflexivity
  interpersonal, 109
  intrapersonal, 109
Reinforcement, 13
Relationships, close affective, 112
Replication, 86-87
Research methods
  advances, 64, 71-72
  ethics, 84, 87-88, 100
  integrative orientation, 133-134
  nonintrusive, 86
  validity, 84, 86, 100-101
Research, cultural context, 87
Rewards and costs, 13
Robbers' Cave experiment, 63

Role conflict, 39
Role expectations
  female, 39
Role theory, 39, 111, 113, 124
  process, 124
  stuctural, 124
Role-taking, 118
  taking the role of the other, 11, 37

S

Scalp-recording research, 117
Schema, 28
Schemata, 28
Scripts, 120
Self, 8, 75, 96, 107
  behaviorist orientation, 76
  cognitive orientation, 75, 109
  looking-glass, 43
  psychodynamic orientation, 75, 109
  role theory orientation, 76
  social, 41
Self process, 7, 76, 109, 115, 119, 131
  theories, 8
Self, "real", 110
Self-actualization, 8
Self-presentation, 109-110, 126
Self-schemas, 109
Self-system, 36
  Mead, 11
Semantic differential, 73, 75
Sensitivity, 42
Sensitivity training, 72
Significant other, 36, 110
Silent organization, 28
Social act, 114, 119-123, 127-128
Social attitudes, 35
Social character, 35
Social comparison, 110
Social contract, 7-8, 10, 13
Social Darwinism, 16, 18, 24
Social development, 108, 112
Social exchange, 111
Social facilitation, 19, 53, 100
Social influence, 18-19, 57, 74, 107, 126
  group pressure, 32
Social learning, 38, 74
Social motivation, 38, 44
Social networks, 110
Social perception, see also Perception,
  interpersonal, 11, 38
Social phenomenology, 43

Social pressure, 55
Social psychiatry, 35
Social psychologists
  applied, 91
  dissident, 105, 106
  humanists and liberal activists, 91
  methodologists and technocrats, 90
  philosophers of science, 91, 92
  psychological, 92, 114
  radicals and revolutionaries, 91
  sociological, 92, 114
  sociologists of knowledge, 91
  traditional, 90, 105
Social psychology
  applied, 66, 70, 72, 87, 100, 108, 110-111
  bifurcation, 4, 67, 79-80, 92, 114
  cognitive, 28
  crisis, 82, 98-99, 102
  cross-cultural, 96, 108, 115
  cultural anthropology's influence, 36,
    38-39
  cultural context, 89, 95
  dialectical, 95
  disciplinary problems, 77
  dramaturgical theory, 36, 126
  ecological approach, 55
  emancipatory, 86
  environmental, 96, 108, 115
  experimental, 25, 52-54, 58, 60, 71, 101
  field theory, 32-33, 74
  fragmentation, 79, 100
  Freudian "revisionists' influence, 34
  Freudian influence, 32-33
  Gestalt, 31
  historical inquiry, 87, 94-95
  in World War II, 63-65
  integrative, 72, 74, 93-94, 104
  interdisciplinary, W. I. Thomas, 43
  metatheory, 101
  neo-Freudian influence, 35
  non-social, 95, 100, 104, 106, 132
  normative, 96
  persistent problems, 6
  phenomenological, 30
  psychological, 4-5, 36, 49,
  scientific status, 52
  sociological, 5, 26, 36, 44, 92,
  sociopolitical biases, 89
  status of, 66, 70-71, 75, 103
  study of interpersonal processes, 35
  theoretical progress, 85, 100
  topics, 1, 2, 54, 100, 103

SUBJECT INDEX

universal issues, 46
value-free, 101
William James' influence, 41
Social Psychology Quarterly, 58
Social psychology, issues
  eclecticism vs. general theory, 78-79
  empiricism vs. social humanism, 77-78
  recognition of significant problems, 78
Social referencing, 110
Social situation, research, 87, 96
Socialization, 38-39, 43
Society, 6, 9, 13, 16-19, 46, 51, 85, 124
  utopian, 17
Sociogram, 57
Sociology
  psychological, 40-41, 44
  sociological, 40
Sociology of knowledge, 51
Sociometry, 57
Status, 39
Status system, measurement, 56
Stooges (collaborative "subjects."), 32
Street-Corner Society, 57
Stress, 13, 14
Suggestion, 14-19
  hypnotic, 18
Suggestion-imitation, 14, 18-19
Supra-individual concepts, 49-50
Survey research, 63-64
Symbolic interaction theory, 42, 113-114
Symbolic processes, 95
Sympathy, 12, 16-18
  Giddings, 10
  Hume, 10, 12
  in contemporary social psychology, 11
  Kropotkin, 10
  McDougall, 11
  Ribot, 10
  Scheler, 10
  Smith, 10
  Spencer, 10

T

T-group, 42, 72
Tavistock Institute, 72
Tension reduction, 13-14
Theoretical orientation
  behaviorist, 25, 50, 104, 112-113, 130
  cognitive, 28, 50, 74, 104-105, 113, 130
  integrative 36, 57, 105, 112-116, 119
  psychodynamic, 25, 32, 34, 50, 104, 112-113, 129
  sociocultural, 50
  traditional, 112-113
Therapeutic community, 72
Time frame, 107, 112-113, 115, 119, 133
Transhistorical generality, 102

U

Unconscious inference, 28
Unit of analysis, *see also* Levels of analysis, 107, 113-114, 118-119
Unitary explanations, 7, 9, 14, 16, 18
Universal validity, 102
Utilitarian, 10, 13
Utilitarianism, 12
  in contemporary social psychology, 13
Utility theory, 13
Utility, principle of, 12

V

Value-free status, 85

W

We-feeling, 43
Weber-Fechner Law, 27

Y

Yankee City Series, 56